Hope and Dread in Psychoanalysis

Hope and Dread in Psychoanalysis

Stephen A. Mitchell

A Member of The Perseus Books Group

Designed by Craig Winer

Library of Congress Cataloging-in-Publication Data

Mitchell, Stephen A., 1946–
    Hope and dread in psychoanalysis / Stephen A. Mitchell.
      p.   cm.
    Includes bibliographical references and index.
ISBN 0–465–03059–9 (cloth)
ISBN 0–465–03062–9 (paper)
    1. Psychoanalysis.   I. Title.
RC504.M54   1993
616.89'17—dc20   92–56176
                                                   CIP

10

For Stanley Mitchell
and in memory of
Lillian Mitchell

Contradiction, conflict, spiraling, reconciliation, a dissolving of achieved reconciliations, new resolutions of dissonances—these are at the center of life and the mind's life.

—Hans Loewald,
Sublimation

Our assumptions about the nature of the world, the way we think the world actually works, so often record our hopes about the world and not the nature of Nature.

—Stephen Jay Gould,
The Individual in Darwin's World

CONTENTS

Preface and Acknowledgments

One of the miscellaneous bits left over in my memory from my undergraduate days is a definition of psychology as "jargonized common sense." I have always tried to make the sense I could offer (common or otherwise) as dejargonized as possible. Because I am, in places, tracing intellectual trends and trying to integrate divergent lines of theorizing, the discussion is at times specialized and detailed. However, in an effort to make the book more accessible to the general reader, I have separated some of the more technical discussions from the text into endnotes. There interested readers will find both arguments with adherents of other positions and an appreciative collection of quotations from others who have taken positions similar to mine. I am an inveterate quote-collector. Where I have found that someone has said something related to my argument in a way I admire, it will appear in the endnotes.

I present two kinds of clinical material. Some of the more specific and limited examples come directly from work with particular patients; I greatly appreciate their permission to use this information. Other examples are composites. There is nothing more essential to psychoanalysis than confidentiality, which makes the use of fuller, extensive case discussions very difficult. By constructing composites, the examples remain true to actual analytic experience but the privacy of individuals is preserved. Thus, there is nothing in any of the examples that did not happen, but I have combined and reorganized material to make possible a fuller picture without compromising privacy.

Although this book is an individual effort, it has benefited from and bears the impact of the experience and the thought of many different people. First and most important, it grew out of my clinical work with my patients over the years, and I owe them a deep debt of gratitude for allowing me to accompany and work with them in their individual analytic experiences. Many of the ideas developed here were born in our struggles to grasp some aspect of their lives or our experience together, and there is no way I can properly acknowledge my debt to them.

I am also grateful to the many students I have taught over the years. Teaching is a great passion of mine, partly because teaching is such an extraordinary opportunity for learning. Virtually all the ideas presented here were discussed, argued about, and continually refined and expanded in courses I was privileged to teach at the William Alanson White Institute; the New York University Postdoctoral Program; the National Institute for the Psychotherapies; the doctoral program of Teacher's College, Columbia University; the Washington School of Psychiatry; and at various local chapters of Division 39 (Psychoanalysis) of the American Psychological Association in Boston, Denver, New Haven, Seattle, and Toronto. I am especially indebted to the members of the reading groups with whom I have been meeting weekly for years, for the unusual opportunity to try out my ideas with them and to absorb and learn from their experience and ideas.

The teaching and speaking I have done around the United States in recent years have been essential in the writing of this particular book in another respect as well. One of my goals here is to capture and portray not just my own personal practice of psychoanalysis but a climate of opinion, a shared sensibility. Psychoanalysis has changed in important and often startling ways over the past several decades, and I have tried to represent some features of that change. Teaching has given me the opportunity to learn about the ways in which clinicians around the country have been thinking about and practicing psychoanalysis, the ideas they find most helpful, the writers they find most inspirational.

A number of colleagues have read various drafts and offered detailed critiques and commentaries, for which I am extremely grateful. They include Neil Altman, Louis Aron, Tony Bass, Jessica Benjamin, Michele Berdy, Margaret Black, Jay Greenberg, Irwin Hoffman, Thomas Ogden, and Charles Spezzano. I am also indebted to William Grossmann and Ernest Wolf for discussions of an earlier version of much of the material that has become chapter 4 (published in *Psychoanalytic Dialogues* 2 [1991]). Responding to their critiques helped me further my own thinking. Earlier versions of portions of chapters 3, 4, 5, 7, and 8 have appeared in various publications. My thanks to *Psychoanalytic Dialogues, Psychoanalytic Inquiry, Contemporary Psychoanalysis,* and the Analytic Press (for material appearing in *Relational Perspectives in Psychoanalysis,* edited by N. Skolnick and S. Warshaw, 1992), for permission to use them.

Hope and Dread in Psychoanalysis

INTRODUCTION

Sophie and the Psychoanalytic Meat Grinder

Expressed in technical terms, he remained potentially analysable. Expressed in everyday, human terms, he never quite gave up hope.
　　　　　　　—Heinz Kohut, *How Does Analysis Cure?*

An air of excitement and expectancy accompanies the resumption of an analysis after a vacation break. The customary routine has been interrupted; the familiarity of the setting has been jostled so as to expand the sense of possibilities. The hopes of both analysand and analyst are sharpened. Their dreads are intensified. How difficult will it be to reestablish the shared consciousness that constitutes the analytic process? How has the work of the analysis held up over the break? How will the living that has occurred during the vacation be viewed and understood in the analysis? Sometimes the dread greatly outweighs the hope.

SOPHIE'S RETURN

After three years of a productive analysis, Sophie, an architectural graduate student in her early thirties, resumes her sessions following my vacation with considerable apprehension and foreboding. In the weeks prior to my departure, she had met a young man in whom she had an intense romantic interest, but circumstances had kept them from spending much time together. In my absence, they have been with each other almost constantly, and she has fallen in love. She is convinced that, after many failed relationships of variable duration, this would be the right man for her, this would be the man she would marry. The problem, as she saw it, was returning to her analysis, where my analytic scrutiny was likely to find fault with what appeared to be an idyllic relationship, to dash her hopes, to rain on her parade.

Sophie had entered analysis with a characterological depression and a history of problematic relationships with men. When we began, she was enmeshed in a long-standing, very stormy, mutually torturous relationship with a man who resembled, in many respects, her depressed and extremely demanding mother, whom she felt bound continually to rescue and buoy up. She felt mired in despair about her ability to find and maintain a relationship with a man who made her happy. She deeply dreaded that her life would always be pervaded by an oppressive sense of heaviness, worry, and obligation.

After about a year of treatment, she ended that relationship, with a mixture of apprehension and relief. She began to date other men, and developed considerable insight into the unconscious neurotic premises and projects that underlay her choices of men and her manner of structuring her involvement with them. These new relationships were all departures for her in one way or another, although none lasted more than six months or so. Her depression lifted, and various other important issues were worked through. Yet as she approached the end of the third year of her analysis, she felt a nagging concern that she would somehow never meet a man with whom she would be happy.

However, here was a man who made her very happy and who did share, to a remarkable extent, her particular talents and interests. Her initial hope that analysis would help her find a richer and more satisfying relationship with a man seemed to have been fulfilled. It felt like the perfect relationship; yet, ironically, she was sure that I, the psychoanalytic version of the grim reaper, would not see it that way.

Sophie grew up in a small midwestern town. Her parents were both teachers of German Lutheran background. Sophie was the oldest of four children; she had two sisters and a brother. Her mother was a very frightened woman with many phobias, who lived always poised on the brink of serious depression. She saw her children as she saw herself— very delicate, different from and far better than other people. Her life was absorbed in protecting and guiding them.

Sophie's father, a very cautious, frugal man, had devoted his life to his wife. He would drive her around, support all her phobias and theories (some of which bordered on the crackpot), never speaking to his children outside of her presence.

Sophie both dreaded and relied on her mother's gaze. The mother would scrutinize the children when they returned home from school, looking for hints of worry or sadness, and interrogate them on their troubles. Sophie had come to feel that it was useless to resist her—she always seemed magically to know if there was something wrong, and would drag it out of her, go over it with her, admonish her on her having left the path of her guidance thereby making herself vulnerable to disappointment and hurt feelings, and wrap her tightly once again in her knowing vision of the future. After any physical absence, she would insist on staring into Sophie's eyes, resurrecting this powerful bond.

From her mother Sophie gained a vision of a world fraught with dangers, one in which most people are alarmingly incompetent and base, and their inadequacies are contagious. In Sophie and her mother's world there is only one correct way to do anything, and near misses are equivalent to complete failure. What distinguishes the good and righteous from the common people is their ability to bypass fun and pleasure in their dedication to duty and excellence. Fun and pleasure are dangerous; onerous obligations and responsibilities are safe and sensible.

Not surprisingly, Sophie entered treatment with a long list of symptoms, including social, interpersonal, and sexual conflicts and inhibitions, and a pattern of getting submissively involved with powerful, opinionated figures who seemed very certain about what would be good for her. It took her a long time to get to treatment. Her mother had warned her against therapy as the ultimate Satanic threat. Therapists lure young people away from their parents, blame their mothers for everything, and control their patients' lives with their own decadent philosophies. Since this is, of course, arguably true, she made a convincing case, and Sophie was terrified of treatment.

As the analysis progressed, Sophie became eager to reexamine all of the major features of her life; analysis seemed to provide her an exhilarating freedom to think for herself about herself. She began to allow herself different sorts of experiences, less encumbered with obligations, both when she was by herself and when she was with others. She experimented with a less solemn, more spontaneous way of living, which both pleased and frightened her. She became aware of how anxious she felt when she caught herself not being anxious, how much the worry and sense of ponderous responsibility, although onerous, also seemed somehow to protect her. She began to realize how the worries about petty details that she had inherited from her parents distracted and buffered her from a deeper dread—a fear of the unfamiliar, a terror of becoming unsuitable for contact with other people, a dread of self-diffusion, and a profound sense of loss and disorientation.

As was apparent in her wariness on returning to analysis following my vacation, Sophie never fully stopped distrusting me, whom she liked to think of as a representative of a way of life more enlightened and better for her than her mother's. She experienced analysis as predicated on a model of interaction similar to her relationship with her mother. She hoped for something different from the analyst than she had with her mother, but in some sense she could envision the analytic relationship only along the lines with which she was familiar.

She felt sure that I, like her mother, had all sorts of ideas about what is best for her. (Whereas her mother made these quite explicit, I tried to hide my directives so that Sophie could discover them "by herself.") But Sophie, who was highly skilled at reading interpersonal cues, felt she could more or less discern my opinions on the "right" course of action. She suspected that I, in fact, intentionally scattered clues, but that it was somehow an important part of the analytic game that she and I avoided openly acknowledging that. There was a pretense that Sophie was discovering the correct and righteous route for herself. Yet mistakes could be disastrous, because I had a great stake in my own wisdom and influence. Unresponsive, uneducable patients were surely discarded for more malleable substitutes.

We explored in considerable detail these transferential themes, which emerged in many different forms and in many different phases of the analysis. There were increasing stretches in which Sophie seemed to be living outside the constraints of her surrender to maternal/analytic authority, both in the analysis and in her life in general. But this central relational configuration was powerfully resurrected in her experience during my vacation and at my return. Sophie felt I had helped her disengage from her previous boyfriends, all of whom she felt I disapproved of. This was all to the good, she felt. But how could she risk my likely disapproval of her new love? In my desire to maintain her in my analytic clutches, I could not possibly share her excitement about him. It was dangerous to return to treatment.

There are many ways to look at this material. Sophie was involved in a manic flight into love; she was using projection to attribute her own doubts and concerns about this man to me and then avoiding me. Sophie was experiencing me as her mother, competitive and jealous of her sexual involvement with a man, wanting to preserve her as an asexual little girl or as her own homosexual love object. Sophie was experiencing me as her father, competitive with her boyfriend, wanting to keep her for myself.

From another angle, Sophie was certainly right in discerning that I did think the boyfriend she was seeing on entering analysis was a drag, with a great deal less vitality and many fewer resources than she. I had to admit (to myself) that I did have certain ideas about what would be best for her. Did Sophie detect my reactions, despite my efforts to keep them to myself? To some extent, her seeming "resistance" was based on an accurate perception and fear of my countertransference.

I think there was considerable truth in all these interpretive hypotheses, and we explored these many facets of this moment in Sophie's analysis. As the work went on, however, I became particularly interested in the question of how she thought I would know whether this man was good for her or not. This led us into some interesting new material concerning her ideas about analysis.

One of her favorite teachers in college was a psychoanalyst. He and Sophie became friends, and, although careful to conceal their identities, the analyst would sometimes talk to Sophie about his patients, describing each one in what Sophie called a "clear, concise paragraph," detailing their histories, dynamics, and likely futures. It was as if psychoanalysis provided a kind of X ray into character, of which Sophie was both admiring and a bit dubious. It was on the basis of such a "clear, concise paragraph" that Sophie figured I would know whether this relationship was good for her or not. Maybe the paragraph theory was a bit of a caricature, Sophie allowed, but was that not how it has worked? She had come to feel very grateful for the help I provided for her. Although rarely commenting explicitly on things, I did seem to have a perspective on her family, her past, and her conflicts that often provided a more reliable guide than her moment-to-moment experience as to what was important, what was "real," what might be in her best interests in the long run. This is why even in this benign view of me, my return posed a realistic threat to her romance. Although she felt she needed me very much, she certainly wanted to enjoy herself a bit more before exposing herself to my somber, objective scrutiny.

Interestingly, she noted that the only person she was less inclined to introduce her boyfriend to than me was her analyst/friend. Her boyfriend was an artist, and the friend had what Sophie considered embarrassingly crude notions of art, all of which he considered reducible to variations on the Oedipus theme. Sophie did not want to expose her boyfriend to what she called her friend's psychoanalytic meat grinder.

Throughout this book I use Sophie's challenging questions about the nature of the analytic process as a taking-off point from which to consider contemporary ideas about what happens in analysis. These ideas have changed very much since Freud's day. I return to Sophie repeatedly in the chapters that follow.

THE ANALYTIC TRADITION IN OUR TIME

Psychoanalysis was born on the cusp of the twentieth century, in the fertile mix of political, cultural, social, and intellectual cataclysms that vibrated through fin de siècle Vienna. This was a time that bridged two worlds: from the faded splendor of the Hapsburg Empire to the nation states of post–World War I Europe; from nineteenth-century science, still based on Newton, to twentieth-century science and the impact of Einstein and Heisenberg; from traditionalism to modernism.

Freud was, inevitably, a creature of his time, one who embodied its hopes and dreads. Psychoanalysis, the intellectual and clinical discipline he founded and shaped over the five decades from the 1890s through the 1930s, bridges the two worlds Freud inhabited: the nineteenth-century world of his childhood, in which he was educated and trained, and the twentieth-century world his own momentous discoveries helped to create. From an offshoot of clinical neurology, a minor extension of hypnotism for the treatment of certain intractable hysterical symptoms, psychoanalysis has become the foundation for virtually all modern psychotherapy as well as a central component in contemporary cultural experience and self-understanding.

Psychoanalysis quickly became a world unto itself. Working at first in isolation and then at the center of increasing numbers of devoted adherents, Freud's enormous energy and brilliance generated an extraordinary sense of discovery, the incremental uncovering of the underlying structures and processes of mind. Freud's hero, the archaeologist Heinrich Schliemann, had electrified the world in 1873 (when Freud was seventeen) by locating and unearthing the ancient city of Troy in the desert of modern Turkey.[1] Similarly, Freud and his coworkers felt they were, by using the analytic method in daily clinical practice, progressively reaching and laying bare the hidden, ancient roots of mind beneath conscious, civilized social existence. New insights developed out of earlier discoveries; the models of the psyche became increasingly complex; clinical technique became more and more sophisticated. For those whose professional lives were spent within the world of psychoanalysis, their discipline had a life and momentum of its own, growing, developing, evolving.

We live now at the far end of the twentieth century. The world is very different from the world in which psychoanalysis first appeared. There have been enormous changes in political, economic, and social structure; stunning developments in scientific understanding; many cultural shifts and cataclysms; striking differences in the ways men and women conceive of themselves, their place in the universe, and their relationships with each other. The patients who seek analytic treatment are different; the analysts who practice psychoanalysis are different. Our struggles, our problems, our sensibilities, our hopes and dreads are, in many ways, significantly different from those of people who lived a hundred years ago.

Psychoanalytic authors have been mindful of these changes in the outside world. New clinical entities have been described and labeled—schizoid personalities, narcissistic personalities—which some consider more prevalent in contemporary society. Many authors have looked to adjacent fields for inspiration: linguistics, anthropology, history, sociology, biology, and, increasingly, literary theory.

Yet there is also a strong sense of self-containment within the way psychoanalysis is thought, written, and practiced. Psychoanalysts see themselves as dealing with universal, timeless dimensions of human experience, currents that run deeper than the surface ripples of cultural change and intellectual or social fashion. For many psychoanalysts, it is important to believe that there has been one revolution—Freud's. All other contributions have been slow, evolutionary, incremental additions to his work. Many psychoanalysts center their identity on a sense of direct lineage from Freud, which provides a connection to and a participation in his authority and genius. For these analysts, it is important to believe that they are digging in the sands of the mind at just the spot Freud himself designated, with better tools, larger numbers, perhaps at greater depths, but all as an incremental extension of Freud's initial vision.

This book is based on the premise that psychoanalysis has changed from Freud's day to ours much more radically than is generally acknowledged and that the seeming self-containment of psychoanalysis tends to obscure those changes. The shifts in the world around psychoanalysis have seeped into its concepts and practice and altered both profoundly. What appear as progressive changes, incremental additions to past discoveries are, in a broader sense, pervasive and often radical responses to major shifts in the world in which the participants in psychoanalysis, both analysands and analysts, live, love, work, and struggle.

The lack of full recognition of the radical nature of recent developments in psychoanalytic thinking is a major factor contributing to the motley state of contemporary psychoanalytic theory and practice. Many fragments of the nineteenth-century features of Freud's original contributions remain, alongside his own stunning and often undeveloped innovations, alongside ideas and concerns that he could never have thought or envisioned.

Do recent contributions in psychoanalytic theory and practice constitute a revolution in psychoanalytic thought, or are they merely elaborations of what has gone on before, the incremental extension of a rich tradition? There is virtually nothing in the problems encountered by contemporary psychoanalytic clinicians and the concepts they have generated in grappling with those problems that was not anticipated, in some fashion, by Freud. And every feature of contemporary psychoanalysis can be traced, from its roots in Freud, through the contributions of subsequent generations of analysts, to its distinctive form in the psychoanalysis of our time.

Nevertheless, I portray these developments as revolutions. My purposes are deliberately provocative. I want to emphasize discontinuities because I believe that an excessive preoccupation with traditionalism has impeded the recognition, working on, and working through of the often stunning changes that have occurred in psychoanalytic thought in recent decades. This failure to recognize these discontinuities between psychoanalysis in our time and the psychoanalytic tradition of prior generations serves to allay the dread today's analysts feel about applying their craft to the deep strains of modern living, with its lack of fixed values, its breathtaking social and technological change, the terrors posed by the threat of extinction and self-contamination. For analysts, on a deeply personal level, psychoanalysis, both its theories and its method, offers meaningful hope. Yet the psychoanalytic tradition, for which I have a deep love and respect, is best served by a framework that balances continuities with discontinuities, preservation with change, gratitude for what has preceded with an openness to moving on.

The love affair psychoanalysis has had with its own founder and its own traditions has obscured just how different the psychoanalysis of today is from that of a century ago. Psychoanalysis is a vibrant clinical process that continues to reinvent itself, finding new meanings for its methodology, as the experience and concerns of its participants change and develop. This book is intended as an aid to an increased appreciation of the development of psychoanalysis as a discipline; although set in motion by Freud's seminal discoveries, psychoanalysis is deeply embedded in and shaped by contemporary experience and thought. I want to paint a portrait of contemporary psychoanalytic thinking and practice, emphasizing the meaning of the process for both participants.

In *Object Relations in Psychoanalytic Theory* (1983) Jay Greenberg and I argued that psychoanalysis, over the course of its development, has been oriented around and enriched by a dialectic between two basic and irreconcilable models of mind: (1) a drive model in which mind is envisioned as built out of sexual and aggressive impulses and their derivatives, and (2) a relational model in which mind is envisioned as built out of interactional configurations of self in relation to others. In *Relational Concepts in Psychoanalysis* (1988) I explored various traditions of relational model theorizing on fundamental psychoanalytic problems and concerns, and I suggested ways in which those traditions can be developed and integrated into a comprehensive relational model, rather than the classical drive model. This book is a continuation of that project. The central organizing thread of *Relational Concepts in Psychoanalysis* was the concept of the relational matrix, a broad, metapsychological notion. The central organizing threads of this book are the experiences of hope and dread in both analysand and analyst and the tensions and reconciliations between them throughout the analytic process.

Psychoanalysis is a process involving, most fundamentally, the hopes and dreads of its two participants. I have begun with Sophie's return to analysis, because it is at such transition points that these issues—expectant, optimistic longings and fearful, gripping terrors—stand out most clearly. The chapters that follow consider many different features of the analytic situation and many different levels of analytic thought. I hope to depict psychoanalysis as operating within the complex tension generated by the deeply personal encounter between the analyst and analysand and the hopes and dreads of each.

The portrait of contemporary psychoanalysis I develop in the chapters that follow is not a singular view of an individual figure, but rather a composite, a kind of family album, with a wide cast of characters, all closely related to each other, viewed from different angles, in diverse contexts, for various purposes.

In Part I, I break down Sophie's challenge about what psychoanalysis offers into two closely related but distinct questions: What does the patient need? and What does the analyst know? Answers to these questions constitute two broad areas in contemporary psychoanalytic thought, developed by two different lines of analytic authors who have operated largely independently of each other.

Contributors to the question of what patients need generally do not follow the implications of their answers with a reconsideration of the nature of analysts' knowledge. Conversely, those who look at the question of what analysts know generally do not reformulate the way patient needs are met in analysis. It is the central project of Part I to trace and explore these two areas of recent psychoanalytic thought. I will argue that each by itself is insufficient for a complete vision and demonstrate how their interconnection provides a distinctly new vision of the search for personal meaning in the analytic process.

Part II offers a very different perspective, focusing on the common tools of analysis by exploring the concept of the self—the central, innovative theoretical construct for addressing personal meaning in most areas of recent psychoanalytic thought. The distinctions between true self and false selves, authenticity and inauthenticity, the dialectic between multiple and discontinuous selves and an integral, continuous self—these have been the basic ingredients out of which a distinctly contemporary version of psychoanalysis has been fashioned. The central concerns of classical psychoanalysis—conflicts over sexual and aggressive impulses—have not been discarded but rather relocated, recontextualized within the framework provided by recent contributions on self. Once again my purposes are expository and synthetic. I trace the major, seemingly disjunctive lines of psychoanalytic theorizing on the self and demonstrate how their integration and extension provide a rich and textured scaffolding for psychoanalysis in our time.

Part III provides yet a third angle on current psychoanalytic thought and practice, more along the lines of action photos, entailing a close consideration of the interactive nature of the analytic relationship. I demonstrate that concepts such as "wishes" and "needs," formally thought to reside "inside" the patient, uncovered through the analyst's interpretations, are more usefully thought of as co-created, negotiated in the interaction between self and other. This requires an examination of the analyst's own wishes and needs and their interaction with the analysand's. I explore the way in which two sets of hopes and dreads, the analysand's and the analyst's, are engaged and the way in which their tensions and reconciliations become the medium within which essential change takes place.

I

THE ANALYTIC SITUATION

1

What Does the Patient Need?

A REVOLUTION IN THEORY

[The ideal termination of analysis has been reached when] the analyst has had such a far-reaching influence on the patient that no further change could be expected to take place in him if his analysis were continued. It is as though it were possible by means of analysis to attain a level of absolute psychical normality—a level, moreover, which we could feel confident would be able to remain stable, as though, perhaps, we had succeeded in resolving every one of the patient's repressions and in filling in all the gaps in his memory.
  —Sigmund Freud, "Analysis Terminable and Interminable"

We are poor indeed if we are only sane.
  —D. W. Winnicott, "Primitive Emotional Development"

Freud developed the psychoanalytic method in the context of a particular intellectual and cultural milieu, which looked to science and its twin beacons of rationality and objectivity to provide the truest and most meaningful perspective on human experience and the world around us. In prior centuries, religion had been the dominant source of orientation and meaning. For those who lived in the nineteenth century, however, "God," as Nietzsche put it, "is dead," and the demise of religion as a reliable, credible perspective brought humankind face to face with the problem of nihilism, the depletion of meaning. Science provided the most powerful and compelling hedge against nihilism. God may not inhabit the universe, but science provides us with the tools to know its secrets, its underlying structure. In the dazzling explosion of technological proficiency in the nineteenth century, the belief was nearly inescapable that the sure knowledge provided by science, and the control it granted us over the world around us and in us, would lead to deeper understanding, wisdom, and a better life.

Copernicus's heliocentric model began to locate us more accurately in deep space; advances in geology placed us in the deep time of the earth's history; and the Darwinian revolution positioned the advent of the human species in the gradual evolution of animal life. Scientific truth had replaced the religious egocentricity that had located humans at the beginning and in the middle of things. We may be latecomers and on the periphery, science told us, but we can see into the underlying structure of things and thereby discern their functions.

Freud, as one of the foremost progressive intellectuals of his day, was very much steeped in this scientific vision. He regarded religion as emotionally compelling, but an infantile, regressive, divisive force.

> Our best hope for the future is that intellect—the scientific spirit, reason—may in the process of time establish a dictatorship in the mental life of man. The nature of reason is a guarantee that afterwards it will not fail to give man's emotional impulses and what is determined by them the position they deserve. But the common compulsion exercised by such a dominance of reason will prove to be the strongest uniting bond among men and lead the way to further unions. Whatever, like religion's prohibition against thought, opposes such a development, is a danger for the future of mankind. (Freud, 1933, pp. 171–72)

In many respects, Freud's genius transcended the limits of his time. He was interested in all aspects of culture, intrigued by the dimensions of human experience that Bettelheim and others have described as "spiritual," and his case descriptions are moving literary portraits and adventures. Nevertheless, the authority that Freud attributed to the knowledge and the interpretations of the analyst clearly derived from his conviction that psychoanalysis was a subsystem within the larger scientific enterprise of his day.

Freud's understanding of virtually every feature of the analytic process was informed by this vision. Underneath the surface of experience is a hidden world of unconscious impulses and fantasies, vestiges from our bestial, prehuman, deep past. Psychoanalysis is a "depth-psychology," its instrument, the psychoanalytic method: "The intellect and the mind are objects for scientific research in exactly the same way as any non-human things." Psychoanalysis is a "specialty science," and "its contribution to science lies precisely in having extended research to the mental field" (Freud, 1933, p. 159). The psychoanalytic method allows us to see beneath the appearance of things and the surface of the mind; by uncovering unconscious thoughts, through the generation of insight, psychoanalysis can transform the mind's unconscious underlying structures. As Freud wrote to Wilhelm Fliess at the beginning of his work with Dora, she was "smoothly opening for the available collection of passkeys" (quoted in Gay, 1988, p. 246).

In contrast to Jung, whose religiosity informed his emphasis on psycho*synthesis,* Freud felt that no synthesis was necessary. (In fact, Freud launched a full-scale attack on religion as a form of infantilism in *The Future of an Illusion* [1927].) To Freud, analysis meant breaking things up into their constitutive elements, taking them apart, grasping their hidden structure. The ego automatically reintegrates itself on a less conflictual, more rational basis: "Where id was, there ego shall be."[1] And rationality does not just integrate the individual but draws humankind together, overcoming the isolating effects of infantilism and primary process mentation.

Through analysis, both the hopes and dreads that the patient brings into the analytic situation are revealed to be based on unconscious infantile fantasies, on illusions of one sort or another. Hopes derive from infantile impulses for oral, anal, and oedipal gratifications and triumphs. Dreads derive from fantasied punishment (particularly castration) for forbidden wishes. Hopes and dreads are transformed, through the analytic process, into rational understanding.

Freud's notion that the ego automatically reintegrates newly analyzed material on a higher, more rational basis was an important component in his basic vision of the analytic process. It made it possible for him to regard the personal participation of the analyst—the analyst's own values, feelings, and beliefs—as unrelated to the analysis. The patient's libidinal energy is released, through the analyst's interpretations, from its entrapment in infantile conflicts. The ego, which operates in terms of rationality ("secondary process"), is now free to employ that energy in more pragmatic, realistic endeavors. The idiosyncratic features—the personality—of the analyst have no influence on the process. This issue of the analyst's personal influence is one of the key features of the analytic process that has been reconceptualized and struggled with in contemporary analytic literature.

Freud was not a particularly cheerful fellow, and his version of the rational, scientific person is not an especially happy person. But that person is stronger, more grounded, more aligned with reality, even if it is a somber reality. "But you will be able to convince yourself," Freud assures us in 1895, "that much will be gained if we succeed in transforming your hysterical misery into common unhappiness. With a mental life that has been restored to health you will be better armed against that unhappiness" (p. 305).

The ambiance of the analytic situation in its classical phase and in some versions of its current "orthodox" practice is, consistent with Freud's sober rationalism, one of abstinence and renunciation. The process of analytic change is often compared with prototypical renunciations such as weaning and mourning, with the patient as the dieter or reformed smoker who, after a period of self-denial, may lose the craving. This renunciatory vision underlies Freud's technical emphasis on the analyst's need to "persuade" the patient to "abandon" particular instinctual strivings (Aron, 1988, p. 10). Freud repeatedly warns the analyst to induce the patient to "adopt our conviction . . . of the impossibility of conducting life on the pleasure principle" (1919, p. 159).

To Freud, renunciation and insight go hand in hand. Renunciation is the price the patient pays for the release analysis provides from the isolating, frustrating, conflictual clutches of the remnants of infantile mental life. The scientific worldview demands, as Freud sees it, a submission to the truth and rejection of illusions. Donald Kaplan has vividly captured this stoical, hard edge to Freud's vision of the analytic process and life in general.

> If people must suffer the loss of their infantile hopes and fantasies, then they should suffer for the fact of this loss rather than for distortions of it in aesthetic bonuses, the empty promises of religion, and the negligible protections of social orders. Unremitting toil in the service of science—naked means toward real ends—was Freud's alternative in *Civilization and Its Discontents,* at least for himself. Any other kind of life was ensnared by illusion, which was but a small step up from neurosis. (1985, p. 291)

In many respects, Sophie's fear of psychoanalysis as a threat to her romantic enthusiasm is appropriate and discerning. If she had read about Freud's treatment of the Wolfman, Sophie would have known that Freud felt free to dispense advice and manage the Wolfman's courtship of his fiancée (1918). If Sophie had read Freud's paper "On Narcissism" (1914), she would have been even more concerned, because Freud viewed romantic love, in particular, as a condition shot through with illusion and irrationality. Romantic love draws on the original pool of primary narcissism, "overvaluing" its objects, in a manner akin to the madman's megalomaniacal overvaluation of self, thereby placing the lover in considerable psychological danger. In this framework, the cold, clear rational light of psychoanalysis is as much of a threat to the narcissistic and oedipal embellishments of Sophie's love as is the striking of midnight to Cinderella's finery. Sophie too could end up in the company of a pumpkin.

Is this a caricature of classical psychoanalysis? Is Freud's somber rationalism merely a personal characteristic, extraneous and irrelevant to the traditional theory of analytic technique? Unquestionably, the emotional tone in which an analysis takes place is a highly personal matter, and there is an enormous variability in the way in which different clinicians conduct analysis.[2]

However, I am not talking just about emotional tone here but about fundamental beliefs—the premise that the analyst knows better, sees more maturely and deeply into the patient's difficulties and into the very nature of life—the premise that the analyst's vision is a rational antidote to the chaotic, infantile, illusion-bound hopes and dreads of the patient's emotional inner world. The analyst has privileged access into the patient's experience; the analyst knows what is real and what is not. To disengage from the compelling clutches of infantile experience and to haul himself toward maturity, the patient needs an infusion of reality in the form of insight.

The belief in the greater objectivity and maturity of the analyst's perspective was necessitated by Freud's deep faith in science and is inextricably bound up with his basic understanding of the nature of the analytic method. The patient, driven by unconscious fantasies to which, by definition, she has no access, is in no position to understand or deal constructively with what is troubling her. The analyst's interpretations provide access into and a blueprint of the patient's unconscious experience. Infantile fantasies are exposed, reexamined, and processed through mature, rational thought: "Where id was, there ego shall be." Darkness is transformed into light; infantilism into a more rational, more mature vision; and the patient gives up and puts away childish things.

The deep conviction that it is the content of the analyst's interpretations that opens the doors of repression—the objective naming, the rational surveillance of the unconscious—is nowhere more evident than in what is to us today the ghastly practice of Freud and other early analysts analyzing their own children. (See Gay, 1988; Grosskurth, 1988.)

In our current psychoanalytic milieu, such an action would border on the criminal, but it would be unfair for us to measure this practice in terms of our times. Rather, this practice dramatically reveals the sharp differences in the meaning of the analytic process in Freud's world and in our own. In the early decades of analytic practice, the message itself was thought to be powerful and transformative. The patient's experience was shot through with the distorting lenses of subjectivity; only the analytic method provided "correct" understanding; it did not matter much who delivered the message.

Contemporary critics sometimes accuse classical psychoanalysis of an inherent authoritarianism. This accusation is unfair. The principle that the patient's difficulties stem from unconscious fantasies leading to irrationality and distortions that are subjected to the correcting influence of the analyst's more objective knowledge was both reasonable and humane within the cultural and historical context of Freud's world. In that context it made sense to consider the patient's difficulties in living as deriving from the impossible hopes and fictitious dreads of childhood, which had, for various reasons, remained intact and embedded within a chronological maturity. It was compelling and humane to feel that what the patient needed was an expansion of the capacity to reason clearly, to dispel illusory hopes and dreads through rational thought. Only as our faith in reason as a singular and linear, inexorable and progressive force has been shaken by contemporary experience has the analyst's claim to greater clarity and objectivity been reconsidered on conceptual, moral, and political grounds.[3]

FROM FREUD'S WORLD TO OUR WORLD

The cultural and intellectual context within which the psychoanalytic method is practiced has changed dramatically since Freud's day. While we are still living in a time of extraordinary and awe-inspiring scientific discoveries, our era is postscientistic—we no longer can maintain a deep confidence that science, objectivity, and technological competence themselves can serve as an orienting framework providing meaning and understanding. Some of the successes of science have come to haunt us, from the awesome destructive power of nuclear arms, to the massive spawning of toxic waste as a by-product of the industrial revolution, to the tangled problems associated with overpopulation and longer life in the age of modern medicine. The key role of science in generating the threats of extinction and self-contamination, the shadow under which we all now live, makes the fully sanguine faith in science held by progressive thinkers of Freud's day a psychological impossibility. Freud could speak, with perfectly defensible optimism, of mankind's "progressive control over the forces of Nature" (1933, p. 177). To those of us living today, with ozone depletion, the greenhouse effect, and other features of the ecological crisis, nature seems a more formidable, less yielding, potentially retaliatory adversary. Our aspirations to control the forces of nature now seem less optimism than a possibly fatal hubris. The problem of nihilism has returned.

Most people of our day still believe in rationality, but the rationalism of Freud and his contemporaries, the faith that rationality places us in a powerful, unique, and irresistible position vis-à-vis the rest of the universe, is no longer possible. Compare Freud's vision of scientific progress discussed earlier with that of a more contemporary scientist, Andrei Sakharov, who, to be sure, also believed in reason, but could make much less ambitious claims for the power and scope of our rationality. Interestingly, Sakharov evokes the "sacred," although not in a strictly religious sense.

> Other civilizations, perhaps more successful ones, may exist an infinite number of times on the preceding and following pages of the Book of the Universe. Yet we should not minimize our sacred endeavors in the world, where, like faint glimmers in the dark, we have emerged for a moment from the nothingness of unconsciousness into material experience. We must make good the demands of reason and create a life worthy of ourselves and of the goals we only dimly perceive. (quoted in Remnick, 1990, pp. 3–4)

The very advances in scientific knowledge themselves have led us to an appreciation of the profound limits of human understanding. First, we have begun to comprehend the enormity of the universe. As the astronomer Timothy Ferris has put it:

> We will never understand the universe in detail; it is just too big and varied for that. If we possessed an atlas of our galaxy that devoted but a single page to each star system in the Milky Way (so that the sun and all its planets were crammed on one page), that atlas would run to more than 10 million volumes of ten thousand pages each. It would take a library the size of Harvard's to house the atlas, and merely to flip through it, at the rate of a page per second, would require over ten thousand years. Add the details of planetary cartography, potential extraterrestrial biology, the subtleties of the scientific principles

involved, and the historical dimensions of change, and it becomes clear that we are never going to learn more than a tiny fraction of the story of our galaxy alone—and there are a hundred billion more galaxies. (1988, p. 383)

Second, we have begun to recognize the embeddedness of human understanding in the very phenomena we are trying to understand. We have become clear as to the impossibility of ever standing outside of nature so as to grasp and describe objectively its underlying structure. Concepts such as quantum indeterminacy, the "incompleteness theorem," the "uncertainty principle," the mystery and inaccessibility of time prior to the big bang—all these suggest that the universe itself does not behave in the accessible, predictable, controllable way Freud and his contemporaries assumed.

Third, the highly abstract, abstrusely mathematical nature of the key concepts of modern physics, impossible to grasp in any direct, intuitive fashion—concepts such as curved space/time continua, antimatter, and hyperdimensionality—removes modern science from the direct, experiential grasp of the average person, making it much more like the religion than the science of Freud's day. Only a couple of decades ago, it was easy to contrast the religious worldview, embracing and enshrining the mysterious and the unknown, with the scientific worldview, illuminating dark corners and solemnly and relentlessly sweeping away the cobwebs of primitive ignorance. Today's physicists spend much time revering the mysterious, and the modern scientific sensibility is less hard and sober than abstract and aesthetic. If today's science is a solution to the problem of nihilism, it is a solution not aimed at full, clear understanding and control but one of appreciation and awe.

As our understanding of the nature and limitations of scientific investigation changed, so has the place of science within western culture in general been transformed. Human knowledge is no longer regarded as an incremental march toward a singular, complete understanding. In the "postmodernism" revolution in thought that has pervaded all the major intellectual disciplines, all knowledge, including scientific knowledge, is regarded as perspectival, not incremental; constructed, not discovered; inevitably rooted in a particular historical and cultural setting, not singular and additive; thoroughly contextual, not universal and absolute.

What does all this have to do with psychoanalysis? Because of these profound changes in the world around us and in us, today we experience the psychoanalytic process in a fashion very different from Freud and his contemporaries, even though we often describe it in the same language. For Freud, psychoanalysis was embedded in the broad, invigorating, reassuring scaffolding of the scientific worldview. He could draw clear and compelling parallels between the analytic process and the child's movement from infantilism to maturity and, ultimately, mankind's gradual evolution from ignorance and primitivism to reason and enlightenment. That scaffolding does not sustain us in the same way it did for Freud and his contemporaries, cannot sustain us; this fact has, in some sense, stranded psychoanalysis, unmoored it from the context that gave it its original meaning. Those who think of analysis in ways similar to our analytic ancestors seem to most of us today more like cultists than scientists.

What is inspiring about psychoanalysis today is not the renunciation of illusion in the hope of joining a common, progressively realistic knowledge and control, but rather the hope of fashioning a personal reality that feels authentic and enriching. This goal does not suggest that contemporary psychoanalysis is individualistic and narcissistic, valuing only private meaning and concerns at the expense of connections to others and society at large. (Many currents within contemporary psychoanalytic thought—object relations theories, ego psychology, interpersonal psychoanalysis—place great emphasis on the importance of relationships with others and the embeddedness of the individual in a social context.) However, whereas Freud could look to rationality as a natural bridge among individuals, reason itself can no longer serve that function. The hope inspired by psychoanalysis in our time is grounded in personal meaning, not rational consensus. The bridge supporting connections with others is not built out of a rationality superseding fantasy and the imagination, but out of feelings experienced as real, authentic, generated from the inside, rather than imposed externally, in close relationship with fantasy and the imagination.

FROM RENUNCIATION TO PERSONAL MEANING

Freud's typical patient was the man or woman otherwise adapted to his or her culture and historical time except for the intrusion of unwanted, often bizarre, symptomatology, such as the Ratman's obsessive fantasies and Dora's hysterical cough. The typical patient in today's psychoanalytic case descriptions is a man or woman, often without bizarre symptoms, whose very adaptation to his or her culture and historical time is regarded as the problem, not the solution.[4]

The type of character pathology most modern analysts are concerned with is seen in people who may be very well adapted to their society, but who are missing something fundamental in their experience of living. They lack something in the very way in which they generate and assign meaning to their experience; these are patients whose subjectivity itself is understood to be basically awry.

Consider Freud's discussion, late in his life, of the goals of analysis in relation to termination. He establishes two conditions that should have been generally fulfilled:

> first, that the patient shall no longer be suffering from his symptoms and shall have overcome his anxieties and his inhibitions; and secondly, that the analyst shall judge that so much repressed material has been made conscious, so much that was unintelligible has been explained, and so much internal resistance conquered, that there is no need to fear a repetition of the pathological processes concerned. (1937, p. 219)

Freud then comments that "external difficulties" may preclude reaching this goal, in which case the analysis would be considered "incomplete." He goes on, in the passage serving as the first epigraph to this chapter, to suggest a much more "ambitious" goal for analysis, a goal that every analyst has likely been able to attain in a few cases: "It is as though it were possible by means of analysis to attain a level of *absolute psychical normality*" (1937, p. 219; emphasis added). For Freud, the goals of analysis are the removal of symptoms by making the unconscious conscious and the attainment of a degree of rational "control over instinct" (1937, p. 229) that makes the formation of future symptoms unlikely. "Absolute psychical normality" is an ideal defined by complete understanding, absence of all repressions and amnesias.

Erich Fromm anticipated the current, strikingly different kind of concern with character and normality more than fifty years ago in his concept of the "marketing personality" (1947). In Fromm's perspective, a blend of psychoanalysis and Marxism, the modern personality is shaped by the necessity for advanced industrial society to generate perpetually changing consumer tastes and fashions; personal meaning and value are determined by social status and material worth.[5]

The most influential recent psychoanalytic account of the pathology of subjectivity has been D. W. Winnicott's concept of the "false self" personality. Although working purely from psychoanalytic data and the observation of mothers and babies, Winnicott arrived at a depiction of the false self personality that is remarkably similar to Fromm's more sociologically derived marketing personality. Winnicott, like Fromm, sees the key problem as the generation of meaning and the organization of experience around compliance and adaptation to externality, what is presented or suggested from the outside, rather than from genuine internal desire or need. Freud's basic conceptual building block, the instinctual impulse, is replaced in Winnicott's theorizing with the "personal impulse," which may or may not be expressed through bodily needs and events. (We consider some further implications of this difference in chapter 5.) Psychoanalysis, for Winnicott, is a treatment aimed at the texture of experience, its richness, its felt reality, rather than at functional capacity. Sanity alone provides a shadowy, empty existence. The well-adjusted person may be missing the central features of experience that mark one's life as a personal life, felt as real, valuable, meaningful. "The false self," Winnicott argues, "however well set up, lacks something and that something is the essential central element of creative originality" (1960, p. 152).

Authors from many different theoretical traditions have become interested in the problem of pseudonormality as, perhaps, the central clinical issue of our time. Some have coined new diagnostic tags: the "normopath" (McDougall, 1985, p. 156) and the "normatic personality" (Bollas, 1987, p. 137). Many authors, especially those influenced by object relations theories and self psychology, discuss what they understand to be disturbances in the development, structuralization, and exercise of authentic, personal subjectivity. What all these perspectives on pseudonormality have in common is a shift from Freud's view of humans as drive-regulating animals to a more contemporary view of humans as meaning-generating animals.[6]

Consider Sophie's difficulties in living. She had a variety of symptoms, including sexual inhibitions, anxiety attacks, and depression. She had a host of conflicts related to sexual and aggressive impulses traceable back to early childhood. However, we came to understand her struggles as involving something more central and pervasive than her symptoms or her conflicts over impulses. In some fundamental way, she had never viewed her life as her own, to be shaped and valued according to her own interests, desires, and goals. Her own experience was hostage to her mother's vision of the world; the mother's image of the most desirable model of adaptation had become Sophie's own vision because there were no safe alternatives. Although Sophie had many specific conflicts, the central problem seemed to be the more pervasive fashion in which she generated all her experiences, always with a focus on caution, remaining her mother's daughter, rather than freely and spontaneously expressing and exploring her own experiences.

Psychopathology, in the contemporary psychoanalytic literature, is often defined not in terms of pieces of conflictual, unwanted fragments intruding into experience; psychopathology is defined by a missing center or lack of richness throughout experience. What the patient needs is not a rational reworking of unconscious infantile fantasies; what the patient needs is a revitalization and expansion of his own capacity to generate experience that feels real, meaningful, and valuable.[7] Although this shift has evolved within psychoanalysis and is generally described simply as a development within the field, it clearly reflects the changing cultural and intellectual context within which we are living. It is part of a search for a new context of meanings to house the psychoanalytic process.

Freud's clinical activity involved interpreting and thereby encouraging the clarification and renunciation of the patient's subjectively embedded, conflictually rent psychic reality. A richer experience of personal subjectivity was the goal, but it was arrived at through what was assumed to be the objective interpretation of unconscious processes.

Analysts today speak less frequently of clarification and renunciation and more often about the importance of accepting, "containing," "mirroring," "holding," embellishing the patient's subjectively embedded psychic reality. Now the psychoanalytic process is described less in terms of correction, illumination, or renunciation of infantile thought and more in terms of confirmation, evocation, expansion, and reconciliation. If the goal of psychoanalysis in Freud's day was rational understanding and control (secondary process) over fantasy-driven, conflictual impulses (primary process), the goal of psychoanalysis in our day is most often thought about in terms of the establishment of a richer, more authentic sense of identity.[8] Although painful symptoms may be the first sign of deeper troubles, the patient's most fundamental difficulties concern the overall quality and texture of experience. There is less interest in discrete unconscious fantasies of early childhood and more interest in such questions as: How does life come to feel real? significant? valuable? What are the processes through which one develops a sense of self as vital and authentic? How are these processes derailed, resulting in a sense of self as depleted, false, shallow?

If Freud's analytic situation consists of a patient caught up in the push and pull of emotions encountering the objective scrutiny of a more rational observer, the contemporary analytic situation is generally depicted as consisting of a patient with a collapsed, weakened, or absent center of personal experience encountering a more receptive, more facilitating human environment. Many patients are now understood to be suffering not from conflictual infantile passions that can be tamed and transformed through reason and understanding but from stunted personal development. Deficiencies in caregiving in the earliest years are understood to have contributed to interfering with the emergence of a fully centered, integrated sense of self, of the patient's own subjectivity. What the patient needs is not clarification or insight so much as a sustained experience of being seen, personally engaged, and, basically, valued and cared about. The "objective" interpretation, the very curative agent in the classical model, can in this view become the instrument for a repetition of the original trauma. Rather, what today's analysis provides is the opportunity to freely discover and playfully explore one's own subjectivity, one's own imagination.

Freud was very suspicious of the imagination, which he linked with the illusion of neurosis, religion, primitive cultures, immaturity, and infantalism. According to Freud, "experience teaches us that the world is no nursery" (1933, p. 168). For many contemporary authors, however, psychopathology results from a premature expulsion from the nursery, not a futile effort to extend it, and psychoanalysis provides a sheltered return, a "new beginning" (Balint, 1968).

Freud's analytic method was aimed toward the rational experience of the capacity "to love and to work." Contemporary authors write over and over again about the capacity to play, about creativity and authentic personal expression. Peter Gay has noted that despite his deep love of culture, Freud felt disdain toward and suspiciousness of creative artists: "Shouting out society's secrets, they are little better than necessary licensed gossips, fit only to reduce the tensions that have accumulated in the public's mind" (Gay, 1988, 322). Many contemporary authors glorify the artistic process; creativity, not normality, has become the paradigm of mental health.

"IN ORDER TO LULL HER INTO SECURITY . . . "

The literature of psychoanalysis is vast, and to substantiate fully broad changes in the discussion of clinical cases would require a volume in its own right. Nevertheless, case material provides the most vivid demonstration of the kind of shift in sensibility we are exploring. So, selectivity is inevitable.

Consider a piece of clinical material from a well-known paper, written by Richard Sterba in 1934 and entitled "The Fate of the Ego in Analytic Therapy." Sterba made important contributions to the classical literature. I have chosen this example because his paper was considered modern for its time and a forerunner of the technical developments in Freudian ego psychology in the 1940s and 1950s. Also, Sterba presented this example of his analytic work precisely because of what he felt was its very ordinariness.

Sterba presents the material as a sketch of a "fairly typical transference-situation such as arose at the beginning of one of my analyses" (p. 363). A woman begins her analysis with a resistant attitude: She was "obstinately silent," had a strongly negative attitude toward the analyst, and constantly threatened to end the treatment. We are told nothing of why this woman is seeking treatment, what she wants or how she sees her difficulties. While this may be a function of the highly selective purpose for which Sterba is using the material, it seems consistent somehow with his attitude toward the patient. Clearly, her own hopes and dreads on entering treatment are not very important; the analyst very quickly determines the reasons for her initial resistance, her central problems, and the course of her subsequent analysis.

The patient spent the first two hours supplying "meagre associations" in "obvious ill-humour" (p. 367). At the end of the second hour, she asked if the analyst had a "cloakroom where she could change her clothes as they were all crumpled after she had lain on the sofa for an hour" (p. 367). She explained in her third session that she had been going to meet a woman friend who would surely wonder whether the wrinkled condition of the patient's dress indicated that she had been rushing from a sexual liaison.

With this revelation, Sterba has all the information he needs to understand this patient's initial hesitance about treatment and to begin to help her understand it as well. "The next thing to do was to explain to the patient the meaning of her defence" (p. 367). Her meager associations and ill humor were a defense, Sterba explains, against her underlying sexual interest in him, the negative feelings and actions shielding her against the positive feelings and erotic intentions. The patient apparently did not immediately accept this interpretation, and it had to be repeated several times. Even then she could grasp it only intermittently, and there was backsliding into efforts to "act out" her instinctual impulses. However, with repeated explanations, "it gradually became possible to enlarge these islands of intellectual contemplation or observation at the expense of the process of acting the unconscious impulses out" (p. 368).

Some time afterward, Sterba reports, an extraordinary memory was revealed. I provide his full account, because of the striking contrast between the dramatic content and the dry tone of the presentation. The memory concerns

> her love for a physician to whom she was frequently taken during her fifth year on account of enlarged tonsils. On each occasion he looked into her mouth, without touching the tonsils, afterwards giving her some sweets and always being kind and friendly. Her parents had instituted these visits in order to lull her into security for the operation to come. One day, when she trustfully let the doctor look into her mouth again, he inserted a gag and, without giving any narcotic or local anaesthetic, removed the unsuspecting child's tonsils. For her this was a bitter disillusionment and never again could she be persuaded to go to see him. (p. 363)

With this memory, Sterba has all the material he needs to chart the basic course of this woman's subsequent analysis. He knows what she needs, and he has total conviction concerning his knowledge. The conclusions, which he presents as if they were mundane and obvious (although to us they may seem remarkable), are as follows. Although this actual experience with the doctor probably had some impact, its meaning was determined by unconscious sexual fantasies from early childhood in relation to the patient's father. "It is hardly necessary for me to point out that the discovery of this infantile experience of the patient with the physician was merely a preliminary to the real task of the analyst, which was to bring into consciousness her experiences with her father and especially her masochistic phantasies relating to him" (p. 368).

The subsequent course of this analysis consists of Sterba persuading the patient of the truth of his conclusion, which is almost too obvious to mention to his readers. Sterba regards the emotional importance of the experience with the physician as deriving from the double use to which the patient was able to put the memory: both as a way of representing her unconscious and conflictual erotic fantasies toward her father and as a rationale for avoiding the threat of revealing those fantasies that the analysis represented.[9]

Sterba describes his interpretations of these processes so that the ego can be brought into harmony with, corrected by reference to, "reality," as represented by his own understanding:

> dissociation had to be induced in the ego, as to separate out of the processes of dramatic enactment an island of intellectual contempla-

tion, from which the patient could perceive that her behavior was determined by her infantile experiences in relation to her father. This, naturally, only proved possible after prolonged therapeutic work. (pp. 368–99)

From Sterba's point of view, the patient's perception of the underlying, infantile fantasies and longings in relation to her father is the heart of the therapeutic action of the analysis. The discovery of these wishes and a rational working through and eventual renunciation of them will set her free.

The clarity of the presentation and the dramatic nature of Sterba's clinical tale highlight the difference between the meaning of the analytic process for the analyst of the 1930s and for many analysts today. One of the most interesting features of Sterba's case is that it raises many of the same questions that have been voiced in relation to that important psychoanalytic classic, Freud's Dora case (1905), without some of the confounding variables. Dora was a teenager who was used by her father as currency in sexual barter for another man's wife. The core of the problem for Freud was Dora's unconscious sexual fantasies and impulses toward her father, not the profound betrayal perpetuated upon her by those she trusted most deeply. Freud spent several months accumulating evidence and trying to convince Dora of her unconscious fantasies, at which point she precipitously left treatment.

Freud has been accused of poor technique and bad timing. Some have faulted him for not acknowledging the reality of Dora's experience of betrayal at the hands of her parents. Others regard the treatment as illustrating and perpetuating the victimization of women at the hands of men, including Freud. Still others have argued that Freud acted out the countertransference in his own exploitation of the patient in hot pursuit of confirmation for his theories.

Sterba's case offers us an identical clinical approach to material, which is uncomplicated by some of the features of the Dora case. There is no reason to think the patient's gender was a factor at all, at least as far as the initial trauma goes. It could just as easily have been a boy taken to the physician for enlarged tonsils. There is no evidence of the kind of countertransference Freud may have been caught up in—the analyst as detective looking for confirmation of his own brand-new and controversial theories. On the contrary, Sterba presents himself as a workmanlike analytic practitioner processing unexceptional clinical material. (Of course, Sterba's personal investment in demonstrating the correctness of the theories he inherited from Freud must be taken into account.) Finally, there is no clear evidence of actual betrayal on the part of the parents. This approach to surgery with children was not uncommon around the turn of the century, when Sterba's patient was operated upon.[10] Let us assume that the physician, with great authority, instructed the parents not to forewarn the child of the operation, and that all the adults involved genuinely believed that such an approach would minimize the trauma and was truly in the best interests of the child. (Certainly parents who have had to decide where to position themselves when some horrifying medical procedure is performed on their child can identify with the dilemma of the parents of Sterba's patient.)

The Dora case is easy to criticize through the lens of modern sensibilities. However, to wrench this treatment from its own conceptual context is to misunderstand it. When the two cases are taken together, it becomes clearer that Freud and Sterba were operating out of an internally consistent model of the analytic process and, on a broader level, a set of premises concerning human knowledge and subjectivity. The problem with these cases is not faulty treatment, but a model of the process that made sense in their day but no longer works in ours.

The approach common to Freud and Sterba's is completely consistent with what they believed the patient really needs. In their framework, psychopathology is generated by the repression of unconscious infantile fantasy; health is attained by the uncovering of these repressed fantasies and, as Sterba puts it, correcting them "by reference to reality" (1934, p. 367). Surely, Dora and Sterba's patient were mistreated, the former avoidably and, perhaps, criminally, the latter perhaps unavoidably and only according to customary medical practice at that time. Neither Freud nor Sterba missed the mistreatment; they did not think it mattered as far as the analytic process was concerned. In the traditional psychoanalytic view, what really matters most deeply, what will determine the patient's chance for subsequent mental health, what is most crucial in terms of both practical as well as humane considerations, is that the patient becomes aware of her infantile sexual and aggressive fantasies and subjects them to rational, realistic control.

Yet, for us, there is something wrong with this picture. Viewed from a contemporary analytic perspective, Sterba's assumptions about both his patient's needs and his own knowledge seem questionable.

To Sterba, his patient's horror of the actual event of surgery without anesthesia by a physician she had been "lulled" by her parents into trusting is less significant for her than her unconscious sexual fantasies toward her father. What seems missing to our contemporary ear is any concern for the patient's relation to her own experience, the meaning of the event to her. She surely needs, we would assume, to be able to relate to her own experience as real, as meaningful, as valued and valuable. Hence we would want to know: How did the patient come to understand and process this extraordinary event of her childhood? What is her understanding of why there was no anesthesia? Where were her parents during all this? Did they lull her into other similar situations? She certainly seems to have come by her wariness honestly! Was her cautiousness in relation to her analyst an unusual, discrete displacement from the past, or a general character style? What was she doing in analysis? Was this treatment for her, or was she being lulled once again? Did she experience the analyst's aggressively interpretive approach, his conviction and certainty, his efforts to remove her diseased infantile thoughts as a reenactment of her childhood experience with the physician? How did she organize this experience into the longings and fears, hopes and dreads of her childhood and subsequent adulthood? These questions, so obvious and important to the contemporary reader, for whom the meaning of experience to the patient is central, do not seem important to Sterba or to Freud before him, with their faith in the transformative power of reason, supplied by the analyst's interpretations. This difference highlights the broad shift in understanding what the patient needs from Freud's day to ours.

Those who do not regard classical psychoanalysis as undergoing or needing to undergo a revolutionary change argue that the problem with Freud's approach (for example, in the Dora case) is not in his understanding of the patient and what she needs but in the whole area of tact and timing of interpretations. One could certainly make the same argument about Sterba. Perhaps the key to his patient's mental health did lie in her gaining access to and rational control over her unconscious masochistic fantasies in relation to her father; but today's analyst practicing good analytic technique would empathize with her plight, the trauma of her experience with the physician, and break the news slowly to her.

Defenders of the classical approach, one very different from the perspective I develop here, offer an alternative understanding of the apparent misfit between much of the classical literature and the clinical problems and sensibilities of our time. In their view, the problem is not in the theory per se, not in the understanding of what the patient needs, but rather in the way that understanding is presented to the patient, a failure to consider "the art of analysis" (Grossman, 1982, p. 931).[11]

According to this perspective, the theory employed by Freud and Sterba (based on the premise that what the patient needs is a rational reworking and renunciation of infantile wishes and fantasies) is still wholly suitable to contemporary psychoanalytic practice. What needs modernization is the delivery. Freud and Sterba rightfully regarded the patient's subjective experience, her sense of meaning and value, as illusory and unimportant, to be replaced by the analyst's rational perspective; what they did not understand was that the patient can be persuaded of this only gradually and artfully.

In my view, psychoanalysis has been undergoing not merely a modernization of its delivery system but a fundamental shift in focus. Freud and Sterba were not clumsy; rather they did not believe that attention to the patient's sense of meaning and value mattered. But in psychoanalysis as practiced in our world, the patient's sense of meaning and value does matter. The articulation of unconscious fantasies is still important but no longer sufficient; what has become central is the emergence, development, and enrichment of the patient's sense of subjective meaning. The problem is not just in in the artistry through which psychoanalysis is applied; psychoanalysis is a method whose meanings have changed radically.

VIEWS OF AUTHENTIC SUBJECTIVITY

Indications of the revolution in theorizing about what the patient needs can be found in many areas and in many forms throughout the contemporary psychoanalytic literature. Its clearest manifestation is in the work of those authors who have had the most dramatic impact on contemporary psychoanalytic thought, those whose work seems to have been most inspirational for current theoreticians and clinicians: D. W. Winnicott, Wilfred Bion, Heinz Kohut, and Jacques Lacan, and, in recent years, such writers as Hans Loewald, Thomas Ogden, Jessica Benjamin, and Christopher Bollas. Each of these authors has, in one form or another, radically reconceptualized the essence of psychoanalysis from Freud's remedy of exposing, mastering, and renouncing infantile longings to a more broadly conceived project involving a reclamation and revitalization of the patient's experience of self, the healing of disordered subjectivity. The contemporary psychoanalytic project would not be possible without the revolutionary contribution of Freud and the tools he bequeathed to us for exploring personal experience. However, analysts today are using his tools in a way Freud himself could not have imagined, with the goal of not merely making the unconscious conscious, but making personal experience more real and deeply meaning-ful.[12]

While there is no uniformity among psychoanalysts practicing today, there are common threads in the visions of the most innovative recent theorists. Because all these authors are concerned, in their own ways, with preserving a sense of continuity with the prior classical tradition, it is easy to miss just how radically different is the way they envision the psychoanalytic process from the psychoanalysis practiced by Freud and his contemporaries.

Whereas Freud was after clarity, explanation, and insight, contempo-rary analytic authors stress ambiguity, enrichment, and meaning. The goal is not clear understanding, but the ability to generate experience felt as real, important, and distinctively one's own. It is not that classical rationalism has been replaced by an irrationalism. Rational thought and the clarification of conflicts are still very much part of contemporary analytic work. But they are no longer at the heart of it. Confusion is now equally valued, the sort of creative disorganization and ambiguity that results from the ability to suspend judgment, premature under-standing, and forced clarity. A sampling of the writers who have had the greatest impact on current analytic sensibilities reveals this common shift in vision.

Winnicott's notion of "transitional experiencing" is a description of the way in which a naturally good-enough parent provides a crucial sort of experience for the young child. The child invests an object—the tradi-tional teddy bear, for example—with special significance. The child ex-periences the teddy bear not as a toy like other toys, but as an extension of the child himself and, at the same time, a part of the mother as well. The child feels he has actually created the teddy bear and controls it completely.

Winnicott points to the crucial importance of the parent not challeng-ing the specialness of the teddy bear (by a forced washing, for example). The very ambiguity of the status of the toy (part of the child, part of the mother; an extension of the child's mind, an object in the real world) al-lows the child an enriched form of experience that is neither omnipo-tent, autistic fantasy nor objective reality, but rather in a transitional realm in between.

Winnicott came to realize that his depiction of transitional space per-tained not only to small children but to the form of experience underly-ing creativity and cultural phenomena in general. The ability to suspend concern with consensual reality and fully explore one's own fantasies is crucial to personal expression that makes originality possible. It is necessary for artists to be able to forget about the outside world, what other artists have done before them, what value the market will place on their productions. Artists work by playing, trying things out without knowing where they will go, as if they are actually inventing not only their own creations but the entire medium as well.

Winnicott's concept of transitional space has provided a powerful vision of the analytic experience. (See Aron, 1992.) Thus Ogden speaks of the "potential space" provided by the analytic situation, in which the patient discovers and explores her subjectivity, which Ogden defines as

> the capacity for degrees of self-awareness ranging from intentional self-reflection (a very late achievement) to the most subtle, unobtrusive sense of "I-ness" by which experience is subtly endowed with the quality that one is thinking one's thoughts and feeling one's feelings as opposed to living in a state of reflexive reactivity. The experience of consciousness (and unconsciousness) follows from the achievement of subjectivity. (1986, p. 209)

Ogden's distinction between subjectivity and consciousness is crucial. Freud took subjectivity for granted. The goal of classical analysis was the lifting of repressions, making the unconscious conscious, filling in amnesias. Contemporary analysts are concerned with psychic processes prior to and underlying conscious and unconscious experience, the creation of personal meaning.

> It is the task of the therapist, through the management of the framework of therapy and through his interpretations, to provide conditions wherein the patient might dare to create personal meanings in a form that he can experience and play with. The therapist working with borderline patients is forever attempting to "pry open" the space between symbol and symbolized, thus creating a field in which meanings exist. (Ogden, 1986, p. 241)

Ogden generally writes about borderline and psychotic patients, those for whom the experience of subjectivity is shattered or missing, and where the analytic process gives birth to the possibility of truly subjective experience for the first time.[13] But his concerns reflect a more general emphasis running throughout innovative contemporary psychoanalytic writing, with patients who are relatively well integrated as well as those who are more disturbed. The analytic process generates a unique form of subjectivity in the interaction between its two participants, "I view the analytic process as one in which the analysand is created through an intersubjective process. . . . Analysis is not simply a method of uncovering the hidden; it is more importantly a process of creating an analytic subject who had not previously existed" (Ogden, 1992b, p. 619).

Benjamin, in her integration of psychoanalysis with feminist thinking and critical social theory, has expanded psychoanalytic concepts of subjectivity in a different way. She argues that recent psychoanalytic thought has become increasingly concerned with the complexities of self-reflection, "the issue of the self's attitude to itself (self-love, self-cohesion, self-esteem) . . . [the] focus was no longer on just the wish that is gratified or repressed, but on the self that is affected by the other's denial or fulfillment of that wish" (1988, p. 19). The expanded sense of subjectivity that Benjamin regards as the goal of the analytic process includes a full sense of the self as agent and an experience of the self as the subject of desire as well as sexual object. Because the experience of self as subject can be arrived at only through recognition by an other (who is experienced as a subject in his or her own right), the development of subjectivity is inextricably bound up with the appreciation of the subjectivity of others. Thus, in Benjamin's vision of the analytic process, intrapsychic and interpersonal processes are intertwined, and the enrichment of the analysand's subjectivity is arrived at through the establishment of a "shared reality" (Benjamin, 1992b, p. 53).

Bollas, also drawing on Winnicott's seminal contributions, vividly portrays psychoanalysis as a process through which the latent structure of subjectivity itself is exposed through re-creations and enactments in the analytic relationship. He argues that the distinctive features of our personalities are laid down in the earliest interactions between baby and caregivers, and that these constitute the "idiom," the personal grid, through which all subsequent experience is registered and generated. The psychoanalytic process is uniquely constituted so that these deepest, nonverbal foundations of personal experience, which Bollas terms "the unthought known," can become known, recognized, and more fully developed.

> This is the "grammar" of the ego, and this deep structure generates the forms of the self's existence-structure, or what we might call the character of the subject. The structure of the ego is the self's shadow, a silent speech that is unheard by the subject until he enters the echo chamber of psychoanalysis. (1987, p. 72)

Kohut's contribution, with its focus on the empathic immersion in the patient's experience, is another way of redefining the analytic experience, from the generation of insight to the development of personal meaning. Clarification, explanation, control over instincts are no longer the goal. Kohut's contributions on "empathy" involve a redefinition of the analyst's role in terms of the creation of a safe domain within which personal experience can be expressed, expanded, and enriched rather than corrected with reference to a rational, objective standard.[14]

Loewald is one of the most interesting contemporary psychoanalytic authors because he has both one of the most radically innovative visions of the analytic process and an abiding concern with anchoring that vision in Freud's own work.[15] Loewald portrays mind as a complexly textured weaving-together of different levels of psychic organization, primary process and secondary process, fantasy and rationality. The problem in Freud that Loewald returned to over and over was the concept of "sublimation," which concerns the relationship between Freud's instinct theory and the realm of culture and the arts. I have noted that Freud, despite his love for culture, locates and explains it vis-à-vis the science of psychoanalysis; he ultimately reduces cultural productions to instinctual derivatives. For Loewald, a theorist in many ways ahead of our time, this approach to the meaning of culture could not possibly work. As our existential center of gravity has shifted from the values generated by the rationalism of science to the values anchored in rational but, necessarily, deeply personal meaning, the arts take on a very different significance. The goal of psychoanalysis is not a renunciation of infantile experience but a reconciliation of different organizations of experience throughout the life cycle.

> Nowadays we seem to acknowledge and yield most readily to the magic of a great work of art. May we assume that this magic is connected with the achievement of a reconciliation—with the return, on a higher level of organization, to the early magic of thought, gesture, word, image, emotion, fantasy, as they become united again with what in ordinary nonmagical experience they only reflect, recollect, represent, or symbolize? Could sublimation be both a mourning of lost original oneness and a celebration of oneness regained? (1988, pp. 80–81)

In contrast to Loewald's straightforward although scholarly style, Bion often writes and speaks provocatively, almost in the manner of the

Zen koan, to jolt both reader and analysand into a more immediate relationship to their own experience. Rationality and "understanding," the hallmarks of classical psychoanalysis, are, for Bion, defensive diversions. Consider this vivid portrait of Bion the analyst in action.

> On one occasion he [Bion] gave me a lengthy but cogent interpretation, to which I unsuspectingly answered, "I think I follow you." His reply was as follows: "Yes, I was afraid of that!" On another interpretive occasion, I replied, "Yes, I understand." To this he retorted, "I don't doubt that you *under*stand, but why didn't you *over*stand, or, for that matter, *circum*stand?" I slowly began to realize that to Bion, "understanding" was akin to possessive idolatry. (Grotstein, 1987, p. 61)

Although delineating the features and development of a full, authentic subjectivity has been the common project of the major visionaries within contemporary psychoanalytic thought, there has been no consensus about the best way to achieve that goal. There are striking differences both about what the most authentic personal experience looks like and about how one might best arrive there, either in childhood or in analysis.[16] We will consider some of the implications of these differences in chapter 5. What I am interested in emphasizing here is not the differences, however, but the similarities. We have been tracing a climate of opinion, a shared sensibility underlying contemporary psychoanalytic theorizing. Because all authors write in their own language, from their own tradition, with their own idiosyncratic formulations, it is sometimes difficult to grasp the common elements in their vision. More often the differences among them have been emphasized and argued about.[17]

The revolution in thinking about what the patient needs sheds some light on Sophie's fear of and longing for the "concise paragraph" of analytic understanding. Within a more traditional psychoanalytic context, Sophie would be understood as needing precisely such a paragraph, an exploration and understanding of unconscious features of her current romance and its triangular (oedipal) implications with respect to her relationship with her analyst. Is she seeking in this relationship gratification for or a flight from oedipal conflicts? Are there neurotic features that need to be brought to light and subjected to a more rational control?

Within a more contemporary psychoanalytic context, the central focus would be on the quality of Sophie's passion. Is she anxiously concealing a relationship of a different sort, felt as more deeply genuine, more freely chosen? Is Sophie concerned with the embellishment of an expansiveness and generativity, felt as fragile and risky? Or is she concerned with the perpetuation, in a new form, of an illusory, fantasied protection, as a dutiful daughter of her mother or a mother substitute? In this perspective, rational inquiry and understanding are not unimportant, but they are not the central project. The goal is not the establishment of a rational normality but the capacity to generate a sense of self and relationships felt as important, meaningful, and deeply one's own.

THE PROBLEM OF ANALYZABILITY

Authors who prefer an evolutionary view of psychoanalytic ideas generally portray the clinical revolution I have been describing as simply an extension of classical theory into work with more difficult patients, reflecting the "broadened scope" of modern psychoanalytic practice. From this perspective, the entire emphasis in modern psychoanalytic theorizing on the development of the self concerns nonanalyzable patients who require a form of treatment different from psychoanalysis in its pure form, as a prelude to real analysis. It is claimed that some patients, those who are "analyzable" in a traditional sense, are able to hear interpretations "as interpretations." More disturbed patients are not ready for this and experience interpretations not in terms of content but in terms of some sort of relational event—an attack, a feeding, a seduction, and so on. These patients require some sort of nonclassical stance, such as mirroring or holding.

This argument is very misleading. These diagnostic distinctions are much more elusive than may appear, often masking a basic shift in clinical practice covered over by a surface loyalty to tradition. Thus, as it has been claimed that traditional analysis is the treatment of choice for "classical neurotics" in contrast to technique informed by object relations theories and self psychology for more disturbed patients, one hears the constant lament that "classical neurotics" are harder and harder to find. In my view, no patient hears interpretations fundamentally as interpretations; interpretations are always most basically relational events, and the meanings of the interpretations are determined by the patient's characteristic patterns of integrating relationships with others.

Consider this description by Betty Joseph, who writes about "difficult to reach" patients who seem to be cooperating with the analyst but who, on a much deeper level, remain untouched.

> I am stressing how often the pseudocooperative part of the patient
> prevents the really needy part from getting into contact with the ana-
> lyst, and that if we are taken in by this we cannot effect a change in
> our patients because we do not make contact with the part that needs
> the experience of being understood, as opposed to "getting" under-
> standing. (1989, p. 79)

The patient, well trained in pseudonormality, seems to be taking in and
working with the analyst's interpretations; yet the patient's deeper hopes
and dreads are never engaged.

The broader question is whether there really are any patients who are
"easy" to reach, or whether the ones that seem easy, such as Joseph's
patients, are more deeply hidden. Joseph stresses the importance of the
immediacy of the interaction:

> Except very near a reasonably successful termination, if I find myself
> giving an interpretation based on events other than those occurring at
> the moment during the session, I usually assume that I am not in
> proper contact with the part of the patient that needs to be under-
> stood, or that I am talking more to myself than to the patient. (1989,
> p. 87)

Freud and Sterba could comfortably assume that in talking to themselves they were also talking to the patient, because the analyst and patient shared, or needed to share, the same world, the same reality, the
same system of meaning and values. For Joseph and other modern analysts, a chasm has opened between the analyst's world and reality and
the patient's world and reality. We can no longer simply assume that the
analyst's interpretive rationality serves as an effective bridge over that
chasm. In our world of multiple meaning and value systems, of a heterogeneity of realities, the analyst's interpretations can no longer claim
an exclusive objectivity and rationality, and the patient's hopes and
dreads can no longer be assumed to be merely subjective and illusory.
The analyst who demands deference to her own "rationality" is, as
Joseph suggests, truly talking to herself. In order to talk to the patient,
the analyst must find herself on the patient's side of the chasm that di-
vides their worlds; analysts must bridge that gulf with the patient, from
the patient's side, from inside out.

The central challenge of each analysis is to find a way out of the
paradoxical impasse in which the potentially transformative is translated into the familiar and static. The analysand and analyst grapple to-

gether with the transference and the countertransference to yield an understanding of the way the patient experiences the analyst's interventions and to find a new way for both participants to speak to each other. The small number of patients who can pass tests of analyzability—who are said to hear interpretations essentially as interpretations, as informational rather than relational events—are sometimes being selected, I suspect, not on the basis of intact egos but on the basis of compatibility with or deference to the analyst's authority and perspective.[18] Yet identification and compliance with an analyst's hopes can often preclude a deep engagement with the analysand's own deepest hopes and dreads. Interestingly enough, the "analyzable" patients are often practitioners in the field of psychoanalysis and related "helping professions," perhaps candidates at the analyst's institute. Whether such patients are truly more analyzable, or whether they are more difficult actually to analyze, remains an open question.

The leading revolutionary voices in theorizing about what the patient needs are sometimes understood as advocating a shift in understanding the therapeutic action of psychoanalysis from an emphasis on insight as curative to an emphasis on the analytic relationship as curative. This understanding of recent contributions presumes that our idea of cure is the same as that of earlier generations of analysts, that the innovations concern merely the routes for getting there. But the revolution charted here entails a change that is both more subtle and more encompassing, a change in the very way we have come to think about what cure or a successful analysis might mean. In Freud's world, rationality—the capacity to think clearly and without illusion—was humanity's best hope for knowledge, progress, and happiness. In our world, rationality still may be our best hope, but its ambitions have been humbled, its luster somewhat tarnished. The search for a safe domain within which the analysand can pursue an authentic, personal experience has taken its place.

2

What Does the Analyst Know?

A REVOLUTION IN METATHEORY

Pay no attention to that man behind the curtain.
— The Wizard to Dorothy, *The Wizard of Oz*

The participation of the knower in shaping his knowledge, which had hitherto been tolerated only as a flaw—a shortcoming to be eliminated from perfect knowledge—is now recognized as the true guide and master of our cognitive powers.
— Michael Polanyi, *The Study of Man*

The psychoanalytic situation is a breeding ground of convictions. As the analyst and analysand explore the details, contours, and textures of the latter's experience, ideas are generated about what is basic and formative, and those ideas often have a very powerful impact on the life of the analysand. The opportunity to be a central part of the analytic process offers the analyst a very rare and privileged position for witnessing the often dramatic role self-understanding can play in transforming human experience.

Psychoanalysis does not always work. Some would-be analysands can never quite be engaged; some analysands find help for problems of various sorts but remain frightened of or lacking in curiosity about the deeper process of self-discovery. But when it takes, psychoanalysis is a very powerful experience for both participants, and a central feature of that experience is the ideas and beliefs the analyst and the analysand generate about the latter's life, present and past. Both participants come to believe they know a great deal about the way the analysand is put together: the role of temperament and particular constitutional resources and deficits; the significant features of early years; major life-shaping events; characteristic patterns of organizing experience; conscious and unconscious fantasies and beliefs, forming a continuity from the past, into the present, and pointing to the future.

When the process is going well, the analyst is able to witness the power of his own ideas as they are taken up by the analysand. Useful interpretations can have an extraordinary impact, sometimes suddenly, sometimes slowly evolving. They can make a profound difference in the analysand's sense of who she is, what she is about, how she came to be the way she is. Perhaps most important, analytically generated understanding can significantly affect her sense of previously untapped possibilities that life offers.

Is it any wonder then that psychoanalysts have traditionally been confident, even sometimes complacent, about the truth of their own theoretical convictions? Sterba's self-assured tone is characteristic of the general attitude in psychoanalytic literature up until fairly recently. Freud, Sterba, and their contemporaries regarded psychoanalytic theory as providing a map of the underlying structure of mind. They believed it was an accurate map because they had been there, in their daily clinical work with many analysands. That map provides analysts with knowledge about the key dimensions and processes of patients' experience, past and present. As Charles Brenner (1987, p. 169), one of the staunchest defenders of classical theory in our times, has put it, "Obviously the person who has the best opportunity to understand a patient's conflicts correctly is the patient's analyst." (It is certainly not the patient!) The analyst delivers these truths to the patient, and the latter, if he is able to consider them openly and unresistantly, is transformed by them. And it works, more often than not.

Therefore, the traditional psychoanalytic literature is filled with claims to Truths. These Truths are there (as Sterba suggests) for anyone with an open and courageous mind to see. The convictions accrued from daily analytic practice take on an obviousness in the mind of the psychoanalytic practitioner and author. As the clinician (of any theoretical persuasion) becomes more skilled at her craft, the data seem to organize themselves automatically into clear and unmistakable patterns. These Truths are often unpleasant and anxiety-provoking; if they are missed, surely it is because the fainthearted reader must be blinded by her own anxieties, her unwillingness to face the unpleasant Truth about human nature. Some theorists believe that "primitive" instinctual sexuality and aggression are at the center of human experience; others believe the core is a profound dependency and helplessness; still others assume a delicate, easily bruised creativity. Whatever the content one assigns to the bottom line, great courage is generally invoked to acccept its implications. Thus, the tone of psychoanalytic literature often reflects a kind of chest-thumping, ideological pride: my view of human nature is the toughest to bear; those who do not see it my way are naive or fearful, resistant or cowardly. The deep conviction that the world corresponds to psychoanalytic understanding, that human nature has been uncovered by the analytic method, was the centerpiece of the hopefulness traditional analysts could derive from their profession and their system of beliefs.

A CRISIS IN CONFIDENCE

The passionate conviction with which analysts have traditionally held their own theories makes particularly astonishing the growing revolution in thinking about what the analyst knows that has emerged in the past ten to fifteen years. This shift in thinking has taken place not on the level of theory but on the level of metatheory: theory about theory. It does not concern questions about what motivates the analysand, the structure of mind, the development of emotional life. Rather, it concerns the question of what the analyst can know about any of these things.[1] This realm of current psychoanalytic debate entails a fundamental redefinition of the very nature of psychoanalytic thought and of psychoanalysis as a discipline.

Whereas earlier generations of psychoanalysts prided themselves on knowing and being brave enough to know, the current generation of psychoanalytic authors tends increasingly to stress the value of not knowing and the courage that requires. A growing chorus of voices from quite different psychoanalytic traditions stresses the enormous complexity and fundamental ambiguity of experience. Consider the following excerpts from three contemporary psychoanalytic authors with very divergent points of view. One of the few things they have in common is their emphasis on how little the analyst can really know, and how anxiety-provoking that is.

The very breakdown of narrative order, the temporary chaos which is provoked, may, in itself, be vital to a creative process: a reorganization of experience into far more complex and flexible patterns.

I am claiming that the real task in therapy is *not* so much making sense of the data as it is, but resisting the temptation to make sense of the data! (Levenson, 1992, p. 189)

One reason that psychoanalysts cling to rules and heroes is the realization that without them they would be set adrift. . . . To suggest that we need neither rules nor heroes nor neurology is perhaps the scariest position of all. . . . We walk through life uncertain and unsure and, yes, a little frightened. The fear is of living in the open without the sense of security that comes from closure. (Goldberg, 1990, pp. 68–69)

When approaching the unconscious—that is, what we do *not* know, not what we *do* know—we, patient and analyst alike, are certain to be disturbed. Anyone who is going to see a patient tomorrow should, at some point, experience fear. In every consulting room there ought to be two rather frightened people: the patient and the psycho-analyst. If they are not, one wonders why they are bothering to find out what everyone knows. (Bion, 1990, pp. 4–5)

Donald Spence (1987b, chap. 5) has noted the similarity between the self-portrait of the analyst in Freud's case histories and Sherlock Holmes in Conan Doyle's detective stories. In both, the brilliant and discerning detective/analyst finds the singular solution to a bizarre and totally confusing quagmire of apparently unrelated details. In more recent psychoanalytic literature the analyst (more like the plodding, seemingly confused television detective Columbo than Holmes) is portrayed less as presenting the patient with the Truth about experience than as challenging the false and overly simplistic truths that the patient brought into the analysis. Other authors and practitioners who still believe they know things are often portrayed as fainthearted worshipers of illusions. In a reversal of traditional psychoanalytic machismo, it now sometimes appears that the capacity to contain the dread of not knowing is a measure of analytic virtue; the fewer convictions, the better and the braver!

The reasons for this very different attitude about theory can be found both outside of psychoanalysis in the culture at large and also within psychoanalysis and its maturation as a discipline in its own right.

I noted in the previous chapter the diminution in the claims contemporary science makes for itself in comparison to the apparently limitless horizons of a century or two earlier. But the radical change in attitude toward what human beings can know from Freud's day to ours is evident not just in science and philosophy of science but in virtually all intellectual domains. The central message of the past fifty years of philosophy in general, and a central tenet of our postmodern worldview, is the impossibility of the clear and certain knowledge of ourselves and the world around us sought by every major western philosopher from the pre-Socratics to Freud's day.

Richard Rorty has been a central figure in establishing the radical discontinuity between earlier philosophy and current thinking. For traditional philosophers, Rorty suggests, to know is to see into the nature of things, and good thinking gives us unmediated access into nature itself. From this perspective, reality is unambiguous, and theories can be adjudicated on the basis of their correspondence to that reality. We "want to get behind reasons to causes, beyond argument to compulsion from the object known, to a situation in which argument would be not just silly but impossible, for anyone gripped by the object in the required way will be *unable* to doubt or to see an alternative" (Rorty, 1979, p. 159).

These are the assumptions that underlay the *Weltanshauung* of Freud[2] and other major thinkers of his day. According to Rorty and, in their individual own ways, according to a large proportion of contemporary philosophers, these assumptions are no longer feasible. Knowledge in our day is considered—can only be considered—pluralistic, not singular; contextual, not absolute; constructed, not uncovered; changing and dynamic, not static and eternal. "We shall no longer be tempted," as Rorty puts it, "by the notion that knowledge is made possible by a special Glassy Essence which enables human beings to mirror nature" (1979, p. 37).

Isaiah Berlin, surveying the history of political and social philosophy, provides another angle on the radical shift in assumptions about human knowledge from Freud's day to ours. He identifies what he characterizes as the "Platonic ideal" that "lay at the basis of all progressive thought in the nineteenth century":

> in the first place, that . . . all genuine questions must have one true answer and one only, all the rest being necessarily errors; in the second place, that there must be a dependable path towards the discovery of these truths; in the third place, that the true answers, when found, must necessarily be compatible with one another and form a single whole, for one truth cannot be incompatible with another—that we knew *a priori*. This kind of omniscience was the solution of the cosmic jigsaw puzzle. (1991, pp. 5–6)

Berlin writes of the compelling power and profound attraction of this ideal, in comparison with the pluralism that he argues is now our only conceptually coherent possibility. One can easily imagine Freud voicing Berlin's mock plea for the now-anachronistic ideal of rationalism (psychoanalytically informed) leading from primary process to secondary process, from the chaos of nature to a singular and inevitable rationalistic progress:

> For if this was not so, do the ideas of progress, of history, have any meaning? Is there not a movement, however tortuous, from ignorance to knowledge, from mythical thought and childish fantasies to perception of reality face to face, to knowledge of true goals, true values as well as truths of fact? (1991, p. 7)

PSYCHOANALYTIC HETEROGENEITY

If we narrow our focus from the culture at large to the discipline of psychoanalysis itself, we find more immediate, equally compelling reasons for the current crisis of confidence within psychoanalytic theorizing.

For most of Freud's life, there was one, and only one, psychoanalysis; it was easy to regard defections as splinter movements, a falling away from an objectively greater, more scientific truth that would ultimately prevail. Now there are many psychoanalytic schools, each with claims to an exclusive possession of objective truth. And that heterogeneity is a constant, looming, often troublesome presence for all psychoanalysts who participate in the analytic community outside their own offices. It is hard to imagine a time when any one theoretical perspective will demonstrate such compelling reasonableness and truth that proponents of the others will change ranks, and psychoanalysis will once again be whole.

Imagine Sterba presenting his clinical material at a case conference set in contemporary times with analysts of different persuasions. He could no longer assume that his conclusions are obvious and almost not worth stating. Sterba's understanding of this material is based on the classical Freudian premise that early childhood impulses and conflicts concerning sexuality and aggression are the formative and ongoing motivational basis of all experience. His interpretation of his patient's initial experience in treatment follows naturally from that premise: Her personality is organized around masochistic sexual longings in relation to her father; the experience with the physician was traumatic largely because it served and serves as a dramatic representation of those oedi-

pal longings and fantasies; she seeks to act out the central oedipal con-
stellation in the transference with the analyst because she still seeks
gratification for her masochistic longings. Thus, this patient experiences
the analytic situation as a setting for seduction about which she has intense conflicts and ambivalence.

This is a compelling interpretive understanding, but, in today's analytic world, it is certainly not the only one. What other hypotheses
would begin to churn in the minds of analysts of other persuasions?

Analysts who tend to think along the lines of object relations theory
(for example, Fairbairnians) begin with the assumption that it is not the
pursuit of gratification that is the basic underlying motivation in human
experience but the pursuit of contact. They would be inclined to assume
that this patient's apparent sexualization of the analytic situation represents the mode of object-seeking and connection to others that was
available to her as a child. It is likely that she experienced her parents as
unavailable to her in other ways, that masochistic surrender, of a quasi-
sexual nature, seemed to be the most exciting and intense form of contact available. It is difficult for her to imagine that she can be loved or
found valuable in any way other than sexual surrender; she maintains
the hope that through masochistic submission, a more genuine connection will emerge. What she seeks, according to this interpretive line, is
love and caring.

Analysts who tend to think along the lines of interpersonal psychoanalysis begin with the assumption that people learn patterns of integrating relationships with each other in childhood, and these patterns
are repeated throughout life. They would be impressed with the deceptiveness and hypocrisy of the parents as well as the physician in the patient's story. Was this characteristic of the way people in this family
acted? Perhaps the story became important because it seemed to be emblematic of the way the world works. From this perspective, the patient
has become very good at giving important people what they seem to
want. What does she believe about the analyst's intentions and interests? Does the analyst expect her to produce sexual material and childhood memories? What does it mean to him? Is the friend who would
suspect her of sexual activity a stand-in for the analyst whom she knows
suspects her of sexual fantasies and longings? Does she produce material for his interpretive scalpel, which seems to make him excited and
gives him a sense of great certainty and mastery, because this is the manner in which she has learned to interact with other important people?
What she seeks, according to this interpretive line, is neither gratification nor caring, but familiarity and interpersonal mastery.

Analysts who tend to think along the lines of self psychology begin with the assumption that the most fundamental motivational thrust in human experience is the maintenance of self-cohesion. They would be impressed with the patient's self-protectiveness at the beginning of treatment and see it as an indication of an endangered sense of self. Here is someone who apparently has learned that the world is not a terribly safe place for her and her needs. People play tricks on you, think negative things about you, invade you, both physically and psychologically. Her initial resistance is a rational response to a real sense of endangerment. She is likely to experience the analyst's formulations not as helpful but as a repetition of the initially assaultive, uncaring parenting she received. What she seeks, according to this interpretive line, is not gratification, caring, or interactional competence but empathic understanding of her deeply felt need for self-protection.

No competent analyst would fix upon any of these formulations with so little data. However, any competent analyst does start associating to clinical data and formulating loose interpretive hypotheses from the start, both consciously and preconsciously. Those associations and formulations begin from assumptions the clinician brings to the material; the data start to organize themselves around those assumptions; and the beliefs and conclusions arrived at are an interactive product of the analyst's manner of listening and thinking and the patient's manner of presenting himself in the analytic situation.

These are all good theories. (Others could have been added as well.) They are all interesting, complex, and work within their own terms. It is precisely this rich heterogeneity of our psychoanalytic world that makes it no longer compelling to think of psychoanalysis as a method for uncovering a singular truth. Rather, this rich heterogeneity that has evolved from Freud's monolithic system makes it much more compelling to view psychoanalytic theory as a group of interpretive systems, each with its own principles, laws, and criteria of verifiability. Object relations theory, self psychology, interpersonal psychoanalysis, Kleinian theory: Each of these fully psychoanalytic systems is a monolith unto itself. But our community of many orthodoxies is a different world from Freud's community of one orthodoxy and several splinter movements (such as Adlerian or Jungian theory).

The shift from the view that the analyst knows the Truth to the view that the analyst knows one (or more) among various possible truths about the patient's experience has created a crisis of confidence in psychoanalytic theorizing and a crisis of authority in the psychoanalyst's self-image. The certainty and its consequent hopefulness that pervaded traditional psychoanalytic theorizing have become inaccessible to contemporary analytic theorists or clinicians. Is this a problem? Is uncertainty a cause for nihilism and dread, or the basis for a different sort of knowledge? If the content of what analysts know is not the Truth, is the authority that analysts can claim diminished?[3]

Among those who have struggled directly with the implications of this proliferation, there have been essentially three strategies (cutting across theoretical traditions): an appeal to empiricism, an appeal to phenomenology, and the hermaneutics/constructivism approach. The first strategy looks outside the analytic process itself for a firmer soil in which to ground psychoanalytic theory; the second strategy tends to diminish the importance of the analyst's theory in the analytic process. The third strategy continues to grant an important role to the analyst's knowledge but calls for a rethinking of the very nature of that knowledge.

RESPONSES TO THE CRISIS: EMPIRICISM

There has been a long-standing tradition of empirical research both on concepts drawn from psychoanalytic theory and on the analytic process itself. An account of this research could fill several volumes. Like most important research traditions, it has generated useful data, new ideas, challenges to existing theory, and many false leads. One popular response to the current heterogeneity of psychoanalytic theories and the crisis of confidence it generates is the hope that one day empirical research will provide a solution, serving as a framework for testing and evaluating psychoanalytic theories, subtantiating some, discarding others.

Freud thought that the analytic method itself was an empirical method, with the analyst as observer uncovering and cataloging data. Today a dwindling number of authors still think this way. For most, the proliferation of different interpretive systems and the inevitable participation of the analyst in what he is observing make the analytic process not an unimpeachable platform from which to determine truths about the patient's experience and life. In our day, in contrast to Freud's, it is difficult to see how the analytic method itself can be employed to adjudicate among the different claims to truth because analysts of different persuasions employing the analytic method are discovering different truths.

Many authors look to empirical research apart from the analytic process itself for the grounding of psychoanalytic knowledge. Such researchers claim that Freud was right to regard psychoanalysis as a science. The problem is that theories have proliferated far beyond our success in testing them to decide which are true and which are false. This very serious problem is solvable only through some sort of extra-analytic empirical methodology and a comprehensive research program to test psychoanalytic ideas and establish their validity. So, many people look to the various extra-analytic methodological strategies for determining the truth value and utility of competing analytic theories and concepts. Their hopes for the yield from empirical studies are extremely high.

Some pin their hopes on the accumulation of data from the comparative study of the course of different treatments.[4] Some look to the study of the analytic process through an analysis of transcripts.[5] Others look to outcome studies. Some regard the analytic situation itself as too messy and prefer experimental laboratory conditions. Still others put great weight on closely related fields, such as infant research, as a testing ground for analytic concepts. These various empirical studies have generated valuable and thought-provoking data about a lot of different things. Yet they do not really help us with the crisis in confidence concerning what it is that the analyst knows.[6]

Those who hope that science will solve the crisis in metatheory seem not to appreciate the difference between science in our time and science in the time of Freud and his contemporaries. Freud could believe that anyone using the psychoanalytic method would gain access to undisputable and clear phenomena, just as the first telescope enabled Galileo and his contemporaries to see, in a clear and unmistakable way, that the apparent smudges in the Milky Way were composed of countless stars. All one had to do was employ the instrument and look.

For Freud, the data that the psychoanalytic instrument yields also speak that directly. The relationship between scientific explanations and actuality seemed simple—Freud felt that what he was seeing had a clear and direct correspondence to reality.

> Its endeavour [scientific thinking] is to arrive at correspondence with reality—that is to say, with what exists outside us and independently of us and, as experience has taught us, is decisive for the fulfillment or disappointment of our wishes. This correspondence with the real external world we call "truth." (1933, p. 170)

Our relationship to reality, both physical and psychical, can no longer be regarded in so uncomplicated a fashion, and this modern sensibility affects our experience of doing psychoanalysis no matter what words we use to characterize it. We may still want to consider psycho-analysis a science, to be empirically tested both within and outside the analytic situation itself. But psychoanalysis can no longer be a science in the way Freud thought about science. It is now a science that yields multiple truths, changing truths, truths that are embedded in the particular interactive context of the analytic relationship.

Empirical testing of various psychoanalytic concepts and psychoanalytic treatments may shed some light on many interesting questions: What sorts of hypotheses are most useful for predicting what will happen next in the analytic process? What sorts of interventions are most useful with certain kinds of patients? How do different metaphors from adjacent fields (child development, artificial intelligence) lend themselves differently to the shaping of psychoanalytic data? And so on. These questions all have to do with utility, not singular explanation; effectiveness, not Truth. These kinds of studies can contribute to the analyst's authority, but they can never resuscitate the belief, possible for Freud and his contemporaries, that the analyst could offer the patient an exclusively correct explanation for and blueprint of his experience and development. Establishing effectiveness does nothing to allay the anxiety of the psychoanalyst of today who may want to believe, as Freud and Sterba justifiably believed, that she has access to the Truth.[7]

Empirical data sometime have had an important impact on the shaping of analytic knowledge. Karl Popper's oft-cited concept of "falsifiability" operates in an informal but important way in the sorting out of theories within the analytic community. The empirical finding in outcome studies of psychotherapy and psychoanalysis that the analytic relationship is more important than the analyst's theory has played a part in the growing prominence of the concern with that relationship in psychoanalytic theorizing. The disconfirmation of the motivational primacy of tension reduction in experimental research on animals and infants (Lichtenberg, 1983) surely has played a part in the abandonment or radical reshaping of the concept of "drive" in psychoanalytic theorizing. And other lines of empirical research have made important contributions as well to the psychoanalytic community and its ongoing generation of analytic concepts.

However, empirical studies have never served as an ultimate test of analytic concepts, nor is it likely that the crisis in metatheory will be resolved by such studies. No experiment or series of experiments will ever be able to serve as a final and conclusive arbiter of the truth of something as complex and elastic as a psychoanalytic theory.[8] Any of the major psychoanalytic theories can account for all the data. They change not because they are disproven, but because they are no longer as compelling or persuasive, because their clinical utility has diminished, or because they have lost their inspirational value.

The hope that empiricism will solve the crisis of metatheory represents a misuse of the contribution of empirical studies. They can never restore the singular Truth that Freud and his contemporaries could believe psychoanalytic theory provided for them. Empirical data make an important contribution to the shape that theorizing takes, but they cannot provide an ultimate standard for choices among theories.

Responses to the Crisis: Phenomenology

An alternative response points to the centrality of the patient's own subjective experience in the analytic process as reason to believe that the crisis concerning the analyst's knowledge is really no problem at all. According to this line of reasoning, what is central to the analytic process is inquiry into the analysand's experience, the analysand's own subjective point of view. The analyst's beliefs are of secondary importance and often operate as a contaminant. The analyst's job is to conduct an inquiry into the patient's experience and what the patient knows, to enable the patient to discover, express, and capture her own experience.

The turn toward phenomenology represents an important dimension of the revolutionary movements we charted in chapter 1. In their debunking of theory, the phenomenologists have helped shift the focus to the patient's perceptions and ideas, to the importance of attempting to envision the world from the patient's vantage point and the centrality of the patient's personal subjectivity. Their contribution also has served as a corrective for the common abuse of theory, for the tendency of analysts to use their own conceptual categories and presuppositions as Procrustian categories into which they neatly distribute the patient's experience. However, the use of a phenomenological emphasis specifically to solve the crisis in metatheory is something else and needs to be considered in its own terms. This strategy has been developed most fully and explicitly by Evelyn Schwaber; we will consider her approach as representative.

Schwaber has developed Kohut's original contributions on empathy and resistance into a critical perspective on the way psychoanalysts listen and the assumptions they make about what is real. She argues that in most analytic work, there is a separation of "two realities, hierarchically arranged . . . the one the patient experiences, and the one the analyst 'knows'" (1983, p. 386). Like many other contemporary authors, Schwaber asks us to rethink the traditional assumptions granting truth value to what the analyst knows and assuming that what the patient experiences is a distortion of reality shaped by his inner conflicts. Schwaber argues that what the patient needs is not a renunciation of his hopes but a recognition and transformative development of them.

> It is not the relinquishment or renunciation of childhood wishes that makes treatment effective, but their discovery and elucidation, the search for their meaning, and the reestablishment of their historical continuity. . . . Analysis is mutative in sustaining that hope, however tentative and defended it may have been, that led the patient to seek help in the first place; for it is ultimately a hope for recognition—of one's feelings, wishes, defences, perceptions, of one's own truth— linked from past to present, articulated by another and by oneself. (1990b, p. 237)

Schwaber argues that reality is relative and perspectival. The analyst's viewpoint, derived from his own theoretical assumptions, is only one among many possible perspectives. The essence of good analytic work is not the superimposition of that perspective on the patient but a listening process that allows the patient's own perspective to emerge and develop. The analyst should be continually alert to the intrusion of his own reality so as to resonate with the "patient's subjective point of view."

According to this approach, the crisis in metatheory is really no crisis because theory is unimportant; in fact, theory is essentially an impediment. What is important for the analytic process is the patient's experience, and that experience is accessible outside of, or unmediated through, the analyst's theory. It does not matter what the analyst believes, or that different analysts may believe different things.[9]

This use of phenomenology to solve the crisis in metatheory is problematic, because it posits, in one form or another, an ideal that is impossible. The notion that the patient's experience can somehow serve as the ultimate standard of truth, independent of the analyst's own ideas and beliefs, rests on several questionable premises.[10]

First, the patient's own experience is assumed to be singular and unambiguous, waiting in the patient for the opportunity to express itself. Second, the patient is assumed to have privileged access to that simple, unambiguous experience, if only unimpeded by the analyst's participation. Third, it is assumed that the analyst can know what the patient's singular subjective point of view really is: "The closer we can stay to their experience of the moment (the closer we stay to the data), the less we are tempted to teach another truth, the more deeply our patients will be able to observe and to face their own" (Schwaber, 1990b, p. 238).

These assumptions fly in the face of some of the most important and enduring discoveries of psychoanalysis over decades of practice: All of us have multiple, conflictual perspectives, many of which are unconscious or preconscious; one's perspective on past and present is always context-dependent and changes according to motivational and affective state; and one's perspective varies a great deal depending on the other to whom it is being spoken and the purpose for which it is being expressed.

Schwaber's assumptions also are contradicted by a great deal of current thinking about how the mind works that has been generated in the field of cognitive psychology and related areas; this research has enormous and exciting implications for psychoanalytic theorizing. Daniel Dennett (1991), for example, points to the "tempting mistake of supposing that there must be a single narrative (the 'final' or 'published' draft, you might say) that is canonical—that is the *actual* stream of consciousness of the subject, whether or not the experimenter (or even the subject) can gain access to it" (p. 113).

Consciousness itself is fragmentary, discontinuous, and much too complex and inaccessible to be captured in a singular, true report. Unconscious experience is, of course, even more problematic in these regards. Further, establishing the patient as the final, unquestioned arbiter of what goes on even in her conscious experience grants her powers she does not have and minimizes the potential contribution of the analyst. Dennett's description of the researcher ("heterophenomenologist") into the conscious experience of another person, and his account of the issues involved in such research, are remarkably similar to accounts from those involved in psychoanalytic inquiry.

If you want us to *believe* everything you say about your phenomenology [Dennett's heterophenomenologist says to his subject], you are asking not just to be taken seriously but to be granted papal infallibility and that is asking too much. You are *not* authoritative about what is happening in you, but only about what *seems* to be happening in you, and we are giving you total, dictatorial authority over the account of how it seems to you, about *what it is like to be you*. And if you complain that some parts of how it seems to you are ineffable, we heterophenomenologists will grant that too.... Later, perhaps, you will come to be able to describe it, but of course at that time it will be something different, something describable. (Dennett, 1991, pp. 96–97)

The phenomenological solution, while decrying objectivism in any form, ironically represents the return of a form of the naive realism of Freud's day. Although the analyst as scientific observer has no privileged vantage point from which to discover the truth, it is assumed that the patient does, and the analyst has the power to know what the patient knows, even if the patient is not aware of it herself.[11] This reinstitution of the assumption of a singular, unmediated reality is at odds not just with contemporary philosophy but also with what psychoanalysis teaches us about the inevitably personal, subjective organization of all experience, including (alas) the analyst's.

There is something profoundly alluring in the longing to contact reality in an immediate fashion. Freud thought his theory gave him access. Those who debunk the pretentions of theory think that by shedding it they gain access. The reality they hope to connect with more immediately is the patient's subjectivity itself. The analyst becomes a kind of portrait painter of the patient's experience, revealing the inner structure of that experience. The problem is that in painting their subjects, portrait painters also are expressing their own sensibility, their own subjectivity, and what they capture on canvas is partly the impact of their own personalities. A personal experience with portraiture recently impressed this point upon me in an irresistible way.

Several years ago, my wife and I decided to contract for a drawing of ourselves by an artist whose work we had admired for a long time. He had done wonderful drawings (I had purchased several prints) and seemed to capture the essence of his subjects. Indeed, he prided himself on just this capacity. He was pleased to take on the assignment and informed us that he would require us to spend some time sitting and talking with him as he sketched us so that he could get to know us better. He felt that to capture the essence of people visually, he had to know something about them: their history, their passions, their beliefs, and so on. This made great sense to two psychoanalysts, so we began enthusiastically.

I can no longer remember exactly how many hours we spent at this project, but I remember it as one of the most tedious and irritating experiences of my life. The artist's idea of getting to know us was to tell us all about himself and what an extraordinary person he was in every respect. I kept reassuring myself that it would all be worthwhile, because I would be able to enjoy his rendering of me for many years to come.

Too many days later, when he showed us the finished portrait, I was absolutely horrified. I could see the resemblance, but it was certainly not what I took to be my inner essence. I looked vacant, devoid of any emotional depth or intelligence. If the artist had, in fact, "caught" anything important about me, I wished it could be thrown back! Out of deference to the money spent, and assuming that, perhaps, his vision was deeper than mine, I tried hanging it up in my dining room. I felt justified in taking it down and burying it in the back of a closet, however, when my three-year-old daughter asked, when she saw it, "What happened to Daddy?"

My initial notion was that the artist had just done a poor job. This judgment changed in a way I found quite fascinating when my wife suddenly realized that, although the portrait seemed not at all representative of me, it did capture something familiar to her. She realized that she had seen the look on my face before; it was my characteristic reaction when trapped in a room with someone I find insufferably boring and offensive. Since in recent years I have become adept at avoiding such situations, she had not seen that vacant, depersonalized stare for a long time—but there it was!

So I was forced to admit that the artist had, in fact, caught something characteristic about me, but what he had caught was me in interaction with someone like him. Would a less intrusive artist have been able to discover and capture something more genuine? Undoubtedly, a version of myself I like better would have emerged, but it is difficult to say whether that version would have been any more genuine. And no version of me would have been separable from the impact of the artist himself. Artists, like psychoanalysts, have a great impact on what it is they are trying to understand, and there seems to be no way to factor out or analyze away that impact. There is no "me," waiting to be captured, either by an artist or an analyst or even by myself. (Problems with the concept of a True Self will be taken up in chapter 5.)

Changes in thinking about what the analyst knows generate a crisis not just in terms of the analyst's knowledge but in terms of the analyst's broader authority. What is it that the analyst can, in good faith, offer the patient, if not a singular explanation for the workings of the patient's mind? Even though empirical and phenomenological approaches can neither reverse nor bypass the crisis in metatheory, they can help us with the problem of the analyst's authority.

Empirical data may eventually make it possible for the analyst to know which kinds of hypotheses are most useful with particular kinds of patients and which theoretical concepts are likely to affect the analytic process in particular sorts of ways. Phenomenological approaches help develop the analyst's expertise in conducting an inquiry, in teaching the enormously complex craft of listening to and experiencing the patient as he presents himself and the personal world he shapes and operates in. These are rich gifts indeed. But they do not alter the fact that today's analyst cannot feel he offers the patient a singular, exclusive explanation in the way that was possible for the analyst of Freud's day. The implications of this difference have been addressed most directly and fruitfully by the authors to be considered next.

RESPONSES TO THE CRISIS: HERMENEUTICS, CONSTRUCTIVISM

The third solution to the metatheoretical crisis has been designated differently by different authors: hermeneutics, constructivism, constructionism, perspectivism. There are many differences among the positions taken, many different forms of these "isms"; they do not, in any way, constitute a consensus. They represent an extended, complex conversation. Entry into the conversation requires a shared sense of the inadequacy of the traditional premise that psychoanalytic ideas correspond, in a direct and immediate fashion, to the structure of the mind. This traditional premise has been designated variously by different authors as positivism, realism, objectivism, foundationalism, and fundamentalism.

Authors struggling with this problem seem to agree that whatever it is that the analyst knows, it is not simply discovered or revealed through the analytic method—it is organized, constructed, fitted together by the analyst herself or, collectively, by the analytic community in its repertoire of theoretical concepts. The analytic method is not archaeological and reconstructive; it does not simply expose what is there. Rather, it is constructive and synthetic; it organizes whatever is there into patterns it itself supplies.

The fundamental assumption in this line of thought is that the patient's experience—the basic data of psychoanalysis, that which is to be understood or "analyzed"—is fundamentally ambiguous. This is an easily misunderstood concept. It does not mean that the patient's experience is necessarily opaque or mysterious (although at times it might be). It does mean that understanding human experience, including one's own, is never simply a process of seeing it, grasping it, or reading it (depending on whether one likes one's metaphors ocular, physical, or linguistic). The elements of human experience are understood only through a process that organizes those elements, puts them together, assigns them meaning, and prioritizes them. The organization that seems most compelling may seem quite accessible and unmysterious; it is still constructed, through an active organizing process, in the person who is doing the understanding.

To say that human experience is fundamentally ambiguous is not the same thing as saying it is complex. (See Sass and Wolfolk, 1988, p. 447.) Freud and his contemporaries regarded experience as very complex indeed, and, as psychoanalytic theory developed and expanded, so did the complexities of understanding. Thus, concepts such as "overdetermination" (Freud), "multiple function" (Waelder, 1936), and "compromise formation" (Brenner, 1982) have been used, quite correctly, to defend the complexity with which the mind is understood within the classical psychoanalytic framework. Any piece of experience may have many different latent meanings and different functions with respect to different psychical agencies. But complexity is not the same as ambiguity.[12]

Within the classical system, any given piece of experience is understood to be determined (no matter how complexly) by a specific and finite collection of motives. There is one correct and comprehensive way to understand that piece of experience. Of course, one analyst may pick up on one meaning, another analyst on another meaning. And both can be correct (because of overdetermination, multiple function, and compromise formation). But each explanation, even though correct, is incomplete. Because all mental events are determined ultimately by a finite set of causes, there is a singular, even if multidimensional, correct and complete answer to the question: What does this piece of experience mean? All the partial answers fit together like pieces of a jigsaw puzzle. (This is a psychological counterpart to Berlin's cosmic puzzle referred to earlier.) Even if we do not completely know what the picture is, the traditional assumption has been (and, according to traditional epistomological principles, has to be) that there is a singular solution to the puzzle. Thus, Freud defined truth in terms of correspondence with what is "out there."

From the hermeneutic/constructivist perspective, we come to know reality outside of us only through our experience of it, which is, inevitably, organized in terms of our ideas, our assumptions, our wishes. In this approach, it is impossible to envision a singular correct and complete understanding of any piece of human experience even as an ideal, because human experience is fundamentally ambiguous. To understand something means to organize it. Since the organization is not solely in the experience to be understood but also in the activity of the understanding, different organizations are possible, different understandings. To say that experience is fundamentally ambiguous is to say that its meaning is not inherent or apparent in it but that it lends itself to multiple understandings, multiple interpretations.[13]

For Freud, the patient's dynamics are in the patient's mind, and the true meaning of those dynamics is inherent within them. The analyst's task is to uncover the fragments of the patient's latent dynamics embedded in the associations and to reconstruct their original configurations, very much as the archaeologists of Freud's time, whom he so admired and envied, uncovered actual remnants of ancient civilization and reconstructed long-buried cities.[14]

Contemporary authors influenced by hermeneutics borrowed from philosophy and literary theory (Paul Ricoeur, Donald Spence, Roy Schafer) have challenged this traditional understanding of the analytic method. They believe that, unlike physical objects, the patient's productions do not constitute a single organizational scheme.

Schafer, for example, argues against what he calls the "official psychoanalytic conception of reality," traditionally positivistic, in which reality is seen as "out there" or "in there," "in the inner world, existing as a knowable, certifiable essence [to be] encountered and recognized innocently." He argues, by contrast, for a view that limits "us always to dealing only with *versions* of reality. . . . One defines situations and invests events with multiple meanings. . . . In this account, reality is always mediated by narration. Far from being innocently encountered or discovered, it is created in a regulated fashion" (1983, p. 234). The patient's experiences, associations, and memories can be integrated or organized in innumerable ways. The organizational scheme arrived at is a dual creation, shaped partly by the patient's material but also inevitably shaped by the analyst's patterns of thought, or theory. The "meaning" of clinical material does not exist until it is named—it is not uncovered but created.

In this view, the analyst's theory has an enormous impact on what he sees in the clinical material, not because it is a sure guide to uncovering structure but because the theory itself shapes and organizes the material. The patient's dynamics and life history do not have an independent reality that can be uncovered or grasped from the outside—they exist in a state of complex potentiality and are actually co-created by the observer's participation. This is a profoundly different view of the analytic process. Frank Kermode, the literary critic, has vividly described some of the implications of this shift from historical truth to narrative truth, from correct understanding to narrative intelligibility.

Pasts, indeed, are not reconstructed; they are constructed here and now. Moreover, since the analyst inserts fictions into the discourse, he might be more usefully thought of as a kind of poet rather than as a kind of archaeologist. What psychoanalysis does is construct "truths in the service of self-coherence . . . it offers no veridical picture of the past." Like the poet, the novelist and the historian, the analyst creates under his specific conditions a past that is really here and now, a fiction appropriate to the present. Any interpretation is true "only in its own analytic space" (Spence). Moreover, it is pointless to call an interpretation erroneous; it works by contributing to narrative intelligibility, and is neither true or false but only a means to an end. (1985, p. 9)

Social constructivism is the term employed by Irwin Hoffman in an important series of articles focusing on the participation of the analyst in the analytic process (1983, 1987a, 1991a, 1991b, 1992). Whereas authors drawing on hermeneutics in philosophy and literature, such as Spence and Schafer, emphasize the impact of the analyst's theory on the process, Hoffman focuses on the analyst's unintended (and often unconscious) participation. The position he has been developing includes some of the following arguments: The patient's experience is codetermined both by the patient's own characteristic organizational patterns and by the patient's perception of the analyst's participation and experience. (See also Gill, 1982.) The patient's interpretations of the analyst's actions and experience are constructions that are usefully assumed to be plausible and anchored in real events in their here-and-now interaction. The analyst's understanding of the patient is also a construction, one among many possible ways of organizing the material generated in interaction between analysand and analyst. The analyst's understanding of her own actions and feelings is a construction as well rather than an accurate rendering, one among many possible (but not unlimited) ways of organizing her experience. The analyst's understanding of both analysand and self is always embedded in the complex interactive matrix that they constitute.[15] Therefore, the analyst's self-understanding is always incomplete and constantly evolving, since it can never free itself from its own current immersion, which, if grasped at all, can be seen only retrospectively, from yet another vantage point.[16]

Traditionalists claim that the analyst, through his theory, has privileged access to the patient's experience. Phenomenologists claim that the patient has privileged access to his own experience. Traditionalists and phenomenologists share the assumption that there is a stream of experience that actually exists in a pristine form, to which either analyst or patient has unmediated access, like the viewer of a film on an interior screen. (Daniel Dennett [1991] describes this anachronistic although pervasive view as predicated upon the assumption of what he terms the "Cartesian Theater.") A central tenet of the hermeneutic/constructivist approach is that there is no stream of experience separable from experience as accessed by someone (either oneself or someone else) at a specific time, for a particular purpose, in a specific context. Thus, experience is constructed on a moment-to-moment basis. At any given point, the patient can only report a particular construction of his experience, which may overlook or obliterate many other important constructions of his experience (which the analyst might be more in touch with). At any given point, the analyst can offer only his own construction of some aspects of a patient's experience, a construction of a construction.

The "only" in the preceding sentence should not be taken as a minimization of the importance of interpersonal understanding. Our constructions of each other's constructions make possible mutual growth and the reciprocally facilitating use of imagination. (How this works in the analytic relationship will be taken up in chapter 8.)

Where does the analyst's knowledge about the patient come from? If the analyst does not have unmediated access to the structure of the patient's experience, if everything that the analyst knows about the patient is mediated through the analyst's own experience, how is it possible for the analyst to feel confident that she knows anything about the patient at all? How can the analyst's beliefs about the patient become relevant and useful to the analysand?

This question is approached in different ways by various authors across the broad spectrum of the hermeneutic/constructivist approach. Let us sample a few representative strategies.

Authors (such as Jurgen Habermas) drawing on hermeneutics in philosophy and literature point to the shared cultural and linguistic categories through which individuals in the same community structure their experience. It is true that I can never grasp your experience directly, but only in terms of my experience, and that, therefore, misunderstandings are common and always a possibility. Nevertheless, the accomplishments of social living and culture are testimony to the likelihood that we do seem to understand each other a large portion of the time. We live in the same physical world, share the same language, enjoy the same cultural traditions, and this communality makes it possible for my understanding of you, formalized in my analytic theories, to be relevant to one or more of your understandings of you or, alternatively, to be a potentially useful and meaningful understanding for you. The analyst's beliefs are likely to be useful to the analysand because the two share, in many respects, a common world.[17]

Schafer grounds the analyst's knowledge in a community more narrowly defined—the narrative tradition developed within each of the major psychoanalytic schools. From this perspective, psychoanalytic theories provide narrative strategies or storylines. They may have relevance to narrative themes within the culture at large (for example, Freud's late nineteenth-century storylines of person as beast and person as machine). However, the analyst's beliefs are rooted most securely in the history of the application of narrative strategies within the analytic discipline. In collaboration with the patient, the analyst provides storylines that have proved useful and powerful in other analytic dyads in terms of generating rich and liberating forms of experience. The analyst's beliefs are likely to be useful to the analysand because she knows ways of organizing and looking into experience that are compelling and freeing.

Yet another approach to the sources of the analyst's knowledge of the patient looks to the more deeply personal experience of the analyst, as reflected in the analyst's own inner life and dynamics.[18] What the patient is experiencing and what the analyst is experiencing are deeply and inevitably intertwined and form a single although very complex dyadic unit. This approach is based on the presupposition that affective experience tends to be highly contagious and that people continually shape each other's experiences in their interactions with each other. Someone who is depressed is likely to "bring one down"; someone who is anxious makes other people anxious; sexual excitement begets sexual excitement; rage and belligerence tend to put others on edge and incite reciprocal hostility; and so on. Affects often work (not always, of course) like tuning forks of the same pitch; vibration in one sets off a resonance in the others.

In classical theory of technique, the analyst's personal, idiosyncratic feelings ("countertransference") are regarded as a contaminant to be eliminated as much as possible. In more current theory of technique, a great deal of value is attributed to the analyst's reactions, to what the analyst feels like when in the presence of the particular patient. In this approach, it is crucial that the analyst not be a neutral observer. It is precisely the analyst's mood, feelings, fantasies, stray thoughts that provide a route to the patient's issues.

Heinrich Racker (1968) was a pioneer in this tradition, and his kind of approach is illustrative.

Let us say that a patient acts in a clinging and accusatory fashion, trying greedily to grasp as much of the analyst's time and/or ideas as he can. The analyst finds himself, despite his best professional intentions, holding onto both his time and/or ideas, protecting them, and, out of anger at the patient's implicit reproaches, finding some satisfaction in the patient's inevitable deprivation.

In the classical analytic model, these feelings on the part of the analyst—countertransference as a response to the patient's transference—would be considered inappropriate. Yet in some areas of contemporary analytic thought, such countertransference can become a powerful vehicle for the analyst's understanding of the patient's experience. As the analyst becomes aware of and reflective about his own retentiveness and sadism, he explores the interaction with the patient for some of its possible sources. His own experience may alert him to ways in which the patient has been clinging and/or implicitly accusatory. He may become aware of the way in which his sense of hoarding and withholding protect him from his own experience of dependency and longing.

In this approach, the analyst makes his way through his own experience to an understanding of the patient's experience and the complementarity of the interpersonal situation they have collaborated in shaping. It is of course crucial that the analyst not use his own experience as if it were oracular, leading to certain knowledge of the patient's experience.[19] When used in a nonoracular fashion, the analyst's personal experience with the patient generates beliefs that are likely to be deeply relevant to the patient's experience or potential experiences.

Viewing the analyst's experience as deeply personal but not idiosyncratic makes possible a grounding of the analyst's beliefs about the patient in the analyst's own subjective experience. Some authors (such as Schafer) see the analyst's organizing role largely in terms of the narrative strategies inherent in their theories. Other authors (such as Hoffman and Stern) regard theory as reflecting (often added on post hoc) something much more personal and spontaneous in the analyst's participation. What these approaches have in common is that they regard the analyst's personal participation in the data, the analyst's personal impact on the patient's experience that both are struggling to grasp and understand, no longer as a contamination of a purer knowledge. Rather, the analyst's participation is understood to be an inevitable element in the subject matter under study and a powerful tool for understanding.

THE SPECTER OF RELATIVISM

Contemporary psychoanalytic writers in the area of metatheory must necessarily steer a course between twin dangers that are so narrow that it makes Ulysses' route seem comfortably lazy and meandering. The Charybdis of modern psychoanalysis is the preservation of the traditional assumption that there is a singular, unambiguous reality "out there," an assumption that is so compelling and powerful that it operates as a conceptual whirlpool from which it is difficult to steer clear. The multiheaded Scylla of modern psychoanalysis is the specter of relativism. In avoiding the assumption of a singular reality, one is confronted by the bewildering possibility of many realities, with no standard or stable framework as a guide.[20]

Does a hermeneutic/constructivist view of psychoanalytic theorizing imply that all theories are equally relative and therefore equally valid? Does the belief that human experience is fundamentally ambiguous suggest that there is no compelling way to evaluate competing interpretations of that experience? Does it leave us, in Levenson's (1992) frightening description, stuck in the "tarpits of constructivism"? Does the abandonment of the belief that psychoanalytic theories correspond, in a direct and linear fashion, to the Truth open the door to the claim that anything goes, that there are no constraints?

Fortunately, psychoanalysis is not on its own in struggling with these questions. Freud's rationalism pervaded the culture in which he lived. Similarly, the postrationalistic, postmodern world within which psychoanalysts must struggle for understanding pervades every intellectual discipline in our time, including the natural and social sciences.

The title of Richard Bernstein's treatise, *Beyond Objectivism and Relativism* (1983), is representative of the direction in which philosophers of science and postempiricist philosophy are moving.[21] The untenability of the belief in a one-to-one correspondence between our theories and Reality has led not to irrationalism but to a different kind of disciplined reason, which Bernstein calls "practical rationality." The critique of traditional objectivism has not left advocates of different theories helplessly out of touch with each other. The critique of objectivism, Bernstein argues, has nothing to do with "relativism, or at least that form of relativism which wants to claim that there can be no rational comparisons among the plurality of theories, paradigms, and language games—that we are prisoners locked in our own framework and cannot get out of it" (p. 92). Practical rationality, as Bernstein describes it, involves rational comparison of theories in terms of their use value, their consensual appeal, their economy of explanation. Practical rationality is essentially dialogic and intersubjective, implying the notion of community. Competing theories are not chosen purely on subjective, relativistic grounds. There is an emphasis on "the role of choice, deliberation, conflicting variable opinions, and the judgmental quality of rationality" (p. 74).

Bernstein argues that his notion of a practical rationality (beyond objectivism and relativism) reflects an emerging consensus in modern philosophy and philosophy of science. In many respects, psychoanalysis of the past several decades—in which theories have emerged, been sorted out, integrated, and discarded—provides some of the best evidence for his claim that rationalism has been replaced not by irrationalism but by a more pragmatic rationality.[22]

The development of psychoanalytic ideas, despite their heterogeneity, has actually been quite orderly. A proliferation of wildly idiosyncratic visions has not occurred. Although the postclassical era has given birth to a number of major independent traditions (such as various object relations theories and self psychology), these traditions have a great deal to do with each other. They can be logically integrated with each other into a comprehensive framework for clinical practice. (See Mitchell, 1988.)

The commitments of modern analysts to different theoretical concepts and systems have not been random and arbitrary. The criteria used for evaluating psychoanalytic concepts have necessarily broadened from narrowly defined empirical verifiability to such considerations as functional utility, intelligibility, and economy of explanation. Empirical data of various sorts certainly contribute to the evaluation of theoretical concepts, but they are no longer viewed as a final, ultimate arbitrator. Empirical data are important for raising questions, challenging explanations, provoking further discussion, contributing to a climate of opinion.

Among the reasons for the current popularity of object relations theories and self psychology is that they are directly useful for the kind of clinical problems that confront today's practicing clinician (feelings of inauthenticity, emptiness, meaninglessness; difficulties maintaining intimate and committed relationships). Among the reasons for the decline in the belief in drive theory (the way Freud formulated it) is that its vision of a human baby is contradicted by contemporary experimental psychology and infant research (Lichtenberg, 1983).

The answer to the question "What does the analyst know?" is not "How the mind works," or "How experience is structured." Rather, the analyst knows a collection of ways of thinking about how the mind works and about how experience is structured that are likely to be useful in the patient's efforts to understand himself and live with a greater sense of freedom and satisfaction in the world in which he finds himself. The state of psychoanalytic knowledge is not anchored in enduring truths or proof, but rather in its use value for making sense of a life, deepening relationships with others, and expanding and enriching the texture of experience.

So, everything is not equally valid. Consider an analogy with visual art. We could all agree that no painting captures reality in an objective, singular, unmediated fashion. Every painting is composed and thereby expresses the artist's subjective vision. Yet it does not follow that all paintings are equally valuable or illuminating. A representational painting strives to re-present something, and the subject matter has a claim on the painting. It is still meaningful to distinguish between good and bad representational art. (In that sense representational art has a responsibility to its subject of which abstract art is free.) Part of any evaluation of a representational painting is in its handling of that claim. Does it capture something about its subject matter, express something, transform something, in a way that is stimulating and captivating, either emotionally or conceptually?

Psychoanalytic theories are not abstract and free-form—they attempt to represent something. In the analytic situation they represent the patient's experience to himself; in the analytic community they represent clinicians' experiences to practicing analysts. Those experiential realities have a powerful claim on analytic theories. Abandoning the belief in a singular, objective analytic Truth (or multiple analytic truths that approach a singular, objective reality) does not lead to a valueless analytic relativism. There are an infinite number of ways to paint a vase with flowers—that does not mean they are all equally moving, that they have equal claims to capture and transform experience.

Ultimately, it is the community of psychoanalytic practitioners who provide the crucial testing ground, in the crucible of daily clinical work, for the relevance and efficacy of all levels of psychoanalytic theorizing. It is ultimately the community of clinicians who end up evaluating the extent to which different theoretical concepts offer compelling frameworks for the experience of both analysand and analyst of life in our time.

When the Wizard warned Dorothy not to peek behind the curtain, he was sure the exposure of the arbitrariness of his claims to wizardry would cost him his profession and possibly his life. Actually, even after his exposure, he was quite helpful to three-quarters of his clientele. (Dorothy required the further intervention of the good witch of the North.) The current revolutionary reexamination of the ground of psychoanalytic knowledge and the analyst's authority has not in any way led to theoretical anarchy or mindless subjectivism. Rather, we have witnessed the development of an orderly, disciplined form of rational theorizing that takes into account the analyst's participation.

3

The Two Revolutions Together

As a psycho-analyst I do not claim to know the answer, but I do not mean, therefore, that those who come to me for analysis know better.
—Wilfred R. Bion, *Brazilian Lectures*

In the previous two chapters I have delineated two striking developments in the recent history of pychoanalytic ideas. On the level of clinical theory, there has been a marked shift in emphasis from the clarification and renunciation of infantile fantasies to the revitalization and elaboration of the patient's sense of personal meaning. On the metatheoretical level, there has been a fundamental redefinition in our understanding of what psychoanalytic theorizing is, from a representation and reflection of the underlying structure of the patient's mind to a construction, an interpretation of the patient's experience.

These two revolutions grow out of the same broad changes in culture and intellectual sensibility from Freud's day to ours. They are essentially two sides of the same coin, the coin being the analytic process, since "What does the patient need?" and "What does the analyst know?" are very closely related questions. The slow and complex process of change in our thinking about one question has been influenced by changes in thinking about the other. Yet the two have not really been pulled together and integrated, despite the fact that each question leads directly to the other and the richness of each is fully developed only in the dialectic between them. One reason they have generally been developed separately is that writers who have introduced advances in theory have often been quite conservative with regard to metatheory, and vice versa.

Why is it important to integrate the two innovative currents we have been tracing? Let us consider the problems that emerge when they are developed largely in isolation from each other.

THEORY WITHOUT METATHEORY

Kohut, Winnicott, and other major figures in the clinical revolution were largely uninfluenced by the metatheoretical revolution. Their challenge operates on a clinical, not an epistemological, level.[1] Kohut and Winnicott locate cure in the rekindling and expansion of the patient's subjectivity, but the stress they place on the importance of reflecting, holding, and affirming the patient's subjectivity is not derived from any doubts about the greater objectivity and scientific validity of their analytic understanding. In fact, it derives from what they regard as advances in scientific understanding of the importance of specific sorts of developmental difficulties. These advances make crucial the affirmation of the child's and later the analysand's subjective experience.

This is why so many people are walking around clutching tightly books such as Daniel Stern's *The Interpersonal World of the Infant* (1985). Although Stern himself is very careful to distinguish his theory from the scattered empirical data he weaves together, the mantle of empiricism is still very important in psychoanalytic culture. It is less dangerous to challenge the tenets of classical theory under the banner of empirical findings from outside the consulting room; it is something else to acknowledge that one is simply hearing the patient differently than Freud did. (The change in the way the patient is being heard, of course, has been influenced by new empirical data.) The discussion gets a little tricky and sometimes a bit disingenuous. It is not that authors within the object relations or self psychology traditions do not claim to know better. In fact, their claim to know better includes a belief that greater knowledge is not what the patient needs right now—so they withhold that.

A further bit of metatheoretical naïveté concerns the belief by advocates of the clinical revolution that so-called correct empathy simply and directly grasps the raw experience of the patient, that "holding" and "containing" actually allow for the emergence of a "true" self, revealed in its original pristine form. Some authors write as if the patient's subjective experience can simply be uncovered, allowed to unfold in a receptive, empathic environment, much as Freud thought the analyst's neutrality allowed the patient's intrapsychic conflicts to emerge in an uncontaminated fashion.² They overlook the extent to which the patient is always speaking selectively to a particular other person for a specific purpose.

If we also take the revolution in metatheory into account, we begin to see that the "self" that the analyst "holds" and empathically grasps in the patient's experience is at least partially a function of what he is looking for and the idiosyncracies of his own mind. Thus, oddly, the clinical shift from clarifying distortions to affirming subjective experience is embedded in a hazy belief that all this is mandated by scientific advances in understanding babies. This leads to, among other things, a tendency to see patients in regressive, infantile terms, to an inattention to the analyst's role in cuing for the seemingly regressed material he finds, and also to a tendency to take theories of early development much too seriously, as fact rather than as fruitful metaphors and mythologies.

Thus, authors and clinicians who embrace the revolution in theory without taking into account the revolution in metatheory regard the revitalization and expansion of the patient's authentic subjectivity within the analytic situation as something they are just facilitating and observing rather than something they are participating in creating. The greatest danger here is the obliviousness this generates regarding the impact of the analyst's own belief system and personal participation and the failure of the analyst and analysand to explore that impact on the patient's experience.

Margaret Little's (1985) moving personal account of her analysis with Winnicott illustrates this problem. Little suffered through two failed analyses (Jungian and classical Freudian) before she found Winnicott. She had her own strongly held conviction that what she required was a deeply regressive experience, a conviction that Winnicott shared. This fit made possible a powerfully transformative analytic experience for Little. But does that mean that Winnicott was right? Was his understanding of what she needed the only approach that could have helped her? What was not considered was Little's obvious awareness of and feelings about Winnicott's beliefs and her apparent eagerness to find herself in them. Because of this omission, the fit between Little's experience in analysis and Winnicott's theories was not considered as possibly containing a dimension involving a reenactment of Little's lifelong pattern of bending herself into a shape corresponding to the expectations of others. (See Bass [1992] for an interesting discussion of these issues in relation to Little's analysis.)

By contrast, Winnicott's book *Holding and Interpretation* (1986) contains a nearly verbatim analysis of a man who did not feel wholly sanguine about Winnicott's beliefs about what he needed. Winnicott's own developmental hypotheses are quite apparent in his responses to the patient. At many points the patient seems extremely exasperated and trying to address what he feels is Winnicott's preoccupation with his own theories.

The patient begins one session by reporting that he is finding it difficult to "produce further material" of the sort Winnicott seems to be looking for.

> Patient: "Sometimes it seems that the deeper material is not so productive. It might be considered too frivolous, too conscious or something. I seem to be trying to produce the right thing. I often feel guilty that I may be wasting the time or fabricating in a way that is elaborate and meaningless." (p. 94)

The patient seems to suggest that he labors to produce material that corresponds to Winnicott's ideas about what is important. Rather than exploring the patient's need to please, his ideas about what Winnicott thinks is important, and his ideas about Winnicott's investment in his own theories, Winnicott responds by recounting his own ideas of the developmental function he is providing.

> Analyst: "All the time there is myself holding you, and further there are the various methods; on the one hand my general management, and on the other hand the interpretations of material." (p. 94)

In another session the patient seems to be addressing the way in which he experiences Winnicott's manner of being with him.

> Analyst: "And at the same time you had no brothers for mutual loving and hating and pushing around."
> Patient: "I feel that that is what I am doing to you, pushing and pushing. I feel though that you would be damnably peaceful, limp like cotton wool; nothing firm. If I hit you, my arm would be left there; it would not come back. . . "
> Analyst: "You never seem to be able to find anyone to match your strength against." (p. 122)

Because Winnicott sees his theories reflecting the patient's inner world (not merely one possible construction of it), he does not pick up on the patient's statements as commentaries on what is taking place between them.

In another session the patient explicitly comments on Winnicott's relationship to his own interpretations, which he seems to experience as regurgitated theory. Notice that there is a pause after the patient comments directly on what is talking place between them. Winnicott does not respond, and the patient resumes by denying that he has just said anything:

> Patient: "I had a curious idea then, that somebody was eating something, like eating ideas, so if you produce something (an interpretation), you are vomiting. Therefore, accepting an idea from you is distasteful. There is the danger that I don't recognize these ideas till they are half consumed, and then I find out and vomit. For a moment I had a very clear picture of all this, of you sitting at a meal, with a plate of food which you eat, and while you eat the food increases, which means that you are bringing it all up, slowly." *Pause* "It seems very difficult, this not talking, it's dangerous, nothing happens. Can you make use of it? It's only too easy never to talk. I remember now, as I left yesterday, I wondered, is it worthwhile to carry on if not talking is life?" (p. 144)

The papers in which Winnicott presented his extremely important and influential contributions to theory contain very little actual clinical material. In them he provides a treasure trove of invaluable insights on the development of subjective experience in childhood and in the analytic situation. He portrays the analyst's role not as largely interpretive but as adapting to and facilitating the expression of the patient's own experience.

Holding and Interpretation, however, provides a unique and very different angle on Winnicott's clinical approach. He speaks a great deal and provides a perpetual stream of interpretations. How are we to understand this apparent contradiction?

It seems likely that Winnicott did not think that all the talking he was doing was interpretive, in the traditional sense of the term. He felt he was providing a "holding environment" that was encouraging the unfolding of the patient's more genuine experience. He must have felt that his talk was providing the patient material with which to "play" rather than interpreting unconscious conflict in the classical mode.[3] Consequently, Winnicott does not consider the specific, formative impact of his own participation on the patient's experience. When the patient is talking about that impact, Winnicott seems convinced that he is reporting internal, intrapsychic states rather than struggling to address the process between them.

Winnicott's approach derives from what remains of the one-person (rather than dyadic or two-person) features of his model of the analytic situation. In his frame of reference, to address the interaction between patient and analyst would be to water down the analytic process, to focus on the shallow, interpersonal dimension rather than on the depths of the patient's regression to points of developmental fixation. In this model, it does not matter if the patient is wrong or right in his references to Winnicott's participation and his relationship to his own theory. What is crucial for the development of the patient's authentic subjectivity is the unfolding of his arrested developmental needs. Winnicott has total confidence that the universal validity and scientific underpinnings of his own developmental theories provide him with an unerring guide to what the patient needs.

In my view, Winnicott's invaluable contributions to the revolution in theory, the generation of ideas about what the patient needs, are greatly enriched by integrating them with considerations raised by the revolution in metatheory. In his work with both Margaret Little and the patient in *Holding and Interpretation,* metatheoretical considerations would arouse interest in the patient's experience of Winnicott's relationship to his own theory and the impact of that on the patient. Ironically, such considerations are extremely compatible with Winnicott's important concept of false self-adaptation to externality. Does Margaret Little's production of material that matches Winnicott's theories so closely suggest only the correctness of those theories, or also the possibility of an adaptation to them in a reenactment of her childhood compliance to powerful parents? Does the patient in *Holding and Interpretation* feel frustrated in his efforts to engage Winnicott because his mother's breast was produced instantly and too perfectly in response to his need (this was Winnicott's understanding), or also because he experiences Winnicott as so absorbed in his own theories about his developmental past as to be completely impervious to his patient's efforts to reach him?

The failure to integrate the implications of the revolution in metatheory into the analytic approach generated by the revolution in theory leads to an emphasis on the emergence and development of the patient's subjectivity as if in an apparent vacuum. As noted in the discussion of phenomenology in the last chapter, this approach does not take into account the analyst's imput into the particular subjectivity the patient has developed and the patient's inevitable conflictual feelings about that participation. By not acknowledging the analyst's active, personal input, it is more likely that the influence of that input will remain unexamined. This approach does not allow the patient to learn that there is always a perspective other than his own subjectivity, that there is always more to say.[4]

METATHEORY WITHOUT THEORY

Those authors who have been the most important contributors to the metatheoretical revolution have been largely isolated from the revolution in theory. Those who have been exploring the hermeneutics wing of the hermeneutics/constructivist movement—philosophers Habermas and Ricoeur as well as Schafer and Spence—all tend to limit their critique to traditional classical theory.

Habermas is interested in the way in which the methodology Freud invented made possible the study of human self-reflection in a new way. He roots Freud's innovations in the philosophical tradition leading up to and developed by Hegel. He argues that although Freud saw himself as providing causal explanations of natural phenomena, he inadvertently developed a methodology for understanding meaning in human phenomena. Ricoeur's concern also has been exclusively with Freud's work. His focus has been on the tension in Freud's thought between causal explanations (drive and energic concepts) and the understanding of subjective meanings.

There are two major limitations in this line of metatheoretical innovation. First, although Ricoeur and Habermas are both centrally concerned with subjective meaning, in their philosophical preoccupation with Freud they do not address the revolution in theory in the work of Winnicott, Kohut, Loewald, and other contemporary theorists, where the problem of meaning and the generation of subjectivity has taken center stage.

Second, both Ricoeur and Habermas lack a clinician's sense of the process of interpretation within the interpersonal context of the analytic relationship. As philosophers, they think of interpretation as a reading, similar to the reading of a text. Their sole concern is with the content of the interpretation. They do not seem to grasp, and therefore do not take account of, what is involved in the actual process of making interpretations, the engagement of the patient. Whereas a text is passive and inert, a patient speaks back, or ought to. Perhaps the most important part of the process of interpreting is the need to discover a way to make analytic self-reflection something that begins to seem interesting and important. Different theoretical content lends itself differently to the problem of engaging the patient in self-reflection. Winnicott, Kohut, and other authors seminal in the revolution in theory stress the importance of speaking to the patient about what feels real and authentic to her.

Spence and Schafer, the two writers within clinical psychoanalysis who have developed hermeneutics with a strong clinical sense, have similarly limited their considerations to classical Freudian thought and have neglected the revolution in theory. Spence has been concerned largely with the epistemological and evidential status of Freud's work. Schafer has developed a compelling view of analytic theories as narrative strategies and enriched our clinical understanding of what we are doing when we make an interpretation. Yet he finds it necessary to insist that Freudian theory is unquestionably the best, the most useful storyline, and he goes to great lengths, over and over, to argue that his profoundly different understanding of the epistemological status of psychoanalytic knowledge has no impact whatever on his practice of psychoanalysis. It seems very improbable to me that, even with identical content, an interpretation that the analyst believes is one of many possible ways to engage the material could be delivered and experienced in the same way as an interpretation that the analyst believes is a correct and exclusive Truth. The nature of the analytic relationship and the analytic process is profoundly changed when one defines oneself as a collaborator in developing a personal narrative rather than as a scientist uncovering facts.

Writers who have been influential in developing the constructivist wing of the hermeneutics/constructivist movement tend to focus on the more personal dimension of the analyst's participation—countertransference, spontaneous reactions, idiosyncratic prejudices and preconceptions. The analyst's theory is not given much importance or is regarded as a post hoc rationale brought in later to justify the analyst's role in the process. (See, for example, Donnel Stern, 1991, p. 75.) Because theory has traditionally been misused by being mistaken for the Truth, it is compelling to regard theory as an impediment to a more genuine inquiry into the interaction between analysand and analyst. In its extreme form, such a position portrays psychoanalysis as purely a methodology with no theory at all (Levenson, 1992).

Clinicians and authors who embrace the metatheoretical revolution without integrating into it the advances of the revolution in theory risk ending up with a methodology that floats in space. The analyst is portrayed as bringing nothing particularly useful to the analytic situation other than a skill in asking questions, analyzing interactions, demystifying the patient's confusions, and "deconstructing" the patient's own understandings (Levenson, 1992). Ironically, an exclusive preoccupation with the analyst's participation can inflate the analyst's importance and detract from an exploration of the patient's experience. Theories that provide possibilities for depicting developmental and structural patterning of the patient's experience, while brought to the interaction by the analyst, can facilitate a deepening of the patient's experience that allows the awareness of the analyst to fade into the background.

Theories of mind such as those of Melanie Klein, Winnicott, Loewald, Kohut, and others do not portray the actual, universal structure of mind, but they do provide emotionally powerful ways to organize experience. Theory has lasted all these years not only for defensive reasons, but because it enables both patients and analysts to construct compelling, growth-promoting patterns out of patients' experiences and memories and out of their here-and-now experiences together. Theory interferes with inquiry only when misused; used properly, with a light touch, concepts derived from motivational, structural, and developmental theory make sense of past experience and open up new possibilities. (See Greenberg, 1991, and Spezzano, 1993, for models of this way of using theory.)

The metatheoretical revolution forces us to be concerned with the perspectivistic, constructive, interpretive nature of all clinical understanding. It encourages a healthy skepticism about what the analyst knows. Thus, Spence argues for the radical skepticism of "know nothing" hermeneutics, always assuming the null hypothesis until a significant deviation from it is demonstrated convincingly. However, the stance of investigator is not wholly suitable to the job of clinician. As analysts we are concerned not only with uncovering arguable understandings of what is and was true but also with the development of a meaningful, authentic subjective experience. These are not identical goals. The investigator who is always questioning both her own and her patient's understandings can sometimes be a provocative and constructive gadfly and sometimes an irritating distraction from the task of facilitating the patient's self-discovery. At times in any analysis a sense of personal conviction is extremely important to protect, and metatheoretical inquiry can become a form of obsessive doubting and timidity.

An exclusive concern with metatheoretical issues tends to minimize an additional feature. The exploration and construction of a personal history with another person is a powerful, transformative interpersonal experience. "History" in this sense does not suggest something arcane, intellectual, and experience-distant. Nor does it suggest a static narrative, rigidly maintained. The reason history has been such a central part of the analytic experience (despite the fading relevance of archaeological metaphors) is that a deep and workable sense of who one is in the present must include a compelling understanding of how one's past has contributed to bringing one here. (Compare Bollas, 1991, and L. Friedman, 1988, p. 468.)

Without memory, there is no self. Meaning in personal experience is composed of narratives. The narratives that the patient brings into treatment are generally stereotyped and closed. A central part of what the analyst adds is imagination, a facility with reorganizing and reframing, a capacity to envision different endings, different futures. If the storylines suggested by the analyst himself are rigid and stereotyped, the analytic process degenerates into sterility and conversion. But if the analyst's contribution is offered as material to be broken down, rearranged, thoroughly digested by the patient, interpretations derived from the analyst's theory play an important and constructive role in the patient's fashioning of personal meaning. (See Aron, 1992.)

Taken alone, the metatheoretical revolution can lead to a preoccupation with epistemological and evidential features of the analyst's participation and knowledge that can detract from the central focus of analytic inquiry—the inquiry into and enrichment of the patient's experience. The danger is that the conceptual awareness of the interactive nature of all experience leads to a technical overemphasis on interaction, where the patient is drawn continually to focus on her experience and perceptions of the analyst and her assumptions about the analyst.[5]

Some authors who emphasize the analyst's participation assume that examining such participation will purge the process of the analyst's influence (Oremland, 1991). This ideal goes back to the earliest days of psychoanalysis, when Freud tried to differentiate the analytic method from hypnotism, which deliberately exploits the analyst's influence. In reality, however, perpetual analysis of the patient's experience of the analyst's participation does not factor that participation out of the process. In fact, the thoroughly interactive nature of the analytic situation suggests that the impact of the analyst is intrinsic to everything that happens, not something that can ever be peeled away neatly. The notion that the analyst's participation can and should be ferreted out, isolated, and removed is a holdover from the classical ideal of a neutral, purely one-person field, in which the analyst's countertransference is a contaminant. It seems more useful to consider the analyst's participation as an intrinsic part of the process that bears continual inquiry and self-reflection, but not an exclusive focus.

I suggested earlier that the metatheoretical advance in thinking about the analyst's participation serves as a corrective for those theoreticians who focus on the patient's subjective experience and who believe that they, in fact, know what the patient needs. The reverse also is true. Theories that provide concepts for describing and tracking the development of the patient's subjective experience can provide a useful corrective for the contributions that have advanced the metatheoretical revolution and our reconsideration of the nature of theory, where there is a tendency to drift into a preoccupation with the analyst's participation and the epistemological status of her knowledge.

THEORY AND METATHEORY TAKEN TOGETHER

The two movements I have charted have developed relatively independently from each other. This is unfortunate. In a fundamental sense, they belong together; they require each other. The two movements have revolved around different questions, but the answer to each question leads enevitably to considerations of the other.

What does the patient need? The answers have moved from insight and renunciation to the development of meaning and authenticity. If we continue in that direction, we end up, necessarily, with questions not only about the patient's subjectivity but also about the analyst's knowledge. How does the analytic process help to generate meaning and to locate authentic experience? What sort of system of meanings does psychoanalytic theory provide? What is the relationship between the analyst and his theory? The revolution in theory that centers on the development of the patient's subjectivity leads inevitably to issues that have been at the heart of the revolution in metatheory concerning the analyst's knowledge.

What does the analyst know? The answers have moved from objective, universal knowledge to interpretive systems and constructions embedded in the personal experience and subjectivity of the analyst. If we continue in that direction, we necessarily end up with questions not only about the analyst's knowledge but also about the changes in the patient's experience and understanding that develop in the analytic process. What does the patient get from the analyst? What sort of self-understanding does the patient end up with? What are the differences between interpretations of self that are paralyzing and fragmenting and those that are vitalizing and enriching? The revolution in metatheory that centers on the nature of the analyst's knowledge leads inevitably to issues that have been at the heart of the revolution in theory concerning the patient's need.

Psychoanalysis is increasingly envisioned as a process that enriches the analysand's subjectivity, a subjectivity that includes an appreciation of oneself as an independent agent among other independent agents (Benjamin, 1992b), a self-reflecting constructor of one's own experience (Hoffman, 1991a), a specifically analytic subject (Ogden, 1992a, b). In this current vision of the kind of experience created through analytic collaboration, the problems of theory and the problems of metatheory, questions of need and questions of knowledge, merge. What the analysand needs includes a particular attitude toward knowing on the part of the analyst. As Benjamin (1991, p. 533) has put it, "In psychoanalysis the question, How do we know? is inextricable from the question, What do we know? since the knowing subject itself is what is in question."

If the revolutions in theory and metatheory are taken together, we end up with a vision of the analytic process that is markedly different from that of its founder. This difference has important implications for clinical practice, many of which have been largely unexplored.

Helping the patient to develop a rich and deeply rooted sense of self is at the center of the modern analytic experience, and the contributions I have termed the clinical revolution have brought this project into sharp focus. The analyst's role is central and crucial in this process, and the contributions I have termed the metatheoretical revolution have enriched our understanding of that role.

The analyst is not a mirror, an inert object, but a complex meaning-generating subjectivity in her own right. The image of himself that the patient sees in the analyst's interpretations is neither an X-ray vision into his true, underlying nature nor an unmodified, accurate reflection of what the patient has expressed. It is a complex reorganization of the patient's productions along highly personal lines, reflecting the analyst's consciously held theory and beliefs, unconscious identifications, accidents of the analyst's own history, and so on. Because of this, the analytic relationship and the analytic process are simultaneously both highly personal and highly interpersonal.

The analytic situation inevitably represents the encounter of two perspectives, two subjectivities, two psychic realities. This dyadic structure is perhaps the most interesting thing about the analytic relationship. How does the patient deal with these two realities? How does the analyst? How does the patient experience the analyst as dealing with her? The participation in and inquiry into this interpersonal dialectic of two subjectivities become a central focus of the work.

The development of personal, authentic subjectivity in the patient and questions concerning the analyst's knowledge become intertwined in another sense. Drawing on Hegel's philosophy, Benjamin (1992b) has argued that the full development of a sense of oneself as subject involves the search for recognition by another subject, that the full development of oneself as human entails a relationship to another whom one experiences as fully human. Aron (1991) has extended this to a consideration of the patient's interest in and search for the analyst's subjectivity in the analytic situation. He argues that a central and necessary feature of the analytic process is the patient's curiosity about, search for, and evolving understanding of the analyst as person. Part of what every patient needs is the freedom to explore the analyst in a very personal way, including the analyst's relationship to what he knows.

RETURNING TO SOPHIE

The revolution in theory regards the development of a sense of personal meaning and authentic subjectivity as the central feature of the analytic process. What light does this sort of approach shed on Sophie's dilemma?

The passion and romance Sophie experienced in her recent relationship is deeper and richer than in any of her prior relationships. Her complex involvement with her mother, her worldview, and her reassuring internal presence previously prevented Sophie from being able to be really excited about any man. Romance, idealization, excitement itself were all experienced as dangerous, because they threatened the interpersonal and intrapsychical moorings that her tie to her mother provided.

Sophie's excitement and erotic expansiveness might usefully be regarded as the growing edge of the self, precisely the kind of vigorous hopefulness and vitality that was not adequately confirmed or engaged by her parents, because it was too threatening to their connection with her. In this view, a central component of what analysis can offer Sophie is a second chance to find and develop the spontaneity of living and loving. Whatever else happens, the analyst ought to find a way to respond to Sophie's anticipation of sober rationality with a passionate identification and resonance with her excitement. In contrast to the more traditional psychoanalytic emphasis on rational understanding of dynamic meanings, a more contemporary analytic approach to what the patient needs would presume that any meanings would need to be anchored in a renewed capacity for excitement and imaginatively enriched passion.

In a traditional analytic framework, Sophie's disinclination to allow the analyst to know and form opinions about her new relationship would be considered as resistance. In the perspective being developed here, this avoidance is in the service of protecting delicate and fragile stirrings of authentic excitement and hope to which the analyst poses a genuine threat. The danger Sophie's resistance is guarding her against is her habitual self-betrayal by allowing herself to be shaped by others' ideas of what is best for her. This perspective suggests a different understanding of the function of resistance, not as an adversary of the analytic process but often, as in this kind of situation, as an ally of the authentic development of the patient's personal experience.[6]

Sterba's patient provides another example of the same problem. The patient experiences a dread of the analytic situation. For Sterba, what is crucial is to bring to consciousness what he believes (because his theory informs him) to be the incestuous wishes underlying her sense of dread. From my perspective, her experience of her dread, her ideas of what is happening and might happen in the analytic situation, her ideas about what the analyst is up to—these are of central and immediate concern. Whether or not the patient herself eventually came to feel that unconscious incestuous wishes underlay her dread of the analytic situation is less relevant than her coming to feel that her wishes, her dread are what matters. Even if Sterba was right about the content (which is not at all clear), his preoccupation with it leads him to circumvent the patient's experience, the structure and textures of her subjective world, which, in a more contemporary perspective, are at the heart of the matter.

Analysts drawing on the revolution in theory exclusively might very well end their considerations of Sophie's dilemma with a sense that what is called for is simply an acceptance of her excitement, the establishment of an analytic presence that unconditionally contains and empathizes with her current romantic state of mind. What about questionable and worrisome features of this new relationship? What if Sophie is overlooking serious problems? What if there are features of this new love that repeat, without her realizing it, neurotic patterns from the past? For those concerned exclusively with the revolution in theory, with the development of Sophie's personal subjectivity, these questions are no longer the central analytic focus. (From Kohut's perspective, for example, the central analytic task is the healing of the self-disorder; later, once Sophie's self has become coherent and durable, she will be able to handle further problems, the pragmatics of relationships, probably mostly on her own.)[7]

I have trouble with this position, partly because it leaves out what the revolution in metatheory has demonstrated in terms of the centrality of the analyst's participation in the analytic process.

No matter how accepting and nonjudgmental the analyst is trying to be, most analysands are quite aware that the analyst has opinions and reactions to important issues the latter is struggling with. Analysands see through the analyst's efforts to be purely empathic and mirroring and feel patronized. Freud early on said, "He who has eyes to see and ears to hear becomes convinced that mortals can keep no secret. If their lips are silent, they gossip with their fingertips; betrayal forces its way through every pore" (quoted in Gay, 1988, p. 254). Surely, although Freud was describing patients, not analysts, this also must apply to the latter group of mortals. If so, then the impact on the analytic process of the analyst's perspective cannot be eliminated by denying its constant presence or apologizing for it when it becomes unmistakably visible in discordancies with the patient's experience, hopes, and wishes.

Further, even if it were possible, the role of mirror, holder, container gives up too much. My participating in such a fashion would enable Sophie to not take me seriously at all, and she would not get what I might have to offer in thinking about this new relationship, or she would get it in a cryptic and dishonest form. Is there a clear, concise paragraph or not? Is Sophie's conviction about that merely a new edition of her mother's gaze? Is denying it double-binding, or a disingenuous false modesty?

Transference/countertransference patterns often involve complementary pairs of choices. In this situation the choice seemed to be the control of Sophie's excitement through exposure to my scrutiny (modeled on the mother's power) or my false acceptance of her excitement and unthinking surrender to her current viewpoint. The latter option was modeled on a reversal, in which Sophie now played the mother's role and I was called upon to purge my mind of any heretically divergent thoughts. The problem seemed to be for me to find a voice in which I could speak, and for Sophie to find an ear in which she could hear, a point of view that was neither an imperative nor a false compliance.

As Sophie and I struggled to get at what we both felt I had been and could still offer her, it became clear that what was missing from her experience was the possibility that I could offer her a perspective, a way of looking at things different from her customary modes that might be of use to her sometimes. In contrast to Brenner's statement cited earlier about the analyst's privileged position, it was clear that, ultimately, Sophie had a much richer and more variegated set of views of herself than I ever could have. What I had added could not be seen as more "correct" or certainly not more comprehensive, but an angle that was new, or one that she had selectively avoided. Rather than a clear, concise paragraph of my own, I had sometimes offered loosely structured, rambling paragraphs, very different in tone and point of view at different stages in the process. At other times I had offered something closer to amendments, editing suggestions and punctuation changes often conveying very different meaning in her paragraphs.

As we clarified how things worked between us, it became apparent to both of us that Sophie had a much more complex view of this new man than she had let on. She actually had become quite observant about many things about him, potential troublesome issues for her, things that seemed to work and also things that did not work. But she still deeply wanted to believe that somehow I really did know better, could predict the future, could somehow really know whether this relationship would work out or not. Sophie had sacrificed her awareness of what she knew to keep that illusion alive. Of course, she also knew that any such claims on my part bordered, like some of her mother's theories, on the crackpot, and felt deep cynicism and bitter resentment about my "psychoanalytic meat grinder." It scared her to come to terms with how unpredictable the future is, how much on her own she really is. It scared me too. But her fears about the future no longer amounted to the deep dread with which she began analysis, and no longer depended on the hope of her finding in the analyst a more benign version of the mother's omnipotent powers. Sophie had become able to ground her hopes in her own considerable resources to deal with her life.

Was the understanding of her past and her parents that Sophie and I arrived at veridical? Would we want to consider it objectively true? In considering this question, it is crucial to move beyond the truth/fantasy dichotomy (parallel to the philosopher's choice between objectivity and subjectivity) that has dominated psychoanalytic theorizing until recent years. The perspective Sophie and I developed on her parents and her early childhood was true in the sense that it fit with a great deal of her experience, both her memories of the past and her sense of who she was in the present. But it was very important that this perspective not be endowed with finality, considered to be the ultimate and unchangeable view of her development.

Perspectives on the past change over the course of treatment and, equally important, long after the treatment has ended. Views of the parents as ideal are replaced by recognitions of them as destructive, which are often, in turn, replaced by a recapturing of genuine love and important moments of connection. There is no formula for these shifting viewpoints. They are neither simply objective nor simply subjective. If they work analytically, they allow the analysand access to previously undeveloped areas of experience in a way that also allows an openness to new possibilities. The process of historical reconstruction in contemporary psychoanalysis represents "practical reason" (Bernstein, 1983) where ideas are offered, compared, and used, always with the assumption that they will be replaced or amended by other ideas.

A central theme in the remainder of Sophie's analysis concerned our mutual effort to work toward a position vis-à-vis each other from which she could take me seriously, but not too seriously, from which she could fully use my interpretations without sacrificing any of her own considerable resources. In that sense, I do not agree with the notion that conflictual interpersonal difficulties take care of themselves once self-fragmentation is healed. The healing of the self and the capacity fully to engage another are necessarily coterminous processes, and constitute the heart of analytic work. I have come to think of the work on this subtle dialectical process as central to all analyses—the capacity to hear, hold, and play with an interpretation, neither surrendering to it as powerful magic nor rejecting it as dangerous poison—not as a criterion of analyzability but as a criterion of readiness to terminate. The development of the capacity for the distinctively psychoanalytic form of self-reflection marks an analysand's readiness to move on.

One of the most important implications of the metatheoretical revolution is that the analyst's experience in general and the analyst's theory in particular have an important presence in the analytic situation. The analyst has a relationship to his theory, which the patient comes to experience in very vivid terms. In one way or another I think Sophie's question is, or should be, every patient's question: What does this person, the analyst, think he is doing? Does he really believe in what he is doing? In what he says? What is his relationship to his theory? To his interpretations? Does he believe them in absolute terms? Is it a claim to knowledge, or an article of faith? Does he play with ideas to enrich experience, or reductively superimpose ideas upon experience? What is it that he wants me to do with these interpretations? What is at stake for the analyst?

A successful analysis results in a much more complex experience of oneself than that with which one began. The analysand learns that there is much more to him than he has previously fully known or been able to use. The analyst's attitude toward her own theories, themselves shifting and evolving products of mental life, becomes an important model in the expansion of the analysand's experience of his own mental life. And at crucial points in any analysis, the analytic method itself becomes the focus of analytic inquiry and, in some sense, needs to be reconstructed, rediscovered in the context of each particular analytic dyad. A central, distinctive feature of psychoanalysis, as Levenson (1983, p. 91) has put it, is that "the method of arriving at the truth is at least as relevant as the truth arrived at."

Analysis does not work unless both analysand and analyst are passionate about the work. Yet this passion, like most passions, has a tragic underside. A passionate analysis, if it is to be maximally effective, must contain an awareness of the limits of the process and the necessary omissions and constraints of this particular dyad. In that sense, termination does not suggest a "completeness" of the analysis but a readiness to move past the limitations and inevitable incompleteness of the current one.

There are major drawbacks in characterizing the analyst's participation in terms of either a claim to absolute objectivity or a postured humility, in which one portrays oneself as merely a container or vehicle for the patient to find herself. Rather, the greater the clarity, meaning, and enjoyment the analyst finds in his own participation, the better able he is to facilitate the patient's ability to expand her own experience while being able to enrich it in interactions with others. What seems to me crucial in enabling the analyst to steer a course midway between claims to objectivity on the one hand and invisibility on the other is a love of the analytic inquiry itself and a deep appreciation of the awesome complexity of the human mind.

REVOLUTION OR EVOLUTION?

One of the most important issues dividing psychoanalytic theoreticians and clinicians today is whether the kinds of changes I have been discussing are best considered revolutionary or evolutionary. There is no right or wrong answer to this question. Almost everyone agrees that contemporary psychoanalysis is different from psychoanalysis ninety years ago and also different from psychoanalysis fifty years ago. It is still psychoanalysis, but it is different. It is the same in some respects; it has changed in others. Calling these changes revolutionary emphasizes the differences; calling these changes evolutionary emphasizes the continuities. Neither view is more correct—it is a question of emphasis. I might have said merely a question of emphasis, but that would be to understate how important the choice of emphasis is: theoretically, clinically, and politically.

A strong case can be made for the evolutionary view, which is conservative in the best sense of that term. Nothing needs to be discarded; everything can be preserved or rennovated. Because Freud's writings are so comprehensive and rich, it can be argued persuasively that there is nothing in the subsequent history of psychoanalytic ideas that he did not anticipate in some form or other. The evolutionary view portrays the development of psychoanalysis as a smooth, continuous expansion and enrichment. There are no bumps, no discontinuities, no hard choices. Further, the evolutionary position brings with it a seeming ecumenicism. All workers can be included in psychoanalysis, as long as they do not argue for the exclusion of the historically common, seminal models of Freud. From the evolutionary point of view, discussions of discontinuities, revolutions in thought, and mutually exclusive alternatives seem unnecessarily contentious and divisive. The guiding ideal is integration and inclusiveness.[8]

Arnold Rothstein (1983) has defended the rationality of what he terms the "evolutionary perspective" with considerable fervor. He regards the development of psychoanalytic thought as a broad, diverse collection of contributions all evolving from Freud's original insights and all comfortably housed within a loose perspective he calls the "structural hypothesis," which "emphasizes conflict that derives from an inner and interminable cauldron of powerful wishes and from the influences of the environment" (p. 2). Rothstein's work is broad and inclusive; he draws on many new currents for adding on and expanding, claiming that all newer developments can be housed comfortably within Freud's structural hypothesis, "a superordinate frame of reference encompassing a number of complementary and resonant models" (p. 28). His major argument is with those who implicitly reject his hospitality and cannot accept his generous offer of housing, those who see their own contributions as revolutionary, as constituting a new and incompatible "paradigm."

The term paradigm is drawn from Thomas Kuhn's overused distinction between normal science, which proceeds through accretion, and revolutionary science, which introduces a novel and discontinuous perspective. To Rothstein, Kuhn disparages the stature of science by suggesting that it is "less than rational" (1983, p. 9).[9] He finds references to Kuhn in various authors, such as Kohut and Schafer, who propose new theories, alternatives to traditional theory, and offers these as evidence that these theorists are suffering from "paradigm grandiosity" (p. 24), leading to the unhelpful practice of "paradigm competition," because they have invested their own thinking with narcissistic illusions of perfection. In his enthusiasm for ferreting out neurotic motives in those who think differently than he does (a venerable psychoanalytic tradition in its own right), he concludes that those who think that psychoanalytic thought is not wholly additive, incremental, and rational are not rational themselves: "To the degree that theories are divested of their narcissistic illusions of perfection, to the degree that creators and disciples mourn their pursuit of these illusionary gratifications, the process of developments in science can be more rational and evolutionary" (p. 4).

Consider more closely the argument of the evolutionaries. It consists of many arbitrary claims, presented as if they were wholly rational.

Evolutionaries claim that the continuities within psychoanalytic thought are more important than the discontinuities. Why? Is it always more rational to focus on commonalities than to stress differences? Is a stress on analytic models as alternatives really any more contentious than an insistence that they all be shoehorned into one or another version of classical theory? Consider Joseph Sandler's description of the traditional style of psychoanalytic theorizing, with its evolutionary stress on continuities.

> Freud's ideas are seen as the core of existing theory, and acceptable later developments are viewed as amplifications and additions, which are consistent—or at least not inconsistent—with Freud's thoughts. Those who think in these terms will, when they disagree with other writers, do so on the grounds that the others have misunderstood, misinterpreted or misapplied Freud, and will turn back to Freud's writings to find supporting evidence for their own ideas. (Wallerstein, 1988, p. 9n.)

Anyone who has labored through traditional psychoanalytic journals is well acquainted with the stultifying impact of the necessity to find the precursors of any thought somewhere in Freud.

It is very important to distinguish conceptual from political issues here, to distinguish attitudes toward integrating theory from those toward freedom of thought. As far as I know, proponents of revolutionary models (such as Fairbairn, Kohut, and Schafer) never argued for the exclusion of those with different approaches to theory from psychoanalytic organizations nor insisted that the latter were not real psychoanalysts. (In fact, these have been the political strategies of many traditionalists.) The evolutionaries seem to feel that their offer of the new inclusiveness should be acceptable to any rational person with an open mind. What they miss is the possibility that someone might regard theoretical heterodoxy as wonderful and enriching for the field and for training and education, and still feel that a postclassical model is conceptually incompatible with the classical drive model.

The evolutionaries claim that the structural model is the best general framework for housing psychoanalytic ideas. Why? The structural model is the most inclusive, since it encompasses body factors (id), regulatory functions (ego), and environmental influences (superego). This is a very compelling argument for people who already believe in the structural model, because it is rich, complex, and infinitely expandable. But evolutionaries overlook the fact that all theorists regard their own theory as the most balanced and most encompassing. Fairbairn's framework also contains body factors, regulatory functions, and environmental influences, all brought together in his own fashion. So does Kohut's. So does Schafer's.

All of us regard our own theory as most balanced, because we each stand at the center of our own (conceptual) world, with the thoughts of others arranged around us, everyone else accounted for. The centrality of each of us within our own horizon is regularly demonstrated when analysts of different persuasions comment on clinical presentations. (See, for example, *Psychoanalytic Inquiry* 7, no. 2, "How Theory Shapes Technique: Perspectives on a Clinical Study" [1987].) All discussants regard the analyst's approach as too narrow and their own approach as encompassing his, but in a broader vision. The presenter regularly thanks the discussants for their partial views, all embraceable within his own vision. It is difficult to imagine anyone who feels she operates within a narrow perspective, unable to account for what is dealt with by others. Each theory can account for all human experience, but in that theory's own terms.

One of the most seductive features in the appeal of the evolutionaries is the suggestion that one can have it all, that it is possible not to choose, that choosing, in fact, is both unnecessary and tendentious. (This is one of Freud's favorite words [*tendenzios* in German] for people who did not agree with him.) But having it all is actually not having any of it in quite the same way. Fairbairn's object relations concepts housed in Brenner's structural model no longer retain Fairbairn's understanding. When Fairbairn said "libido is not pleasure-seeking, but object-seeking," he was establishing a motivational framework for viewing human experience that was dramatically different from and incompatible with Freud's. Someone else can surely say "Well, we can have them both, pleasure-seeking *and* object-seeking." That is a perfectly defensible choice, but it is no longer *Fairbairn's* vision. Fairbairn cannot really be himself in Brenner's domicile.

Let us shift the metaphor from the residential to the gustatory. A stew (the evolutionaries' structural model) is different from a smorgasbörd (mixed models perspective: a different theory for different patients), and both are different from a seven-course dinner (a purely classical or purely relational perspective). These are different meals, and the experience of eating them is different. With theoretical perspectives, as with meals, taste is important. It is not possible to decide which is better on purely rational grounds. (This does not mean that the theories themselves are irrational.) A great deal depends on whether the theory speaks to you. A crucial factor that the evolutionaries miss is that the current Freudian stew simply does not move many people in the way that Freud's theory moved people fifty or ninety years ago. Many contemporary clinicians, patients, and general readers find that it does not explain them to themselves in a way that is at all compelling.

A final point about evolution. In biological evolution there are points, of course, when a new species has emerged. In some respects, the evolutionaries of psychoanalysis are really using the term in its nineteenth- and early twentieth-century sense: as change taking place very gradually and incrementally. (In biology, evolution takes place through many minor chance genetic variations subsequently selected for adaptive advantage.) Some contemporary biologists, such as Stephen Jay Gould, argue that many very important changes in the evolution of species have not emerged gradually over long periods of time but more or less discontinuously and suddenly in relation to changed circumstances. It is a central argument of this book that psychoanalysis, as practiced and understood by many contemporary clinicians and theorists, is a different, although closely related, species from its ancestor, and that this is masked by an often contrived preoccupation with continuities.

One of the major reasons that psychoanalysis can be seen in terms of both continuities and discontinuities with its founder is that Freud himself was such a complex and, in some respects, conflicted genius. He was both a man of his own time and one who anticipated and helped create our time.

Consider Freud's conflict between the free play of his imagination and what he felt was the necessity for scientific discipline. The latter concern led Freud, as his biographers have pointed out, to keep watch on his own speculative flights, to keep his philosophical wanderings on a short leash. But what extraordinary flights they were! Freud was a scientist but also a philosopher and literary master. He was concerned with the biological underpinnings of mental life but also with spirituality (broadly defined). Freud's conflicts have extended themselves to his interpreters and define many of the current controversies in the field.

Some think that Freud regarded himself as a scientist dealing with empirical facts. Among proponents of this view, some (such as Brenner) approve of Freud the scientist and some (such as Harry Guntrip) disapprove of Freud the scientist for neglecting more humanistic and spiritual concerns. Others regard Freud as fundamentally unscientific. Among proponents of this view, some (such as Bruno Bettleheim) approve of Freud's unscientific temperament because they see him as dealing with more spiritual matters. Some (such as Robert Holt and Adolf Grünbaum) disapprove of Freud's unscientific failings because they feel they reduce psychoanalysis to suspicions and speculation. Freud clearly does not fit tidily into any of the standard categories, and his own conflicts are now writ large by contending parties in controversies about whether psychoanalysis is a science or not.

Another alternative might be called the modified evolutionary position. Habermas (1968, p. 246), for example, regards Freud as suffering from the "scientistic self-misunderstanding of metapsychology" whereby he fundamentally misunderstood himself. In this view, Freud founded "what is in fact a new science of man while always considering it a natural science" (p. 246). Recently Jonathan Lear (1990) has further developed this line of approach, treating Freud as a patient. His book

> takes up and develops certain salient themes in Freud, themes that from the perspective of this interpretation are his theoretically symptomatic acts. It pursues connections, insights, consequences of Freudian thoughts that Freud himself did not pursue, and of which he remained unaware. In this sense, the book is about the Freudian unconscious. (pp. 15–16)

Lear has Freud making statements whose unintended meanings (presumably coming from his unconscious) sound a lot more like someone writing today.[10]

I have two problems with this kind of approach. First, I think it is very unfair to Freud, who is being blamed for not knowing (or rather knowing but repressing!) what we think is important. (Freud also is granted prescience, since he is portrayed as anticipating what we think is important, even if he did not know that was what he was doing.) Second, by seeing the real Freud in the part of his vision that corresponds to our current ideas and sluffing off the rest as easily detachable and discardable artifacts of his milieu, we distort Freud's own vision. As I have suggested in chapter 1, Freud's belief in the scientific nature of psycho-analysis as a discipline had an enormous formative impact on the way he thought about the analytic situation and on many of the basic princi-ples he established in his theory of technique. To portray him as basi-cally interested in personal subjectivity in a more contemporary sense and merely clothing that core interest in the scientific fashions of his day seems forced and unpersuasive. It distorts Freud's own thought, and it also impedes a clear exploration of his legacy in current psychoanalytic thinking. Thus, modified evolutionism buys continuity at the price of obfuscation.

Jessica Benjamin (1992a) suggests a closely related but much more honest and clarifying approach, drawn from the German tradition of critical social theory. The best way to approach theoretical revision, she argues, is to "recognize precisely what phenomenon or problem the old theory was trying to explain and to show how that problem can be un-derstood better with a different analysis. The purpose is also to unfold from within the contradictions or inadequacies within that theory" (p. 417). Thus, Benjamin and other like-minded revisionists draw a great deal on Freud's concepts, such as "penis envy," the "Oedipus complex," "drives," and "regression," which they explicitly reinterpret, revise, and rework along more contemporary lines. The reinterpretations generally involve a shift in understanding the meaning of physical processes and body parts not as inherent in their anatomy but as a function and reflec-tion of social and interpersonal relations.

> My purpose . . . may have been to turn Freud upside down, that is, to reverse his biological materialism, to give psychology a larger role in development. But in the process of overturning great thinkers, we are not simply discarding their thought; we are reformulating it, and looking to see what falls out of the pockets that is still usable. Bodily metaphors are among the usable parts, when they are understood to represent certain relationships rather than as things in themselves. (Benjamin, 1992a, p. 418)

This approach strikes me as very constructive. Certainly it is essential that psychoanalysts never discard Freud's thought, the study of which generates perpetual insights into our own problems and choices. Many relational theorists, in their eagerness to distinguish themselves from Freud, have neglected the importance of bodily experiences, particularly in relation to sexuality and aggression. (This issue is addressed in detail in chapter 6. See also Mitchell, 1988.)

However, there is an important difference between the aesthetics of preserving pieces of the past in the abstract activity of constructing theories and the pragmatics of clinical theorizing for analytic work. Reworking the contents of Freud's pockets has an enormous appeal with respect to modernizing and revitalizing psychoanalytic tradition and its seminal texts, but it may lead to the preservation of anachronistic concepts that no longer speak directly to the clinical experience of practicing analysts. For example, many analysts do not see compelling indications of "penis envy" in their analytic work with most female patients (although it certainly does speak to the experience of some). Although that concept can be reworked along relational lines, it is not clear that it is clinically useful to do so. (See Schwartz, 1992, for an extended discussion along these lines.) It may be clinically helpful to recontextualize some of Freud's concepts as metaphors rather than anatomical destiny. Yet many of the contents of his pockets are more usefully preserved as pieces of history rather than as building blocks. "Found" art can be fun, but sometimes it is better to start with a fresh canvas!

II

SELF IN PSYCHOANALYSIS

4

Multiple Selves, Singular Self

These [more "intimate reactions"] I have always found it difficult to commit to paper—at least for the eyes of others. Perhaps I was too much of a coward: too conscious of the fragility of the individual's innermost identity; too respectful of that identity's need for and right to privacy; too accustomed to view this as a privileged inner chamber, cluttered with fragile objects, into which the clumsy finger of the outsider could not be thrust without creating breakage and havoc. I preferred, I thought, to leave all this to the novelist or the poet, whose greater brutality, in the one case, and more natural use of the allusive rather than the explicit, in the other, permitted a bolder penetration into these dangerous premises.

—George Kennon, *Sketches from a Life*

Language cannot be separated from the world, from others, and from ourselves. It is not an alien enclave that can outwit me or subvert my purpose; it is me, so that I am nearer to being myself when I am farther away—with others and among things; it is the indissoluble reciprocity of men and their struggles together embodied by the internal relations of this linguistic whole that has neither door nor window, where we can neither go in nor come out, where we are.

—Jean-Paul Sartre, *The Family Idiot: Gustave Flaubert*

The two passages serving as epigraphs for this chapter suggest sharply contrasting views of self.

George Kennon, the historian, political theorist, and diplomat, ex-

plains in the preface to his autobiographical *Sketches from a Life* that
he has held back his more personal self, his "innermost identity," which
he preserves in a "privileged inner chamber," protected from his readers' view. This is a view of self as layered, with a singular inner core, its
exposure or concealment operating fully under the subject's control.

Sartre, the philosopher and political theorist, explains early in his bi-
ography of Flaubert that self exists in relations with others. There is no
hidden chamber, nor does the subject maintain control over exposure or
concealment. Self is woven into reciprocal interactions between the subject and others, particularly in the language that is the common medium
for those interactions. This is a view of self as multiple and embedded in
relational contexts.

These two very different ways of thinking about self also have appeared in the psychoanalytic literature of recent decades. They provide
powerful and compelling frameworks for organizing clinical data. Both
speak directly to the experience of patients.

ROBERT AND THE VOLCANO

Robert, a writer in his late twenties, sought analysis because of a
chronic sense of inadequacy and anxieties and inhibitions with respect
to sexual functioning. It was difficult for him to experience a securely
anchored sense of his own sexual potency and masculinity.

At times Robert could successfully complete intercourse with a
woman only with great anxiety and difficulty. He would begin to lose
his erection during coitus, and could regain it only by conjuring up an
image of a hypermasculine, macho type of man—sometimes drawing on
the cigarette advertisement of the "Marlboro Man." (This was quite a
few years ago, when cigarette smoking was not generally regarded as
being suicidal, and often homicidal, in the way it is today.) Robert was
worried about the possible homosexual implications of this fantasy.
However, the fantasy seemed to work not by generating erotic excitement about the man but rather by making possible an identification
with his imagined potency.

Robert was the older of two sons born to a couple who seemed, according to his accounts, oddly unsuited to each other. His mother was a
librarian in a small, rural town in New England; his father had apparently
been a ne'er-do-well, largely unemployed and alcoholic, who had abandoned the family when Robert was eight years old. Robert never saw him
again and found out in his early twenties that he had died, apparently

from alcoholism. Robert and his brother were raised in relative isolation by their competent but very depressed and overprotective mother.

During the course of treatment, early memories emerged of his mother's administrations of enemas to him when he was a small boy. One memory was particularly vivid. He suffered episodically from constipation and, on this occasion, was in the bathroom trying to move his bowels. His mother had decided to administer an enema and entered the bathroom unannounced. Her eyes focused on his penis, which was resting on the rim of the toilet. He sensed her recoiling, and felt enormously ashamed. He tucked his penis underneath the rim of the toilet, as if removing the offensive organ from her view, and offered her his anus for her cleansing ministrations. We came to realize that this early memory was emblematic of Robert's chronic sense of his need to disclaim his masculinity by surrendering to his mother's powerful, encompassing, purifying care.

Consider one other bit of family life. When mother and sons would go out to dinner as a family, it was never possible for the two brothers to go to the men's room together—each would quietly slip away and return as quickly as possible. When Robert and I explored this taboo, he realized that he believed deeply that for the two boys to participate with each other in as important an activity as urinating, outside the mother's purview, in the men's room, no less, would have been exceedingly painful for her.

After several months of cautiously testing the analytic waters, Robert became intensely involved in the analysis. He began to focus on a deep and painful longing for his father, which had secretly dominated most of his life. It seemed very difficult for him to allow himself to have these feelings when around his mother, and his mother seemed to be always around (either actually, or as a kind of internal perpetual presence in his experience). He had a belief, which we traced through various manifestations throughout his development, that other men knew something, had something, that he did not, because it was never given to him by his abandoning father.

I spent considerable time exploring and questioning his assumption of an effortless communion that he assumed other men felt with each other. I frequently pointed to his tendency to disclaim his own substantial resources and actual potency, in many forms, to keep alive the hope that an ideal father would someday return, rescue him, and properly confer manhood upon him. I think partly as a result of those interpretations, there was a very dramatic and moving session in which he experienced himself as a frightened little boy and imagined crawling across the room to lie, curled in a fetal position, at my feet. It was not long after that phase, about two years into the analysis, that he reported the following dream.

> I was looking out across a great expanse of flat land—an enormous plain. Way in the distance was a big mountain, very far away. As I was looking, I noticed a wisp of smoke coming from the top of the mountain, and realized that it was a volcano. As I watched, the smoke thickened and it became apparent that the volcano was about to erupt. It was so far away that I did not feel threatened, although I was fascinated. After a while a crack appeared down the sides of the volcano, and it split in two, with the two halves falling away to reveal inside a giant ball of molten lava, reddish-orange in color. Losing its containment in the mountain, the ball began to collapse and flow down onto the plain. It was so far away that at first I still did not feel threatened, but little by little the lava began to flow across the plain in my direction. I began to get very anxious and was looking around for a way to save myself. Everything was very flat and therefore unprotected. The red-orange of the lava was a brilliant, terrifying color, which began to dominate everything. I started to panic. The dream gets hazy after this, but I think there was a man who appeared and showed me a way to escape through a woods with a stream.

We lived in that dream landscape for many months. One of the most important associative paths developed from the color in the dream, which led him back to the small bedroom he shared with his brother before the father's departure. The room was painted red-orange and was near enough to the living room to allow him to hear his parents' arguments at night when they thought the children were asleep.

As I encouraged him to enter into the feelings and textures of the dream, he uncovered a memory, undoubtedly partially a screen memory, of the particular night when his father walked out. His parents were fighting, but this fight was much more explosive. He was afraid that his father would hurt his mother; he wanted to protect her but felt impotent. He was enraged at his mother for making life so difficult for his father; he was enraged at his father for what he felt was his verbal brutalization of his mother. His father smoked cigarettes, although it is not clear whether they were Marlboros. (Remember the smoking volcano.) As Robert reconnected with those memories, he reported a sensation that our room seemed to be glowing a red-orange color. The visual image in the memory, my office, his own insides—all seemed to be joined in this glowing, smoldering, terrifying color.

How are we to think of the organization of Robert's experience of self? His tentative sense of sexual potency and masculinity? His chronic sense of weakness and inadequacy?

Is Robert's singular, true self, his innermost identity, hidden and isolated (in the volcano of his dream) under the necessity for his adaptation to his mother's worldview? The familiar sense of self that developed during his childhood feels real enough, but weakened, empty, needful of resources and sustenance. He sometimes experiences himself as layered and hidden, with a deeply buried, smoldering core.

Or is Robert's self variable, organized in different ways at different times, embedded in each of his relationships with significant others? There seems to be a smoldering rageful self, in close identification with his father's eruption. There is a passive, yielding self, longing to be penetrated and cleansed by his mother's controlling ministrations. There seems to be a disclaimed masculine self, tied to his discredited father, waiting for another, credible father to grant him his rightful place in the community of men. His self-organization, as it unfolds in the analytic process, appears as multiple patterns grounded in different, prototypical interactions with others.

Are these two approaches to self fundamentally irreconcilable, or are they integratable? This is the major question I explore in this chapter. I will return later to Robert's experience in analysis to explore different ways in which self is understood, explored, broadened, and enriched in the analytic process.

SELF IN PSYCHOANALYSIS: SPATIAL AND TEMPORAL METAPHORS

The self has been the central and most important concept in psychoanalytic theorizing of the past several decades.[1] The most striking thing about the concept of self within current psychoanalytic thought is precisely the startling contrast between the centrality of concern with self and the enormous variability and lack of consensus about what the term even means. The self is referred to variably as: an idea, or set of ideas in the mind; a structure in the mind; something experienced; something that does things; one's unique life history; even an idea in someone else's mind (Shane and Shane, 1980); and so on. Khan (1963), whose central concern has been the self, admitted that no one has defined self experience successfully (p. 303), and even Kohut, whose theory is named after the term self, acknowledged difficulty in clearly defining what he meant by it (1977, pp. 310–12.) Why is something so clinically important and affectively central so conceptually elusive, so hard to grasp?

One radical and tempting answer is that self as such does not exist, that it involves a mistaken use of language. John Stuart Mill pointed to the ease with which language can cause us trouble.

> The tendency has always been strong to believe that whatever received a name must be an entity or being, having an independent existence of its own. And if no real entity answering to the name could be found, men did not for that reason suppose that none existed, but imagined that it was something particularly abstruse and mysterious. (quoted in Gould, 1981, p. 185)

One might argue, as do Gilbert Ryle and Ludwig Wittgenstein, that the treatment of the "self" as an entity is a reification, a misuse of the reflexive pronoun referring to the person in question. "Myself," "your-self," "oneself"—these are ways of talking in which we refer back to the person concerned; perhaps taking "self" out of that context and setting it up as if it were a phenomenon in its own right is merely a trick made possible by the ambiguities of language. Perhaps contemporary psycho-analytic concepts of self are like a hall of mirrors in which distorted re-flections create elaborate and fantastic images, appearing "abstruse and mysterious," out of the simple, everyday person.[2]

Yet activities involving "self-definition," on many different levels, have always been a central human concern, even more so for people liv-ing in our time. Sass (1988, p. 552), in surveying the contemporary in-tellectual scene, notes that "according to many historians, concern about the self is *the* central theme of the last several centuries of West-ern culture." What does it mean to be a person? What sort of persons are we? How are we connected and related to each other? This sort of self-reflection has become a preoccupying concern: on a global level, in the face of self-contamination and self-annihilation; on an interna-tional level, in the wake of astounding shifts in the way nations are po-sitioning themselves vis-à-vis each other; on a national level, in the con-text of shrinking economic and political horizons; and on an individual level, in the wake of historically unprecedented shifts in social, eco-nomic, and gender roles. The central focus on self in psychoanalytic theories of the second half of the twentieth century reflects these con-cerns, very different from those of Freud's patients, who lived in a much more stable, hierarchicalized society.[3] Psychoanalysis, as a set of ideas, a process of discovery, and a worldview, helped to create our contemporary western concepts of self. Psychoanalysis, with its lan-guorous pace, its fascination with the textures and shadings of experience, its profound privacy, remains one of our most precious methods for understanding, protecting, and developing our sense of self, both individually and as a culture.

The diverse ways in which psychoanalysts have written about self are separable into the two different models or accounts of self advanced by Kennon and Sartre and illustrated by Robert's analysis: self as layered, singular, and continuous and self as multiple and discontinuous. These two different ways of thinking about self and mind in general are based on two fundamentally different metaphors.

There has been considerable interest in contemporary philosophy and linguistics in the way metaphor shapes understanding and experience. Concepts as vague and insubstantial as "psyche," "mind," or "self" are impossible to grasp in precise, denotative terms. We understand and come to experience them in terms of other, generally more concrete kinds of experiences and activities. (See Lakoff and Johnson, 1980.)

The view of the self as layered, singular, and continuous is grounded in a spatial metaphor: The mind is a place where things happen; the self is something in that place, which is composed of constituent parts or structures. This way of thinking comes directly from Freud. (Freud did not invent spatial metaphors for thinking about mind; they have a long history in western philosophy. (See Ryle, 1949, for an extended critique of this way of talking about mind.) In both the topographical and the structural models, Freud grounds his theorizing in a clearly defined spatial metaphor: "The hypothesis we have adopted for a psychical apparatus extended into space" (1940, p. 196). If we think about mind in terms of spatial metaphors, as if it existed in space, with structures, within a topography, then it makes sense to approach it as we would an onion, to try to locate its singular "core" or "heart," to delineate its layers, to differentiate its authentic pieces from its false, protective covering, and so on.

Some of the more careful psychoanalytic theorists have taken pains to point out that the concept of psychic structure refers not to something substantive but to recurring patterns of experience and behavior over time.[4] Yet, in common usage, deriving from Freud's manner of talking about the psyche as occupying spaces with structural properties, the spatial metaphor pervades psychoanalytic discourse on self.[5]

The view of self as multiple and discontinuous is grounded in a temporal rather than a spatial metaphor: Selves are what people do and experience over time rather than something that exists someplace. Self refers to the subjective organization of meanings one creates as one moves through time, doing things, such as having ideas and feelings, including some self-reflective ideas and feelings about oneself.

In *The Magic Mountain,* Thomas Mann (1927) draws a contrast between the spatial properties of bodies and the temporal properties of life (or self), anticipating the widespread current interest in narratives as the form through which self is experienced and develops.

> For time is the medium of narration, as it is the medium of life. Both are inextricably bound up with it, as inextricably as are bodies in space. Similarly, time is the medium of music; music divides, measures, articulates time . . . Thus music and narration are alike, in that they can only present themselves as a flowing, as a succession in time, as one thing after another; and both differ from the plastic arts, which are complete in the present, and unrelated to time save as all bodies are, whereas narration—like music—even if it should try to be completely present at any given moment, would need time to do it in. (p. 541)[6]

People often experience themselves, at any given moment, as containing or being a "self" that is complete in the present; a "sense of self" often comes with a feeling of substantiality, presence, integrity, and fullness. Yet selves change and are transformed continually over time; no version of self is fully present at any instant, and a single life is composed of many selves. An experience of self takes place necessarily in a moment of time; it fills one's psychic space, and other, alternative versions of self fade into the background. A river can be represented in a photograph, which fixes its flow and makes it possible for it to be viewed and grasped. Yet the movement of the river, in its larger course, cannot be grasped in a moment. Rivers and selves, like music and narratives, take time to happen in.[7]

As we explore the spatially grounded approach to self as singular, layered, and continuous and the temporally grounded approach to self as multiple and discontinuous, we will discover that their apparent contradiction actually provides a creative tension that makes possible a more complex and useful view of the place of self within experience and the transformations of self in psychoanalysis. In the following two chapters, I extend this perspective on self to the problem of the core or center of the self (chapter 5) and the ancient controversy over the nature of aggression (chapter 6).

MULTIPLE, DISCONTINUOUS SELVES

Consider the experience we have all had that is reflected in the statements "I am not myself today"[8] or "I am not all here today." For the clinician, it is not just the absence that is important in that experience, but also the presence of some other experience of being. "Who are you today?" and "Where else are you?" might become important questions. The everyday observation of different organizations in our experience of ourselves, discontinuities in our sense of self, has become a crucial dimension of contemporary psychoanalytic theorizing, particularly within British object relations theories. Like most important psychoanalytic understandings, this line of thought began with Freud.

Freud's portrayal of the relationship between the ego and the superego (in the structural model, introduced in 1923) is the original paradigm from which derives much current psychoanalytic theorizing. To highlight this link with later developments, I am going to describe the structural model in an unusual fashion, shifting from spatial to temporal terms.

We sometimes operate and/or experience ourselves as the active agent of our experience, a way that Freud called the "ego"; we sometimes operate and/or experience ourselves in a different way, taking ourselves as an object and overseeing and judging ourselves, a way that Freud called the "superego." Our ego way of being and our superego way of being are oriented toward each other, Freud suggested, rather like a relationship between two independent people.

For Freud, the underlying motivational source of all experience derives from the formless energy of the id. Our ego way of being and our superego way of being, and their relationship to each other, develop out of the encounter between the id's impulses and the real world and are superimposed, in Freud's vision, like a membrane on the surface of the id. Thus, ultimately, Freud still considered the relationship between the ego and superego, a very novel way of thinking about mind, to be shaped by the need to gratify or defend against the id's ceaseless pressures. The very purpose of mind is the discharge and/or control of that energy, and the experience of self is derivative of that function. To be a person is to struggle with powerful asocial impulses, to check, divert, or sublimate them, to reconcile them with internalized parental presences. Freud's image of the id, drawn from Newtonian physics and Darwinian biology, remained, throughout his writings, one of raw, unstructured energy and explosive bestial passions.

The key transition to postclassical psychoanalytic views of the self occurred when theorists began thinking about the id in a different way, as structured rather than formless, as directed rather than explosive. They began to think of the repressed not as disorganized, impulsive fragments but as constellations of meanings organized around relationships. Thus, they began to conceive of the id as involving a way of being, a sense of self, a person in relation to other persons, bringing it much closer in nature to Freud's portrayal of the ego and superego. (Melanie Klein, Fairbairn, Edith Jacobson, Loewald, Lacan, Otto Kernberg—all in their own ways and in their own language portray the id as a person or collection of persons in passionate relationships to other persons or parts of persons.)

Since Freud's death, in a halting, diffuse, and informal fashion, his structural model has been largely replaced (often not terminologically, but conceptually) by different versions of a relational model. Freud pictured conflict as the clash among impulses (id), regulatory functions (ego), and moral prohibitions (superego). In a growing sector of contemporary psychoanalytic thought (often connected with the term object relations theories), the joints of the mind are located at the borders between different versions of self. Conflict is now envisioned as the clash between contrasting and often incompatible self-organizations and self-other relationships.

The model of self to be found in object relations theories, in their emphasis on multiplicity and discontinuity, portrays experiences of self as inevitably embedded in particular relational contexts. Because we learn to become a person through interactions with different others and through different kinds of interactions with the same other, our experience of self is discontinuous, composed of different configurations, different selves with different others. But that is not all. There are times when I experience myself as myself in relation to a significant other—a dependent child cared for by a solicitous mother, for example. But there may be other times when I organize my experience and sense of meaning around my image of that other in relation to me (my identification with them)—for example, as a solicitous maternal figure taking care of a dependent child. Each relational configuration yields two ways of being in the world; each actual relationship may contain multiple self-organizations; and there may be many such relationships.[9]

The result is a plural or manifold organization of self, patterned around different self and object images or representations, derived from different relational contexts. We are all composites of overlapping, multiple organizations and perspectives, and our experience is smoothed over by an illusory sense of continuity. Ogden (1986) has compared the subjective sense of self as unified and continuous to the manner in which the mind weaves together the discordant visual images from our two eyes into an apparently seamless, unitary visual field. The relationships among these different versions or organizations of self are complex and depend largely on degrees of conflict and issues of loyalty in the real, external relationships from which they derive.[10]

Variations in the use of language often provide a dramatic indication of variations in self organizations. Studies of bilingual patients suggest that, especially when one language is learned at a developmentally later point than an original language, the different languages reflect very different organizations of self. A person feels different when speaking and thinking in the language learned in early childhood; there are enormous differences in nuance, affective tone, and often access to memories, coded and filed in one rather than the other language (Foster 1992). Studies of children speaking to other children suggest that the syntax and grammatical structure of their spoken language is quite different when children are speaking to an older child than when they are speaking to a younger one (Snow and Ferguson, 1977). The language differences seem to reflect discontinuous, variously organized, developmentally sequenced versions of self.

There is some evidence to suggest that different versions of self may be not only encoded in different language systems, but that they may be accompanied by and experienced in different physiological states as well. It has been documented that the different identities in patients who suffer from multiple personalities often have strikingly different physiologies, including cardiovascular function and blood chemistry. In non-multiple personalities, different states of mind are clearly associated with different bodily states, creating complex cycles of mind/body interaction. Depression is physically enervating, slowing down activity, which in turn constricts emotional experience. Joy is invigorating, encouraging activity, which in turn makes new experiences possible. Happy versions of self are often distinctly different, both emotionally and physically, from depressed versions of self.[11]

Is the degree of discontinuity among different versions of self a measure of the degree of psychopathology? Does the analysand end treatment with a more unified, more homogeneous self? Certainly psychopathology might well be measured by degrees of dissociation of important versions of self. Yet it seems mistaken to assume that a digestion and blending of different versions of self is preferable to the capacity to contain shifting and conflictual versions of self. Mixing colors together does not increase their intensity or beauty; it washes them out into a featureless gray. Discontinuities in self-organization are part of what enriches life, enabling conflicted domains of experience to be developed without the pressure of continual moderation and integration.[12] (The issue of integration versus discontinuities in versions of self will be taken up again in the next two chapters, in connection with authentic versus inauthentic experience and loving and hateful versions of self.)

Emerging from a very different context, American operationalism and the development of interpersonal psychiatry, Harry Stack Sullivan also stressed repeatedly the illusory nature of the self we ordinarily take ourselves to be—singular, unique, in control of our self-revelations and self-concealments—which he felt was at enormous odds with what we actually do with other people. In contrast to this illusory, subjective experience of self, Sullivan suggests that the same person may be quite different with different people or integrate a relationship in very different ways with the same person in different contexts. We operate, he suggests, in "me-you patterns," never singularly, always in relation, and we tend to form very different, discrete "me-you patterns" in different circumstances. Sullivan (1938) came to regard the experience people have of possessing a unique personal individuality as essentially a narcissistic illusion—"the very mother of illusions"—in the service of allaying anxiety and distracting attention from ways in which people actually operate with others.

Thus, Sullivan too arrived at a view of self as manifold. Although we experience ourselves as transparent to ourselves and much the same person in our dealings with various other people, we are, in a fundamental sense, quite different persons at different times. Of course, in some obvious way, we are the same person; I am putting it this way to stress Sullivan's point that at any given time we operate out of a particular way of representing ourselves to ourselves, in relation to a portrayal of a distinct sort of other with whom we are engaged—"me-you patterns." These different forms of self-representation may be quite fully developed, cognitively and affectively, entailing a full sense of personhood, yet they are likely to be discontinuous, one from the other. We are not generally aware, Sullivan suggests, of this discontinuity.

Common to both Sullivan's interpersonal theory and object relations theories is a view of the self as multiple and discontinuous.[13] The interpersonal approach focuses on what people actually do with each other and the strategies they have learned for being a person with other persons. It is a view of self as action. The basic mode within the interpersonal approach to the analytic process consequently involves questions and detailed inquiry: What happened? What was the precise sequence? Who did what, when, and to whom?

The object relations approach focuses on phenomenological units, the kind of person one experiences oneself as being when one does what one does with other people. These phenomenological units are understood to derive either from how one felt with a significant other in a particular context or from one's sense of how it felt to be that other in relation to oneself. The basic mode within the object relations approach to the analytic process is, correspondingly, not so much an active inquiry but the facilitation of a kind of unraveling. The protection and timelessness of the analytic situation, the permission, or even the injunction to free associate, to disorganize, allows the sometimes smooth but thin casing around the self to dissolve and the individual strands that make up experience to separate themselves from each other and become defined and articulated.

Interpersonal theory might be regarded as a depiction of the transactional manifestations of internal object relations; or, conversely, it might be regarded as a depiction of the implicit and largely unconscious senses of self underlying interpersonal transactions. Both types of theorizing presume a multiple, discontinuous, and relational view of self.[14] (Joyce McDougall [1985] has elaborated this view in her metaphor of mind as theater.)

THE SELF AS INTEGRAL AND CONTINUOUS

We began our consideration of the psychoanalytic view of self as multiple and discontinuous with the experience captured in the statement "I am not myself today." Let us return to this statement and proceed along a different route. In this sentence, self is being represented in two different ways. There is a variable "I" that has changeable content, that feels different today from most days, and that contains different suborganizations. Yet despite the discontinuities, I still recognize all these differences as versions of a more or less invariant "myself." I do not, even for a moment, consider the possibility that I actually have awakened as someone or (Kafka notwithstanding) something else. There is a sense of self that is independent of shifts over time, connected with the function of self-reflection, providing continuity from one subjective state to the next. I can represent that enduring sense of self as "myself" and assign it specific content, which my current experience can either match or not match, and which enables me to feel either very much "myself" or "not myself." But even when I am not myself, I experience a continuity with previous subjective states.

This experience of self as integral and continuous also has been very much illuminated within contemporary psychoanalytic thought. Among the antecedents of this approach is William James's notion of a central

self or a "self among selves," and Carl Jung's (1933) notion of an arche-
typal predisposition for people to form a singular, integrated sense of
self. The most important contribution to this perspective on self in recent decades has been Kohut's self psychology, in which the effort to organize and maintain an integrated sense of self has been assigned a primary, superordinate motivational status.

Kohut does speak of subordinate selves, trapped in what he terms
vertical and horizontal splits, but these are seen as quite pathological.
The central thrust within mind is viewed as integrative, and that continuous line of subjective experience forms the core of the self. To Sullivan,
the idea of uniqueness each of us maintains is the greatest psychological
impediment to constructive living; he believes that an appreciation of
our commonality with others, not our distinctness, holds the key to a
richer life. In self psychology, it is not possible to connect with others in
a way that is vital and alive without first being centered in and deeply
connected with one's own distinctive subjectivity. In this approach to
the self, the analytic process is not viewed as an unraveling. It is as if
there is one thread or one voice within the textured complexity of the
patient's experience that represents the patient's true subjectivity. The
analyst, in her "empathic attitude," finds and mirrors that core subjectivity, and this confirmation constitutes the key therapeutic action of the
analytic process.

A crucial premise in this perspective is that whatever else is going on
at any particular moment in the analysis, the patient is also struggling to
locate and express the center of his own subjectivity. A key feature of
this self-forming and self-articulating process, in the self-psychological
view, is the patient's search for long-sought healthy experiences with an
Other, a perpetual effort to find a constructive bridge over developmental impasses, the search for a "new beginning." The task of the analyst
is to locate and ally herself with that hopeful self-expressive, self-
forming process. That constructive hope, that positive developmental
striving is the voice among the others that Kohut feels needs to be
found, amplified, and warmly responded to if the damaged self is to be
repaired.[15]

Kohut was getting at something very important in the analytic
process that tends to be overlooked in perspectives that emphasize the
multiplicity of self. What distinguishes multiple personalities from the
rest of us is precisely that in multiple personalities, there is no sense of
continuity from one self-organization to the next, no recognition of a
continuous, enduring subjectivity. The discontinuities are too discontinuous. Kohut was addressing the sense of self as integral and continuous

(as did Winnicott in a somewhat different language). At every moment, people create subjective meaning out of the context in which they are operating. The content of the meaning created may vary relatively widely (as organized according to different internalized object relations or "me-you patterns"); yet there is a sense that the "I" that is creating meaning today, processing and organizing experience, is a continuation of the "I" that created subjective experience yesterday and the day before. By recognizing the "I" that organizes my experience, I recognize myself as myself.[16]

We each have some sense of our own particular style or aesthetic or pattern of self-organization, our personal "signature" (Donald Spence, 1987), our "idiom" (Bollas, 1987). This personal sense of self is deeply private and ultimately ineffable, much easier to feel than to describe. The content I select in trying to represent my idiosyncratic patterning of experience today may be very different from the content I chose yesterday, or the way I would represent myself to myself tomorrow. Yet except for patients who suffer major dissociative states, the experiences all feel like "mine." Thus, Ernest Wolf (1991) refers to "my conviction that I am the person who was born in a certain place at a certain time as the son of the parents whom I knew and that I am the person who has had a history in which I can identify the 'I' of yesteryear as the 'I' of yesterday and, hopefully, of tomorrow" (p. 169).

Another aspect of experience closely connected with the concept of self as integral and continuous is the sense of agency. Kohut (1977, p. 99) described the self as "a center of initiative"; this continuity in action also is at the heart of the centrality Schafer (1976) assigns to "agency" in his "action language." All of us, Schafer argues, generate all aspects of our experience through our actions. Many of our actions are disclaimed, so that we feel our experience is happening to us rather than created by us. The processes of psychoanalysis unmask disclaimed actions, revealing the person as the singular agent of her experience.

It is very tricky, however, to separate out subjective from objective features in this assignment of integrity and continuity to the self as agent. It may be that I do everything that I do, but I may do certain things in a very different experiential context than I do other things. The I that does these different things is a quite different I at different times. In fact, as Ogden (1991) has argued, the very sense of being an agent who does things may be missing in more disturbed patients (living in the paranoid-schizoid position); they experience feelings and thoughts as happening to them rather than as generated by them. Over the course of treatment, the patient often learns to wrap a sense of agency around states previously experienced more passively. But it seems strained to assume that the self (agent) that is experienced after analysis has facilitated the integration of experiences was there, although disclaimed, all along.

Adherents of the view of the self as singular and integral sometimes claim that such an experience of self is somehow wired in human biology and develops in sequential stages. Wolf (1991), for example, argues that there is "a biologically given need of the subject to organize experience into patterns that make sense as the bedrock from which springs the emergence of the self as an organization of experience" (p. 169n). This assumption that the self of self psychology is biologically mandated is often connected with what is termed a developmental point of view, in which such a self unfolds in a preordained, universal sequence. (See Philip Cushman's [1991] critique of Daniel Stern's work along these lines.) Compare this claim with the following statement from the anthropologist Clifford Geertz (1979) in a paper entitled, interestingly enough, "From the Native's Point of View":

> the Western conception of the person as a bounded, unique, more or less integrated motivational and cognitive universe, a dynamic center of awareness, emotion, judgement, and action organized into a distinctive whole and set contrastively both against other such wholes and against a social and natural background is, however incorrigible it may seem to us, a rather peculiar idea within the context of the world's cultures. (p. 59)

To assume that there is a sequence of universal developmental needs or self-object experiences leading to a form of life consistent with our ideas about mental health is as ethnocentric as Freud's assumption, along with most other intellectuals of his day, that so-called primitive societies could be arranged in a hierarchical fashion, leading to the acme of human development—late-nineteenth-century upper-middle-class Viennese society.

In light of the previous discussion of multiple versions of self, one might argue that the feeling of continuity in self experience is thoroughly illusory. Although at any moment I may experience myself as always having been the self I am currently experiencing, the self changes continually over time. In some sense, I am never "myself" today. Yet most of us do seem to have, and perhaps need to have, such an experience of self. The experience of self as singular and constant serves an important adaptive, psychological purpose. (In nonwestern cultures, the concept of the supraindividual, invariant group carries much of this burden.) Without a sense of self as constant and unaffected by time, as continuous and unvarying (even though from a temporal perspective it is discontinuous and continually changing), we would have no way to prioritize our goals, motives, and impulses—we would be all over the place (Minsky, 1985). So we need to feel we have an "innermost identity," as George Kennon (1989) puts it, and act accordingly, even though the content of that identity may change considerably over time; we claim and commit ourselves to some experiences and disclaim and avoid others. What may have begun as an illusion often becomes an actual guide to living by virtue of our necessary belief in it.[17]

SELF AS INDEPENDENT AND SEPARATE FROM OTHERS

One of the most appealing features of the view of the self as integral and continuous is its seeming separability from its interactions with others. As the excerpt from Kennon at the beginning of this chapter illustrates, Freud was not alone in thinking of the mind in spatial and topographical terms; we all have some sense of our most personal self as an entity residing deep inside us, revealed to or concealed from others at our will. The sense of intimacy with another is often forged precisely out of such revelatory experiences. It feels as if our personal self is ours in some uniquely privileged way; we control access to its protective layers and its "core"; only we know and understand its secrets. It feels as if the self is not inevitably contextual and relational but has an existence and a life that is separate and autonomous from (perhaps even, as Winnicott [1963] argues, inevitably unknown by) others. Yet the self that seems so personal and interior is, in a broader perspective, deeply embedded in relations with others.

Consider the sort of access one has to oneself. Can one experience oneself in a direct fashion, unmediated through relations with others? We cannot look at our complete physical selves directly with our own eyes: We have to rely on reflections. In some ultimate sense, we do not really know what we look like; we know how we appear in particular contexts, depending on the nature, quality, and conditions of the reflecting substance. But perhaps the self has more mobility than our eyeballs, trapped forever in their sockets. When we speak of "self-observation" and "self-reflection," does not the self stand outside itself, taking itself as its own object? Does not this capacity to objectify ourselves, to play both subject and object, establish our independence from other people? Is it not this very possibility of establishing our own inner dialogue that serves as the grounding for the sense of privacy of the self?

Yet when one considers the categories, the basic language in which one observes and reflects upon oneself, the self as subject loses some of its seeming mobility and independence. That language derives from past interactions with others, past reflections; the very terms and categories in which we experience ourselves, in which we represent ourselves to ourselves, embody a social history, a family history, a complex interpersonal history. It has been argued that thought itself is interiorized, inhibited speech (Dennett, 1991; Ryle, 1949, p. 27), and it is not just within contemporary psychoanalytic theory but also within current thinking in neurophysiology that the individual brain and mind are regarded as organized through social interaction.[18]

One of the most consistent themes in the "independent group" of the British psychoanalytic world has been the deep privacy and interiority of the self: Winnicott (1963) speaks of the true self as "incognito"; Khan (1963) speaks of the "privacy of the self"; and Enid Balint (1991) considers some of the deepest forms of experience as simply unable to be organized into language, and hence ineffable. However, when it comes to the separability of the self, it is crucial to distinguish between the subjective experience of interiority and the theoretical understanding of how that experience comes about and how it operates.

Paradoxically, when we feel most private, most deeply "into" ourselves, we are in some other sense most deeply connected with others through whom we learned to become a self. Thus, Winnicott (1958) argues that the very capacity to be alone is first established in the experience of being alone in the presence of another, whose nonintrusive receptivity makes it possible for the baby to surrender to the flux of the spontaneous stream of "going-on-being."

Melanie Klein believed that we each experience the world around us as the inside of our mother's body. Recent infant research on the communication of affect between mother and infant makes it possible to think about this concept in a somewhat different way. The mother's emotions "become" part of the baby's emotional experience, supplying the tone and the contours that make up the world in which the baby lives. Thus, the child's sense of the world and its contents literally derives in no small measure from the contents of the mother's affective life. There are people whose life's project seems to be the creation of experiences that give meaning and form to affective states inherited from parents (for example, grief connected to losses before the child was born, common in children of survivors of catastrophic tragedies like the Holocaust).

The dialectical play between self and other pertains not only to past relationships. The pragmatic requirements involved in operating as a person amid the enormous complexities of our daily lives make self-observation always a limited affair. Of course, we usually have some idea of what we are up to, but it is very difficult to become aware of and articulate the complex array of our motives and concerns. It is not uncommon for people to have a sense that they do not fully know what happened in some complex interpersonal situation and that they do not as fully know "themselves" until they have had a chance to "process" the events in an intimate relationship with someone else. This is partly because awareness often comes from the opportunity to put inchoate feelings into words; partly it is the chance to overcome subtle, inevitable self-deceptions. The opportunities for what Sullivan termed "selective inattention" are too great for people to slide through complex experiences by translating events into old categories. It is too easy to collapse new situations into recurrent scenarios in which one always turns out to be one's fondest version of hero, victim, or perhaps both. Psychoanalysis with another person is a very different experience from self-analysis, no matter how faithfully attempted. It is often not until the other person's participation is felt—the questions, feedback, skepticism, support—and the participation of the other breaks up the facile, habitual categories in which one's own experience is automatically packaged, that one arrives at a richer, fresher sense of oneself. Is the self-understanding before such a conversation more "personal" than the self-understanding arrived at through dialogue? That which is most deeply personal is often arrived at only through interaction. It was not there and revealed through mirroring; it was created through dialogue.

There is another important sense in which the very nature of self is necessarily dialectical and interpersonal. Self-definition always implies definition of others. In the very process in which I decide "This is me. This is the sort of person I am," I am delineating and deciding the sort of person I am not. Thus, the self is defined and experienced largely through contrasts and in relation to others. Children define themselves vis-à-vis parents; siblings define themselves vis-à-vis each other; men and women shape their gender identities vis-à-vis images of the so-called opposite sex; one defines oneself in the present vis-à-vis images of the past and future, developmentally earlier and later selves (Greenberg, 1991). "I" always implies "you," in the same way that "light" implies "dark" or defining "day" implies a definition of "night." The self forms itself through processes of inclusion and exclusion: "This is me." "This has always been me." "This is no longer me." As one moves through time, one selects different content, including some, excluding others. Self and not-self are created in the same process, and not-self becomes others. Jung's (1933) concept of the "shadow" refers to the inevitable counterpoints and exclusions that accompany self-formation. Inclusion and exclusion are characterized in a different sense in the Kleinian depiction of introjection and projection, taking in and extruding. We are often involved, in our experience of others, with discovering and enjoying in them or revealing and controlling in them aspects of ourselves that have been underdeveloped and/or disallowed.

Experience is never completely communicable to or knowable by another. The mind is extremely complex, and therefore revelation and recognition are always highly selective processes. In that sense, the self, although formed continually in a relational field, is always in some sense immutably and profoundly private. Further, we generally spend most of our time being conscious, not self-conscious, being aware of ourselves as an ongoing process, without objectifying ourselves in an active effort to grasp or understand or communicate. Bromberg (personal communication) refers to a sense of "interiority," which derives "from being conscious of oneself without thinking about oneself." The capacity to take oneself for granted derives from experiences with others; it is the kind of experience one may have in the presence of others; yet it is impossible ever to represent or communicate the texture or contours of these most private dimensions of experiences to others.

The experience of the self as distinct and separable from relations with others—the "individual's innermost identity," as Kennon (1989) puts it—is a central feature of human subjectivity, at least as it is lived within western culture; it is, perhaps, a psychological necessity. Yet contemporary psychoanalytic theorizing has expanded our understanding of the relational and temporal context within which that phenomenology takes place, and that expanded, enriched vision of the ground of personal subjectivity is part of what the patient gains from the analytic process.

MULTIPLE SELVES, INTEGRAL SELF

The portrayals of self as multiple and discontinuous and of self as integral, continuous, and separable seem to be at odds, mutually exclusive. They are not. People act both discontinuously and continuously; people organize their experience into both multiple and integral configurations. Any given piece of experience can be looked at and felt both in terms of a particular relational context, a particular self/other integration and, at the same time, in terms of a larger, variegated, singular process that forms itself into different patterns at different times. At any given moment, a person operates out of a particular relational context (internally and/or interpersonally); at the same time, that very version of self contributes to the shaping of a continuous sequence of experience that has its own distinctive characteristics. Thinking about self in temporal as well as spatial terms makes it possible to account for both continuities and discontinuities as they appear, disappear, and reappear over time.[19]

Think of self as operating like cinematic film, composed of discrete, discontinuous pictures that, when run together, create something very much continuous and integral. Of course, with both film and selfhood, in a literal sense the experience of "motion" and continuity is an illusion. Yet this is an extremely dull and misleading literalness. The "illusion" creates an experience that has a powerful subjective richness of its own, creating a larger, "moving" picture, very different from (and much more than) the simple sum of the discrete pictures. Each frame is both a discrete, discontinuous image and a subunit of a larger, continuous process that takes on a life of its own. The most interesting feature of contemporary psychoanalytic perspectives on self is precisely the creative tension between the portrayal of self as multiple and discontinuous and of self as integral and continuous.[20]

Psychoanalysis fosters experiences of self as both an array of multiple, discontinuous relational configurations and as an integral, continuous process. The analyst implicitly or explicitly asks the patient, "How do you experience yourself today, in this particular transference-countertransference situation? Don't worry about yesterday; don't bother with tomorrow. Don't concern yourself with explaining it or reconciling it; let's just trace its outlines and learn its ways." It is precisely the timelessness of the analytic siutation that fosters the unraveling and makes learning about and connecting with multiple self configurations possible without having to account for oneself in the way one has to in ordinary life. The suspension of time and continuity in each individual analytic session allows the patient to find herself in the phenomenological "space" of the moment.

Yet the analyst, whatever else she is struggling with in terms of her own reactions and feelings, also attempts to hold on to the content of the sessions over time. The analyst accompanies the patient at each moment in the various ways of generating their own subjectivity. It is that

experience over time that helps generate a sense of the self as function-
ally dependable across discontinuities.

One of the great benefits of the analytic process is that the more the
analysand can tolerate experiencing multiple versions of himself, the
stronger, more resilient, and more durable he experiences himself to be.
Conversely, the more the analysand can find continuities across his various experiences, the more he can tolerate the identity diffusion entailed
by containing multiple versions of self. The analyst helps to enable him
to find and recognize himself when he is experiencing and behaving
"out of character," and it is that re-cognition that opens up the possibility of a more complex, richer experience. Robert captured this process
in an ironic quip in the middle of his analysis. He had come to treatment with many sexual and social inhibitions, and now, quite some time
later, he reported going up to a woman on a train, managing to meet
her, and securing her phone number. "And that," he noted emphatically,
"is precisely the kind of thing I do not do."

Satisfaction and the relative richness of life have a great deal to do
with the dialectic between multiplicity and integrity in the experience of
self, the balance between discontinuity and continuity (Harris, 1991;
Dimen, 1991). Where there is too much discontinuity, there is a dread
of fragmentation, splitting, dislocation, or dissolution. (Sullivan, 1958,
spoke of a dread-filled dimension of experience he termed the "not-
me.") Where there is too much continuity, there is a dread of paralysis
and stagnation. Meaningful hope is often generated in analysis precisely
when a sense of continuity begins to emerge from within disconnected
fragments of experience or when a compulsive, rigid character armor
melts into a new freedom to discover the self in different forms.

Parallel to the development of the experience of self is the experience
of others. This also involves a dialectic between multiplicity and singu-
larity. Earlier developmental theorizing portrayed the infant as
swamped by multiple, discontinuous images of the mother, forming a
consistent sense of "object permanence" only slowly over time. Some
more contemporary authors suggest that the infant is capable of per-
ceiving both self-invariants and invariance in others from the earliest
months (Daniel Stern, 1985). Yet both young children and adults have
difficulty throughout life reconciling different experiences of others, different "sides" of caregivers and other significant others. Not necessarily
on a cognitive or perceptual level, but rather on a deeper emotional
level, children have very different and often discontinuous images of
those closest to them: angry father, gentle father, excited father, and so
on. In one sense, these are all the same father; in another sense, these are

quite different fathers, and will always remain so. From the earliest interactions between infant and caregiver to the complex relationships between adults, experiences of others, like experiences of self, operate in a perpetual dialectic between multiplicity and integrity, change and continuity.

RETURNING TO ROBERT

What does the patient need to learn about himself in analysis? How will the analytic process make that learning possible? What sorts of participation are required by the analyst? How do different ways of understanding self translate into different forms of analytic engagement?

Robert's capacity to sustain a positive sense of himself as effective and powerful was compromised as a result of chronic interpersonal deprivation in early experiences with both parents. His mother was able to tolerate in her sons no independent viewpoint or source of initiative. We came to understand his early memory of the enema as emblematic of this central feature of his relationship with his mother. If he could conceal his active sexuality, his potency, his manhood, his sense of his own autonomy, his mother would take him over and nestle him in her protective care. His father offered no compelling alternative to Robert's efforts to find his own voice, to ground his own experience in a subjectivity that was uniquely his. The father seemed to have totally abandoned the boy and offered no refuge. He was interested only in his own autonomy, which he gained at the cost of destroying everything that Robert loved.

Robert was easily bruised and very vulnerable to feeling unprotected and endangered. One important dimension of his experience in analysis was the discovery and belief in the voice within the complex textures of his experience that was forced go underground, to conceal its rightful claims. My participation as analyst included helping him find and value that voice, through a sustained and detailed exploration of his feelings, his fantasies, his ideas. From this perspective (along self-psychological lines), analysis helped Robert reclaim a sense of centeredness, continuity, and integrity of experience.

Robert also needed to learn that what he experienced as his separate, distinct self is actually composed of complex forms of being with others. In continually reconstructing a sense of himself as weakened and in need of purification and bolstering, he was perpetually resurrecting his mother's protective care and reassuring her that he had not left the domain of her power. In his passive surrender to others to whom he attributed great power, he was maintaining a sense of his own connection both to the enema-bearing mother and to the powerful but dangerous father, whose return he was continually longing and preparing himself for. In maintaining his rage in a distant, smoldering container, he was protecting his tie to his father from the fearful, leveling intrusion of his mother (and his tie to her) and, at the same time, protecting his mother (and his identification with her) from both himself and his father. In recreating painful, unsatisfying relationships in his current life, he was enacting his devotion to both parents, "exciting objects" who seemed to promise a great deal but who always managed to remain unsatisfying and unresponsive.

From this perspective (along the lines of object relations theory, especially Fairbairn's), Robert needed to loosen the tight constraints within which he experienced himself, to hear the echoes of other voices, to feel other presences of earlier selves and earlier experiences of others. He needed to be able to surrender his hold on the misleading, apparent continuity of his experience, to discover its discrete and discontinuous subplots and worldviews. My participation helped him feel safe enough to unravel, to suspend continuity, to discover the hidden worlds embedded in his experience.

A very crucial dimension of Robert's analysis was learning about his tendency to draw others into repetitive enactments of his early relationships with his mother. He engaged others in a way that suggested a very discerning activity on his part, drawing on his own considerable intelligence and resources. His entire focus came to be on the other's beliefs, values, expectations. A subtle but pervasive molding of his own experience around the other was accomplished, which left out his own self-direction and also fueled and perpetually replenished his considerable resentment toward others. He ended up experiencing himself as passive, weak, at the mercy of the other's expectations, as if he were simply being dominated by virtue of some chronic weakness on his part. Other people, including me, tended to become controlling in either a misguidedly benign or sometimes malicious fashion.

From this perspective (along the lines of interpersonal psychoanalysis), Robert needed to come to appreciate that he was much more effective than he knew. He needed to become intrigued by the highly complex although unwitting fashion in which he enacted situations from his past, selected an appropriate supporting cast, taught them their roles, and reviewed and reported on events to himself always along preselected lines. He needed to become a skeptical detective in pursuit of his own operations. My participation included a modeling of that appreciative/skeptical inquiry.

A final but extremely important dimension of Robert's analysis was the development of his appreciation of his projective use of others as a vehicle for managing his own experience. He had great difficulty in consciously owning the more spontaneous, more sexual, and more aggressive dimensions of himself, all of which seemed extremely dangerous. He feared becoming fully immersed in his own sexuality or aggression for fear that he, like his father, would destroy the world and damage his mother, which he both wanted to do and also desperately did not want to do. He experiences these disowned aspects of himself in others and then tries to control these qualities in them by controlling and distancing them. Thus, it seemed much safer for him to experience power, potency, and aggression in others to whom he could passively surrender, and thereby control, than to contain these feelings within the borders of his own sense of self.

From this (Kleinian) perspective, Robert needed to discover the permeability of the boundaries between his experience of self and others and to appreciate what is often the exchangeability of the contents assigned to each. He needed to understand that what he was drawn toward and repulsed by in the Marlboro man, the analyst, and others were disclaimed and undeveloped aspects of his own experience. My participation included an illumination of these processes, both through interpretive description and through efforts to delineate, understand, and work out of the roles Robert and I alternatively enacted.

Consider these different dimensions of Robert's analysis with respect to the dialectic between multiplicity and integrity of self experience. The interpretive work on Robert's quest for an ideal father, played out in his actual relationships and in his manipulation of fantastic images in his mind, revealed an experience of self as helpless and profoundly dependent on me, the analyst. The expression and containment of that experience in the analytic relationship, in turn, seemed important in allowing him access to a very different version of himself—explosive, dangerous, and powerful—which the dream prefigured. That previously inaccessible internal domain, in turn, became the space in which we now worked (as the color of the lava, the color of his memory, became the color of the analytic room). Intrapsychic becomes interpersonal; interpersonal transforms intrapsychic, in a perpetual cycle of expansion and enrichment. New versions of self emerge and are embellished; an ongoing sense of self as more resiliant, variable, and dependable is established.

An additional feature of the analysis was a loosening of the unidimensional images Robert had maintained of both his parents. His convictions about both his mother's power and intolerance of his autonomy and his father's neglect and abandonment—these were all convictions that Robert had come to have an investment in. They sustained his subjective world as he had constructed and maintained it. The images of others he constructed and controlled in his reenactments of these dynamics with others were partially a product of his projections. As he became more able to contain other ways of experiencing himself, he came to be able to tolerate other dimensions of his parents and important people in his current life. Over the course of the analysis, other features of both parents emerged.

In every analysis, the analyst participates in a variety of ways, which lead to different sorts of experiences of self in the analysand. These forms of participation entail the use of language in different ways. These contrasts are not distinct and mutually exclusive; there are subtle, tonal emphases deriving from the very different purposes to which language can be put.

In the kind of inquiry emphasized by the interpersonal analyst, language serves to clarify, to articulate distinctly, to illuminate.[21] In the "empathic stance" developed within self psychology, "understanding" assumes priority over "explanation," and language serves not to illuminate but to convey a sense of accompaniment, an "attunement"; the goal is not clarity or detail but the sense of "being-with" the other.[22] In the form of participation that facilitates the unraveling of the multiple versions of self, as suggested by many object relations authors, language has a distinct and somewhat different function—neither to illuminate nor to accompany, but to establish and embellish a resonance with dimly felt, often developmentally earlier self-organizations. Here the aim is to use language to evoke original feeling states and earlier versions of self in relation to significant others. In this case, the evocative use of language dissolves its consensual dimensions to allow hidden resonances to be heard.[23]

Although one or another form of participation tends to be stressed by each school of analysis, most practicing clinicians find themselves interacting with their analysands in quite different ways at different times, facilitating a broad range of experiences. Of course, different types of patients with varying forms and degrees of psychopathology require very different weightings in the way these experiences are balanced. Subtle shifts are made all the time, from clarifying, to accompanying, to evoking.

I want to stress that I do not think these shifts tend to be made through conscious, deliberate choices by the analyst—nor should they be. Rather, analysand and analyst draw each other into patterns of interaction whose constructive and destructive, novel and perseverative features can be sorted out and understood only slowly over time (Gill, 1982a; Hoffman, 1987a; Levenson, 1983; Racker, 1968).

New forms of experience of self cannot be taught to the analysand in didactic fashion. Rather, they are learned only by being lived in, through participation in the psychoanalytic process, in a variety of different ways: through the analyst's interpretations, curiosity, and other features of a distinctly analytic presence; through the atmosphere created by the structure of the analytic situation; through the profound form of intimacy created and protected by the structure of the analytic relationship; and, finally and perhaps most important, through the model of the analyst's sense of herself, in the countertransference, as a container of multiple versions of self, providing a vehicle for understanding the manifold intricacies of relatedness.[24] It is here that the revolution in theory (What does the patient need?) and the revolution in metatheory (What does the analyst know?) most fully converge—in the analyst's use of her own participation in the process to facilitate an enriched sense of personal subjectivity in the analysand.

Nowhere is the inadequacy of the medical model approach to psychoanalysis more apparent than when one considers the experience of self that is generated by the analytic process. This is not a return to "normality," some premorbid standard of health, but rather a form of being, an appreciation of one's own subjectivity, that has its own unique qualities. Nor do I think it sufficient to designate what the analysand gains in terms of a particular function, such as a capacity for self-observation or self-reflection or self-analysis. Rather, psychoanalysis, at its best, makes possible a more variegated experience of self: Past and present, fantasy and actuality, interpenetrate each other; the phenomenology of the self as independent and separable is illuminated by an awareness of the self's embeddedness within a relational matrix; the experience of the self as layered in space is expanded by an appreciation of the self as continually regenerated in time; and an appreciation of the multiplicity within the integrity of self-organizations enriches the tapestry of subjective experience.

It is a great irony of the psychoanalytic experience that, in some respects, the patient is actually less known at the end of analysis than at the beginning (Graham Bass, personal communication). Early on, the patient's sense of who he is reductively collapsed and stereotyped: the

self as heroic, the self as monstrous, and so on. Much of the analysis involves a slow and painstaking revelation and articulation of these configurations, in the process of which the patient comes to feel very deeply
and profoundly known indeed. At the end of analysis, the patient's ways
of representing himself to himself tend to be much more fluid, complex,
subtly textured. He experiences himself in many more ways than can be
conveyed in the three or four or five analytic sessions per week. He becomes aware of how highly selective the presentation of self within
analysis really is. The freedom and loneliness of that realization are an
important part of termination.

5

True Selves, False Selves, and the Ambiguity of Authenticity

His desire to set a beginning to the chain of events to which he belonged encountered the same difficulty that it always does: the fact that everybody has a father, that nothing comes first and of itself, its own cause, but that everybody is begotten and points backwards, deeper down into the depths of beginnings, the bottoms and the abysses of the well of the past.

—Thomas Mann, *Joseph and His Brothers*

Revelation is addictive because the pursuit of the esthetic—at the expense of the accurate—is essentially coarsening. Ordinary, fragmentary truth, on a more modest scale, appears by contrast trivial and inadequate—appears, in short, untrue, since it so conspicuously lacks the splendor and intensity of feeling by which one has come to recognize the validity of revelations. In this way one's assumptions about truth fasten on the revelatory, and this habit of discovery quickly becomes addictive.

—Leslie Farber, *Lying, Despair, Jealousy, Envy, Sex, Suicide, Drugs, and the Good Life*

The major influences on Freud's thought include not only the rationality of the eighteenth-century Enlightenment, which laid the philosophical foundation for the modern scientific worldview, but also the powerful romantic vision of nineteenth-century poets and painters. Central to the vision of the latter was a call for the shedding of the trappings of civilization and a return to the power and immediacy of the "natural" world. For Freud (1940), the embodiment of the "natural" world in man is the "id," where he locates the instincts, at the core of the self; they represent "the true purpose of the individual organism's life. This consists of the satisfaction of its innate needs" (p. 148); the ego and the superego are secondary formations, social adaptations, formed on the surface of the id. For Freud, an understanding of the body-based instincts makes psychoanalysis a "depth" psychology, grounded in the most central, most "primitive" wellsprings of the individual.

The commitment of many contemporary analysts to Freud's drive theory is based on their belief that only by appreciating drives can the deepest understanding of the individual be found, underneath the more superficial, cultural, adaptive overlays. Just as society requires us to wear clothing to cover our physical nakedness, social necessities create layers of regulatory and defensive adaptations to cover our true animal motives and nature. Robert Waelder's (1960) homage to what he called the "imperative, majestic, power of Trieb" (p. 98) is emblematic of the elemental and elevated primacy attributed to the drives.

From this viewpoint, by abandoning the theory of drives, various relational theories, including self psychology, interpersonal psychoanalysis, and some versions of object relations theories, have lost the basis for an understanding of the individual in any depth. They have given up the tools for exploring true, passionate, authentic individuality, in contrast to the more superficial, shallow, interpersonal, and social overlays. In fact, many European analysts see the movement away from an exclusive focus on drives in contemporary American Freudian theory, exemplified by ego psychology, as an abandonment of the individual, personal depths of human experience, a denial of the unconscious. The call for a "return to Freud" and much of the contemporary loyalty to classical theory derive from the concern that the increasing emphasis on relational factors in recent psychoanalytic theorizing threatens to eliminate the personal, the uniquely individual, which Freud located in the body-based, sexual, and aggressive impulses of the presocial id.[1]

Where is the core of the self within a relational perspective? This is a real problem. As we saw in the last chapter, in most relational theorizing (consistent with most contemporary infancy research as well as with contemporary linguistics) it is assumed that the self cannot exist in isolation. The very capacity to have experiences necessarily develops in and requires an interpersonal matrix, and the organization, the patterning of all experiences is an extremely complex product of the interactions between the baby (with its temperamental sensitivities and thresholds) and the semiotic and interactive styles of the caregivers. There is no experience that is not interpersonally mediated. The meanings generated by the self are all interactive products.[2]

But where is the center, the heart, the core of the individual in such a perspective? How can we find a place in the self where the individual qua individual might be thought to begin or reside? With the relational emphasis on attachment, interpersonal relations, identifications, and so on, how can psychoanalysis fail to become a form of sociology or social learning theory in which the individual is viewed as a product of the social environment? If there are no body-based drives to represent "nature" at the intrapsychic core of the individual, how does psychoanalysis retain its most important and precious legacy as an instrument for inquiry into the depths of personal experience? The distinction between the true self and false, between the superficial and the more deeply felt, between conformistic adaptations and the more truly personal, between the authentic and the inauthentic: These distinctions are crucial to the analytic enterprise, and they seem to require that we locate the core or center of the self for use as a reference point.

THE SEARCH FOR THE CORE

There have been various attempts to deal with this problem instead of retaining Freud's outmoded concept of drives as preexperiential, prelinguistic archaic, phylogenetic residues.

One strategy has been to grant primary importance to the body, its parts and processes, and particularly to infantile bodily experiences, yet without Freud's notion of "drives." Why would the body be important if not for drives? There might be many reasons. Schafer, whose identity as a Freudian despite his disavowal of drive theory is based largely on the importance he places on infantile sexuality and aggression, believes that infantile body parts and experiences are the cognitive paradigms for organizing all experience (1978, p. 196). Our early life is dominated by powerful and absorbing physical events—eating, urinating, defecating, arousal, quiescence—and these events and processes become the basic categories, the underlying metaphors through which all subsequent experience is patterned.

This approach makes possible an interesting and valuable reinterpretation of Freudian and Kleinian concepts of instincts from energic into cognitive and linguistic terms, and characterizes some of the most important contemporary contributions to psychoanalytic theorizing. (See

Ogden [1986, 1989].) Yet it does not help solve our problem of locating the core of the self. Freud thought that body parts and processes are represented directly and invariably in experience; that the ego is first and foremost a body ego; and that "anatomy is destiny." This made sense within the context of drive theory, because the bodily tensions drive the mental apparatus, because instinctual experiences are the sole motivational energy for the mind, and because the self as a whole is derivative of and superimposed upon the vicissitudes of body-based drives. But if we eliminate drive theory as a motivational substructure, how do we understand the *meaning* that body parts and experiences take on for the individual? They must derive to a significant degree from the mutually regulatory, interpersonal, linguistic, and cultural matrix into which the individual is born.

In most relational approaches, in contrast to drive theory metapsychology, it makes no sense to talk about raw bodily experience, which is subsequently controlled or regulated through cultural processes. As George Lakoff and Mark Johnson (1980), who have made important recent contributions to our understanding of the metaphorical structure of language, argue:

> what we call "direct physical experience" is never merely a matter of having a body of a certain sort; rather, *every* experience takes place within a vast background of cultural presuppositions. It can be misleading, therefore, to speak of direct physical experience as though there were some core of immediate experience which we then "interpret" in terms of our conceptual system. Cultural assumptions, values, and attitudes are not a conceptual overlay which we may or may not place upon experience as we choose. It would be more correct to say that all experience is cultural through and through, that we experience our "world" in such a way that our culture is already present in the very experience itself. (p. 57)

It is also true that individuals experience culture through their own bodies. In that sense, all experience is also bodily through and through. The cultural input can sometimes be factored out, because it appears across individuals and its transmission is often visible and apparent, as in a particular cultural value system, such as American individualism or Victorian attitudes toward sexuality. Bodily experience only becomes known in necessarily social experience with others, and the very terms and categories through which it becomes known are shaped by linguistic and social experience. Thus, there is no way to ascertain what it is like to have a male as opposed to a female body, apart from a particular culture and its gender definitions within which the meanings of those bodies are shaped.[3]

The physical structure of the body probably provides constraints on body-based elaborations of meaning. The penis probably lends itself to a somewhat different, although overlapping, array of possible meanings and metaphors than either the clitoris or the vagina, although this is impossible ever to really determine. Within the framework of drive theory it made sense to think one could separate out the universal from the socially elaborated in bodily experience and assign the core of the individual to the former. Without the presumption of primary drives as the underlying motivational push, it makes no sense to think about the distillation of a pure, "natural" dimension of experience.

Another way to relocate the importance of the body within a relational framework is to argue that intense bodily happenings—such as sexual arousal, orgasm, eating, defecating, perhaps rage—have a preemptive physical claim and explosive power that inevitably places them at the core of personal experience. This is a very useful approach, but once again, it does not help us with the problem of locating a core self.

In Winnicott's writings, for example, the self is derived from interactions between the baby and the mother. "Instinctual experiences" (the phrase Winnicott often uses for intense bodily events, which has very little to do with Freud's drive theory) can facilitate and vitalize the self, but they also can operate totally outside it. Winnicott warns that the baby can be "fobbed off" by a good feed. What does that mean? The self does not develop out of instinctual experiences such as feeding but rather out of the subtle dialectic of maternal responsiveness. If feeding occurs in the context of good-enough mothering, it becomes a vehicle for growth of the self. If the mothering is inadequate, the power of the feeding experience actually detracts from self-development. The meaning of the bodily event depends on its position vis-à-vis the self.

There are people who experience sexual desire, or hunger for food, as a welcome sign of vitality. Others experience desire as a toxic impingement. Still others have no idea at all when they might be desirous of sex or food but decide by the clock. Finally, others never seem to experience desire or hunger at all. The location of experiences of anger or rage in relation to the self is similarly crucial; anger can vitalize, intrude upon, or deplete the self. The meaning of these bodily events, the psychological significance they contain regarding self, derives not from their inherent properties but from the way early relational patterns have structured them vis-à-vis the self. Such physical experiences cannot represent the core of the self, since they operate rather as vehicles to self experience, in either authentic or inauthentic ways.

Another aspect of constitutional, bodily factors—temperament—has been similarly recently appropriated as a route to finding the core of the self. In their eagerness to jettison the concept of innate drive, early relational theorists often wrote as if all babies were the same and as if the course of development derived purely from environmental input. Critics now correctly argue that babies are quite different from each other and that these temperamental differences have major implications for development. These differences have been amply demonstrated empirically over the past several decades, and recent models of infant-mother interactions stress the "fit" or lack thereof between particular mothers and particular babies. Bollas (1991) has explored and extended this factor in stressing the importance of constitutionally based temperamental differences leading to a particular personality style or personal "idiom" and to a sense of "destiny."

Differences in temperament, although extremely important, are nevertheless a problematic place to locate the core of the self. Temperament is not in any obvious sense motivational, and it is not represented directly in experience. The experience and meaning of temperamental differences are interpreted, often through identifications and counteridentifications. What is "high energy" in one family is hyperactivity in another. What is "sensitivity" in one family is weakness and inadequacy in another. Temperamental factors, like bodily configurations and processes, can be used by the self to fill out and represent various self-expressions and self-definitions. But they do not in themselves lead to particular forms of self-formation outside of complex social interaction.[4]

There have been other attempts to search for a new locus of individuality apart from the body per se, but located in very early experience. In the place previously occupied by Freud's id, Kohut (1977) puts a preprogrammed "destiny"; Guntrip (1969) places a regressed, schizoid baby; Winnicott designates a creative omnipotence; and so on. Each theorist wants to divide the content of the self, to cut up the pie into socially negotiated segments and something else, which exists prior to social interaction and which can be considered the core of the self.

This approach is closely connected with a linear perspective on development and developmental arrests. The infant is presumed to begin life with a whole, or integral, self, at least in potentiality; that self is either facilitated by the human environment or blocked and thwarted in some fashion. If the self is blocked, the potential for authentic experience is frozen at that developmental point, and a reanimation of the true self is possible only through a regeneration of those developmental needs. One artifact of this strategy for locating the core of the self outside of and prior to the relational field is that it leads to a regressive cast in theorizing. Earlier is presumed to be somehow more primary, more personal, more "primitive," as if the core of the individual existed preverbally, even pre-experientially before the infant encountered others.

One way in which this sort of developmental approach is framed is to speak of the self of the child-to-be as existing in potentiality in the infant and intuited and reflected by the mother (Kohut, 1977; Loewald, 1960). I have no problem with this notion if it is understood that the child has many potentialities with respect to self-development and that the one intuited by the mother is regarded as also partially a reflection of her own subjectivity.[5] The father, after all, may very likely intuit a quite different child in potential. In fact, it is precisely because the mother's child is somewhat different from the father's child that conflict between different organizations of self is generated so universally. Thus, to speak of the core of the self as existing in potentiality is to beg the question. Either it exists in already organized fashion and unfolds in a receptive environment—a notion I find implausible—or unorganized, temperamental differences that exist are organized and selected through interaction with caregivers. This brings us straight back to the problem of locating the core of the self.[6]

TEMPORALITY AND THE PROBLEM OF THE CORE

In the last chapter I suggested that the apparent contradiction between a view of self as multiple and discontinuous and a view of self as integral, layered, and continuous was due to the tendency to employ reified spatial metaphors in thinking about self. We saw that regarding self in temporal as well as spatial terms was helpful in establishing a constructive dialectic between these two lines of theorizing.

Thinking about self in temporal terms also is helpful in providing a fresh look at the problem of locating the core or "true" center of the self. The common subjective sense of depth, or plumbing a core to one's self, is created through the spatial metaphor, and arises at any particular moment in time when experience is generated in a more spontaneous fashion, less focused on externality. If conceptualized in objective terms, however, this project is necessarily ill-fated and futile. Subjective experience is an important but not infallible guide (as discussed in chapters 2 and 3) to generating the most helpful understanding of the factors that make those subjective experiences possible. Thinking about self in terms of time rather than space provides a more useful way of approaching the important issue that the search for the core of the self was meant to solve—the need to distinguish among degrees of authenticity in experience.

All the strategies for theorizing about the "true" or "core" self that we have considered employ, explicitly or implicitly, a spatial metaphor in their attempt to locate the elemental and essential from the superficial features of the self, to locate its center or foundation. They want to get underneath the adaptations that the self has made in its negotiations with others, to get at its beginnings, its true, presocial essence. This search for a core is what continues to make Freud's id and its romanticization of a pure, animal nature so compelling.

But if the self moves in time rather than exists in space, it has no fixed core. Rather, it has many different ways of operating. The pursuit of an invariant core or true self entails a removal of self from time, a misguided effort to make the shifting organizations of self experience static. As I mentioned earlier, spatial metaphors capture the sense of self at particular moments, like a snapshot of a river. But any effort to fix a core to the river, as one can determine the center of a snapshot, is doomed to fail.

Daily clinical work entails comparisons among different versions of self: Some seem spontaneous and constructive, some tortured and hidden; some more truly expressive of the individual, some a strategic adaptation for defensive purposes. How does an account of self as temporal make possible the necessary comparison among these different versions of self?

Some of the ways in which I operate and express myself I consider more "authentic," more important to or representative of "me" than others. Although these are difficult discriminations, we are all involved in making them a good deal of the time. At times I feel more "myself" than others, feel I have presented my thoughts and feelings accurately and succinctly, been comfortable enough to allow myself to reveal more of my spontaneous repertoire. At other times I feel less "myself," jumbled, unable or unwilling to make myself clear, too awkward or too constrained to reveal myself in anything but a stereotyped or constricted fashion. We all operate in this range of possibilities. The extreme form of inauthenticity is deliberate lying. When I am lying, I am misrepresenting my feelings or events and am being less authentic than when I am trying to represent myself and events more accurately.

In differentiating authenticity from inauthenticity, the crucial difference lies not in the specific content of what I feel or do but in the relationship between what I feel and do and the spontaneous configuration and flow of my experience at that point in time. A particular act or self-expression—a piece of self-revelation, for example, or a sexual overture—may feel extremely authentic at one point and extremely inauthentic at another. In the first case, it feels "right," suits both the external, interpersonal context and the internal emotional context. In the second case, it feels "off," forced, contrived, out of "sync" interpersonally, internally, or both. The degree to which an act or feeling represents or misrepresents the personal self depends not on its content (not on what is in it) but on its place in the context and configuration of experience as it is continually organized, disorganized, and reorganized in time.

In using the terms authentic and inauthentic, are we not measuring our experience against some implicit standard, some preconceived idea of what is "me"? Do these terms also not imply a "core" or "true" or "real" me that exists somewhere (smuggling back the spatial metaphor)? No. One has a sense of one's experience over time. One can measure a new experience in terms of continuity or discontinuity with the past and present; a new experience can represent and express one's history and current state or deny and betray one's history and current state, or reshape one's history and current state in a new and enriching way. The sense of authenticity is always a construction, and as a construction, it is always relative to other possible self-constructions at any particular time. Speaking of authenticity versus inauthenticity or true versus false experience frees us from the spatial metaphor in a way that speaking of a true or false self or a "core" or "real" self does not.

It is important to note that a sense of authenticity and inauthenticity is complexly related to the intricate textures of experience as it is composed of multiple versions of self. What may seem authentic in the context of one version of self may be quite inauthentic with respect to other versions. (Remember my reaction to the portrait painter, subsequently unrecognizable to my ordinary sense of self.) There are also times that an action that seems inauthentic with respect to preceding experience becomes more authentic over time, as one grows into and fully identifies with a new possibility. We will see in the final chapter that the constructive use of imaginative interpretations in analysis often works in precisely this way.

INTERNALITY VERSUS EXTERNALITY

Consider Winnicott's (1960, 1963) depiction of the earliest feeding experiences, which he establishes as the basis for the split between true and false selves. In pathological feeding, he suggests, the infant takes its cues from impingements from the outside. The baby's own impulses and needs are not met by the mother, and the baby learns to want what the mother gives, to become the mother's idea of who the baby is. Authentic feeding experience, on the other hand, derives from the baby's spontaneously arising gestures, which the good-enough mother meets and actualizes, creating what Winnicott terms the "moment of illusion."

What is the content of these spontaneous gestures? Even in the earliest feedings, Winnicott suggests, the baby's "readiness" to imagine a breast leads immediately to experiences in the real world out of which develops the baby's idea of the breast, which is further matched by the mother's responsiveness. It cannot be the content that differentiates authentic from inauthentic experience; the image of the breast in the two experiences is virtually the same. What is crucial is the point of origin of the idea at any given time, and that makes all the difference. At one moment a movement toward the breast occurs spontaneously in the baby; at another moment it is a response to the mother's idea of what the baby wants, a compliance with external impingement. Does the idea of the breast at a particular moment come from the baby or the mother? Does it arise spontaneously in the baby, or is it suggested or even coerced from the outside? This is the crucial issue for Winnicott, and it is a very useful starting point for thinking about the problem of authentic individuality in general.

The individual discovers himself within an interpersonal field of interactions in which he has participated long before the dawn of his own self-reflective consciousness. The mind of which he becomes self-aware is constituted by a stream of impulses, fantasies, bodily sensations, which have been patterned through interaction and mutual regulation with caregivers. The experience and meaning of all these have been established and continue to be established, through the physical and mental handling and holding of significant others.[7] With the gradual dawning of self-awareness, that mental content becomes more fully one's own and can be used in various ways—it can be spontaneously expressed; it can be collaboratively coordinated in interactions with others; it can be deceptively packaged, disingenuously presented; it can be compromised; it can be betrayed.

In classical psychoanalysis, the central and most important question to be asked of the individual is: What are the patterns of gratification, frustration, and sublimation that shape this person's life? In contemporary psychoanalysis, in the work of its most visionary contributors, the most important question to be asked has shifted to: How meaningful and authentic is a person's experience and expression of herself? Richness in living or psychopathology is the product not of instinctual vicissitudes but of truth or falseness with respect to one's own experience. Why is the self so easily and commonly falsified, so routinely betrayed?

The self operates in the intricate and subtle dialectic between spontaneous vitality and self-expression on the one hand and the requirement, crucial for survival, to preserve secure and familiar connections with others on the other.[8] Spontaneous self-expression serves as the ground for an array of authentic experience; the need for security leads to a concern with the impact of one's self-presentations on others. If I spontaneously express my feeling or thought or state of mind, do I make the other on whom I am greatly dependent anxious, angry, likely to withdraw? Do I have to conceal my spontaneous experience? Disguise it? Package it in a particular way, perhaps differently for different significant others? It is the necessity for mindfulness (both conscious and unconscious) and some degree of control of one's impact on others that makes inevitable for all people at one time or another a whole array of inauthentic experiences. It is not differences in content that distinguish the authentic from the inauthentic; it is the way the content is organized, particularly in terms of the balance between internality and externality and the purpose to which the content is being put at any given moment.

Deciding what is true and what is false when it comes to self is a tricky business. Although Winnicott's idea of the "true self" is often used in a concrete and reified fashion, he himself suggests that "there is but little point in formulating a True Self idea except for the purpose of trying to understand the False Self, because it does no more than collect together the details of the experience of aliveness" (1960, p. 148). Khan (1963), who wrote of the "privacy" of the self with such eloquence and subtlety, suggests that the "true self" is a conceptual ideal, known concretely mostly by its absence (p. 303).

We are often quite aware when we are being false or betraying ourselves, but authenticity does not often announce itself in such a stark and unambiguous way. In fact, a lack of self-consciousness, posturing, self-arranging, self-presenting, narcissistic pulse-checking is often the hallmark of a truer form of experience, in which the self is taken for granted, unheralded and without banners. The patient who struggles to reveal his "true" feelings or disclose what he is "really like" may reveal a conflict- or shame-ridden aspect of experience, but this is hardly the whole story.[9]

Consider the enormously delicate clinical problem involved in the psychoanalysis of victims of childhood abuse, sexual or otherwise. There are moments when to speak of anything else is false, inauthentic, a denial of what has taken place. Yet there are other moments when the account of the victimization is serving the purpose not of making oneself known but of creating an impact, making a claim, often turning the tables via an identification with the original abuser (Davies and Frawley 1992). In such moments, which Sandor Ferenczi (1988) termed the "terrorism of suffering," the content is true but the intent is laced with falseness. Any statement about the self and one's past can, and inevitably does, begin to serve other purposes in the present. This is what Sartre (1958) meant by his argument that we are all continually struggling to emerge from "bad faith." Yesterday's insight becomes today's resistance; yesterday's hard-fought self-understanding becomes today's familiar and comfortable refuge.

RECONCILIATION: INSIDE AND OUTSIDE

The seductiveness of discovering one's "true self" is, as Farber suggests in the epigraph to this chapter, both addictive and reductive. This is necessarily so, because of the temporal nature of self and the dialectic between the multiplicity and integrity of the self explored in the previous chapter. There are many conflictual versions of self-organization, and these emerge in and bear on experience in succession over time. At any particular point in time, one may be experiencing and employing a version of self in a true or false fashion, and the sudden, unselfconscious discovery of previously inaccessible aspects of self can be a powerful and transformative experience. However, the self-conscious designation or coronation of one version of self as the true self brings with it an inauthentic foreclosing of experience and an arbitrary claim made both on oneself and on others.

Part of the trickiness of distinguishing "true" from "false" experience is that both the distinction between internality and externality and the distinction between self and other become more complex the more closely they are considered. Winnicott's use of these distinctions for the infant vis-à-vis the breast provides an important starting point, but this is too simplified a situation when we consider adult experience. All personal motives have a long relational history. If the self is always embedded in relational contexts, either actual or internal, then all important motives have appeared and taken on life and form in the presence and through the reactions of significant others.

Let us say a little girl decides she will become a physician through a mixture of motives that we could divide into two groups. Group A includes genuine interest in the workings of nature in general and bodies in particular, sexual curiosity, a concern with helping others, and counterdependent defenses against being sick herself. Group B includes a strong desire to please her parents' thwarted longings to be educated as professionals, identification with their social class aspirations, their anxieties about their daughter's future security, and so on. Let us assume that the little girl sensed the importance of this career path to her parents from the moment they gave her her first Fisher-Price doctor set. How do we evaluate the authenticity versus inauthenticity of this choice and life course? Since the motives in group A reflect internal concerns and those in group B reflect external concerns, the obvious starting point would be to assume that the balance between truth and falseness in this choice would be determined by the balance between motives A and B. But a closer look suggests a greater complexity.

Group B motives began as external considerations. The girl likes to make her parents excited and happy by parading around with her toy stethoscope. But by the time she is applying to medical school, she has long since left home—her parents may even be dead. Externality now means something different. She certainly may still make the choice in order to please her parents; yet her parents are not actual people at this point but internal parents, internal objects. In making the choice to go to medical school, she feels a deep and pervasive connection with her parents, and her feelings of closeness with them perpetuate them as emotional presences in her experience. So these formerly external objects now operate internally.

Conversely, although group A motives seem to be purely self-generated, they cannot be wholly so. Allowing for the importance of constitutional, temperamental factors in terms of activity level, intellectual gifts, and sensibilities, we would have to assume that qualities such as interest in nature, bodies, sexual curiosity, helping others, and counterdependent defenses could not emerge in an interpersonal vacuum or flower in a simply mirroring, facilitating environment. They must have identificatory meanings embedded in interactions with important others, complex reverberations and resonances within various relational configurations. Group A motives, like group B motives, are complex blends of both internal and external factors.

It is not so easy, therefore, to parse self from other, to neatly divide internal from external considerations. The extreme stickiness of this problem is one of the reasons why theories claiming to have located a center of the individual outside the relational field are so compelling.

Probably we all have had the very private experience of connecting with ourselves in solitude in a way that is not possible in the presence of others, the "incognito" subjective core of Winnicott (1963). And there is the experience of refinding what one really feels or wants to do through a sudden realization that one has been too concerned with the opinions and reactions of others. These considerations suggest that the core or foundation of the individual self is egoistic and discoverable only in isolation.

Yet there also are experiences of losing oneself in private ruminations, self-alienation in solitude, and a sense of refinding oneself through engagement with another. There is a difference for most people between the relative hollowness of masturbation and the fullness of sex with another that probably has something to do with the perpetuation of the species. In sex with another, externality, compromise, and compliance are clearly features. If there is too much concern with externality, there is no spontaneous desire, and the experience lacks depth and passion.[10] On the other hand, if there is no sense of externality, there is no awareness of the other except as a masturbatory vehicle.

The richness of experience is generated in the subtle dialectics between internality and externality, desire and concern, destruction and reparation, self and other. Human beings use each other not just for safety, protection, control, and self-regulation; we also come alive, develop capacities, and expand personal consciousness through interaction in a way that is not possible in isolation. The simple distinction between internality and externality, although a very useful starting point, is not sufficient to distinguish true from false experience.

As I noted at the beginning of this chapter, Freud's notion of the id prior to, buffered from, and uncompromised by social experience reflects a long-standing, romantic tradition in which human freedom is located in an escape from social compliance and constraints.[11] However, the strategy of defining freedom in terms of independence of society and culture is not limited to drive theorists. It is central to the vision of Erich Fromm (1941), who regards the threat of social ostracism as the fundamental obstacle to authentic experience in the self-definition of the individual. Fromm once commented that the reason he never had children of his own was that "children make one hostage to the culture" (David Schecter, personal communication). Anyone who has had children understands immediately what Fromm meant. Concern about a child's peer and school adjustment begin to limit, or at least introduce, considerations of restraint and caution into one's own freedom of speech and expression. Nevertheless, for this to be a reason not to have children suggests the limitations of defining authenticity solely in terms of freedom from social constraint. A more meaningful (although less pure and romantic) definition entails a process of working through social considerations and constraints to a deeply personal, individual experience. What is crucial is the extent to which internal and external considerations, self and other, have been balanced and reconciled.[12]

What is central to the analytic process is precisely an overcoming of the sense that one has to choose between being oneself in the "use" of others or betraying oneself in adaptation to others. Psychoanalysis becomes a struggle to find and be oneself in the process of atonement[13] and reconciliation in relation to others, both actual others and others as internal presences.[14]

Let us return to our would-be medical student. Most clinicians, regardless of ideological persuasion, would be concerned with the following considerations when thinking about her career deliberations: Is this choice consistent with enough dimensions of her personality to represent and work for her in a meaningful way? Will she use enough of herself, or does it draw her away from too much that is important to her? Is she anticipating pleasure in this work, or primarily a fantasied security or fantastic solution to infantile anxieties? These considerations could be translated into different theoretical terms: Have the original motives attained sufficient secondary autonomy? Is she motivated by satisfactions or security? Are the identifications primarily superego or ego identifications? Are her superego and ego reconciled or at odds? Are her internal objects happy? All these questions are concerned, in one way or another, with the way in which what was formerly external has become internal, the extent to which externality and internality have become reconciled or are pulling against each other in different directions, and the degree to which past interpersonal negotiations have been metabolized into nutriment for further growth and development.

Consider other kinds of experiences that provide for some people a deep sense of authenticity: athletic activities or artistic creation. If I am just learning to play tennis, the effort will feel unnatural, inauthentic, modeling, or posturing, not representative of me: "Grip the racket just so; position your feet perpendicular to the net; keep your eye on the ball; keep your weight moving toward the net; swing through the ball." In learning the game I am learning a complex discipline created through a long history by a community of others. Some people are "naturals" with respect to sheer athletic ability, but no one can play tennis naturally, at least not very well. The techniques are essential if you are to get where you want to go.

Yet if I have played tennis for a long time, I may feel truly and deeply myself when I play. When I play well I am likely not only to feel free of any attention to technique or discipline but also to feel free of self-consciousness altogether, playing "in the groove," or "out of my mind." The same techniques so painfully and awkwardly practiced over many years are now a part of me and make possible kinds of experiences not attainable in any other way. Tennis is a set of complex, social conventions that make possible an individual, deeply subjective experience of potentially profound personal significance. Authenticity reflects the use of the interpenetration of internal and external to represent and express myself; inauthenticity reflects the use of the interpenetration of internal and external to create and manage impressions of me in others.

SPATIAL METAPHORS IN EXPERIENCE OF SELF

Certain kinds of experiences—different ones for different people—are difficult or impossible to risk displaying with others. It is as if they exist in secret, hidden recesses of being, and they can feel as if they constitute a core or center of the self. Other ways of being feel stereotyped, facile, and easily conjured up; these ways of being seem to provide a protective buffer, a shell under which or within which more vulnerable, more hidden, and more authentic forms of experience can be concealed.

For some people, sexual responses are impossible to express and integrate in interactions with others and have a "true" or pure quality to them, precisely because their sexuality has rarely been modulated through social interaction. For others, dissociated rage has a pure, deep quality about it, in contrast to the chronic characterological submission that may govern all other interactions (necessitating the dissociation of the rage in the first place). For others, a pure joy or spontaneous laughter remains hidden and unexpressed behind a dour demeanor or a hyperresponsible version of adulthood. For still others, certain kinds of preverbal experiences have been preserved as a refuge for the self, while language in general has been co-opted by deception and self-betrayal. These experiences are sometimes organized into the representation of the thwarted spontaneity of the self as baby, hidden behind the empty, conformistic adaptations of adulthood.

Clinical psychoanalysis, unless it becomes a sterile exercise in "rationality," operates within the phenomenology of the self. Analyst and patient enter spaces, explore recesses, traverse topographies. Previously inaccessible experiences, running the gamut from totally dissociated to concealed, to conflict-ridden, often make themselves known through personalized metaphors: animals, babies, explosions, elemental forces, closets, demons. These experiences can come alive in the analytic situation only in their own terms. The experience of self as a preverbal baby cannot be talked about, because it is the very corruption of language in the dynamics of particular families that initially makes it impossible for the patient to feel alive through words.[15] The experience of the self as explosively rageful or demonically sexual cannot be translated into polite conversation, because it was precisely the disembodied and mannered forms of familial discourse that created the sense of rage and sexuality as dangerous and primitive. The metaphors around which versions of self are organized generally come in complementary pairs (see also Wachtel's [1987] concept of cyclical psychodynamics): the needy baby/the pale and joyless adulthood; the beast/the civilized citizen; and so on. Versions of the self are states of mind accessible only on their own terms, and the collaborative struggle to discover and create these terms is a crucial dimension of the analytic process.

Ironically, only as the analytic process enables the patient to live in what are felt to be secret, hidden, core spaces within the self does she begin to experience these states as versions of herself, among many other versions, that emerge and are shaped over time. As this capacity to experience self in deeper and richer forms develops, the temporal and spatial dimensions of self fully complement each other. Spatial metaphors often are necessary for any given experience to be expressed and developed. As the temporality of the self is more fully experienced, spatial patterns become less static and confining.

Thinking about self in temporal as well as spatial terms forces a reconsideration of the relationship between body and self. I have argued elsewhere (Mitchell, 1988) that it makes more sense to think about body-based experiences such as sexual desire or rage not as continual, primitive, endogenous pressures located in a place within the psyche (like the "id"), but as reactions to stimuli, internal and external, always in particular relational contexts. From this perspective it makes no sense to say that desire and aggression are any more "primitive," basic, or fundamental than laughing or painting. It is not the content that is important, because no content is more central or primary than any other. What is important is the function of the content in the larger context of experience. Does the desire, rage, laughter, or painting derive from and express spontaneous reactions to both internal and external stimuli, or is it contrived to manage self states (for example, by warding off depression) and other people (for example, by pleasing or impressing them)? Body-based experiences of self are no more primary than verbal ones; rather, different ways of organizing experience are coterminous and in dialectical relationship with each other.[16] It is a mistake to think of one form of experience as more basic or deeper, because experiences are not layered in space; rather, they shift back and forth as forms of self-organization over time. The common subjective sense of greater depth that accompanies some experiences in contrast to others should be understood to derive from their relative spontaineity and freedom from attention to their immediate reception by others in the present, not from a deeper origin in some objectively layered psychic structure.

An additional facet of the relationship between the body and self concerns the issue of gender. If one assumes, as did Freud, that "anatomy is destiny" and that the drives constitute the core of the psyche, one would think of the self and of experience in general as gendered. (Freud felt that the array of component drives makes us all bisexual, so that both genders are represented in each psyche.) In contrast, if one assumes that the self is organized in different ways at different points in time, some of those organizations may be gendered (monosexually or bisexually), while others may not. It may be developmentally necessary for a little boy or a little girl to feel very much like a little boy or a little girl, but very unnecessary and enormously constricting for adult men or women to need to experience themselves continually in a gendered way (Dimen, 1991; Goldner, 1991; Harris, 1991). Gender identity, or a gendered identity, is, for most people, extremely important to establish. In fact, the most important function of sexual activity for many people is not the pleasure or release per se but the establishment of the sense of oneself as a woman or as a man. (See Person, 1980; Simon and Gagnon, 1973.) Yet a gendered sense of self may not always underlie experience. In fact, the capacity to organize experience in many ungendered (not bisexual) ways, without a compulsive need to evoke a gendered identity, might be considered a feature of mental health (Goldner, 1991).

REGRESSION: DOWNWARD OR OUTWARD?

The concept of "regression" has been used traditionally to suggest the movement, in the psychoanalytic process, from more developed and integrated layers of the self to earlier, more "primitive" dimensions.

Within the traditional embedded spatial metaphor, the earlier experience is assumed to underlie later, less deeply personal, roots of the self. In my view, regression can be thought about more usefully not as a movement down, into the heart of the self, but as a movement out, as an enrichment and overcoming of constraining self-organizations.

Bollas (1987, p. 218) speaks of patients who seek him out looking for a "Winnicottian" analysis, envisioned as a regressive return to total dependency, a letting go of what they feel are their inauthentic yet perhaps highly effective ways of functioning in the world. The quest of these patients is clearly consistent with one aspect of Winnicott's contribution. (Little [1985] notes that Winnicott "spoke of patients having to 'queue up' sometimes to go into such a state," to wait for their turn at "full regression" [p. 23].) Yet Bollas points out the importance of not assuming that the functional self and the person's resources are any less "true" than the image of the regressed and wholly dependent infant the patient longs to be. The original reasons for someone to become resourceful and effective might well have been "inauthentic" and some distance from where the person genuinely was at the time. Nevertheless, what is crucial now is the use or misuse to which those capacities are put. The idea that one's "core" or "true" self is located in developmentally earlier states is both overly simplistic and also very compelling, as evidenced by the popularity of "the child within" in much mass-market popular psychology. The claim to be helpless and the disclaiming of one's actual resources, although very understandable (it often operates as a testament to hope and an avoidance of coming to terms with irreversibly lost opportunities and experiences), nevertheless serve current purposes that are no longer simply authentic.

Develpmentally prior self-organizations often emerge in the analytic situation; one's experience of oneself, the world, and relationships to others is felt to be patterned in a very different fashion from one's ordinary adult life. In many ways the analytic situation is structured precisely to pull for such "regressive" experience in the transference relationship to the analyst. However, the idea that the developmentally earlier versions of self underlie, or are more fundamental than, later versions of self fails to appreciate the flow of different versions of self in time. Again, it is crucial to distinguish subjective phenomenology from theoretical clarity.[17]

Another kind of "regressive" process concerns not so much a return to developmentally earlier self-organizations, but the emergence of pieces of experience never integrated into a coherent self-organization and, perhaps, never represented and made real through language. This kind of regressive experience consists of a kind of constructive disintegration, in which the ordinary contours of self experience become less guarded and more permeable, allowing an opening to and eventual integration of less controlled forms of experience not possible before, such as fusion and surrender (Ghent, 1992). Once again, regression seems an ill-chosen term for such experiences, which are not a return to anything as much as a reclaiming of lost potentials, not a retreat but an expansion.

ONE-PERSON/TWO-PERSON?

As relational theory has become more and more prominent over the past several decades, one finds increasing discussion in the literature about the relationship between a two-person, interpersonal perspective and the more traditional one-person, intrapsychic perspective of classical theory. There have been several ways of approaching this problem.

One strategy (developed most explicitly by Levenson, 1983, 1992) has been the establishment of a "radical interpersonal" position, which is thoroughly two-person and eschews all intrapsychic concepts. In this view, everything important is happening in the interpersonal field. There are no mysterious dynamics inside the patient; rather, the patient and analyst enact the important dynamics in their interactions with each other. The patient's problem is not the father or mother but the analyst, who will inevitably act like the father or mother. To speak of internal object relations, inner worlds, even identifications, is to compromise a radically interpersonal perspective with residues of traditional intrapsychic theorizing and, ultimately, to deny what is most important, the enactment of crucial dynamic issues in the analytic relationship.[18]

The counterpart to Levenson on the other end of the continuum are more traditional Freudian authors who regard psychoanalysis as essentially the study and treatment of one person.[19] The analyst is merely an observer or technician; her personhood has nothing to do with it. For these authors, the "interpersonal" is as much of a contaminent and danger as is the "intrapsychic" for the "radical interpersonalist." The patient's problem is with the father or mother. It is ultimately irrelevant whether the analyst does or does not act similarly. The analytic field is merely the empty stage upon which the internal dynamics of the patient come to life.[20]

I regard approaches located on both extreme ends of the one-person/two-person continuum as unnecessarily reductive and narrow.

On the one hand, isolating any aspect of human experience or the analytic relationship outside of its embeddedness in an interactive, relational matrix starts one off on the wrong footing. On the other hand, to consider only that which is currently interactional for fear of intrapsychic ghosts is a massive and unfortunate overcorrection. The human psyche, in my view, is both intrapsychic and interpersonal, simultaneously both a one-person and two-person phenomenon. (See Benjamin, 1992b, for a similar view.)

Is there something problematic or difficult to grasp about regarding mind in both intrapsychic and interpesonal terms? Some writers (such as Arnold Modell) have suggested that this amounts to bringing together two essentially incompatible frames of reference and therefore constitutes a paradox. Since Winnicott has made the concept of paradox acceptable (even fashionable!), maintaining both the intrapsychic and the interpersonal in a contradictory but complementary juxtaposition is thought to be possible.

This position often reflects an effort to preserve the particular version of the intrapsychic as developed in the classical tradition while adding to it interpersonal considerations. The intrapsychic within Freud's drive theory is constituted by a priori, preformed instinctual organizations; to combine that version with a more interpersonal vision is truly paradoxical. However, the intrapsychic as envisioned by many relational authors (such as Fairbairn, Loewald, and Racker) is itself the residue of prior interactions. Here we have an intrapsychic that is, in its basic constituents, interpersonally derived. In this sort of framework, not only are the intrapsychic and the interpersonal not incompatible, they are natural extensions of each other.[21]

To consider the relationship between one-person and two-person psychologies as paradoxical is to beg the question of exactly what sort of one-person psychology is being advocated. In my view, the intrapsychic and the interpersonal are perpetually interpenetrating realms that continually fold back into each other. The process of self-discovery generally leads to the discovery of past relationships, and in encountering others, one frequently also discovers oneself. There is nothing fundamentally paradoxical about the relationship between the intrapsychic and the interpersonal, or one-person and two-person frameworks, any more than there is something paradoxical about being both an individual and, simultaneously, a member of a couple or family. Surely, sometimes one might be acting solely on one's own behalf, at other times for the couple, and at other times on behalf of the family. But there is nothing contradictory and therefore nothing paradoxical about these different dimensions. The fundamental authenticity of self experience rests precisely on the reconciliation and effective transversing of these different realms.

THE ANALYST'S AUTHENTICITY

In puzzling through the ambiguities of authenticity, I have used career choice and tennis as examples. To highlight other features of these issues, I would like to consider the problem of authenticity in relation to the experience of the analyst. This issue is becoming increasingly important in the analytic literature as we move farther into the postclassical era of psychoanalysis. Is the analyst true to himself and being authentic when being an analyst? This question provides an interesting complement to the problems we have been struggling with in connection with establishing authenticity with respect to the patient.

Even to pose the question of authenticity in terms of the analyst's experience makes no sense in most traditional views of the analytic process. In the classical model, the analyst is essentially playing a role, serving a particular function. In the "handling of the transference" as Otto Fenichel (1940) puts it, "'not joining in the game' is the principle task" (p. 73). The patient experiences a range of different sorts of passionate feelings; the analyst experiences the feelings consistent with their observing, interpretive function. Thus, Schafer (1983), in his generally classical approach to technique, describes doing analysis as entailing a "subordination" of the analyst's personality; this tradition lays a great emphasis on control and restraint in descriptions of the analyst's experience (for example, Abend, 1986; Silverman, 1985). To ask whether the analyst's true self is being expressed in this process is a meaningless question, akin to asking whether the analyst is being authentic while driving a car across a mountain pass on a rainy night. The analyst is doing a complicated, hazzardous job requiring great concentration; self-expression has nothing to do with it. Consider this representative but especially vivid description in which the role of the analyst seems rather like Ulysses resisting the sirens, tied to the mast of neutrality:

> If the analyst is indeed immersed in the intense emotional interchange that the analytic situation is designed to provoke, he is subjected to powerful pressures to abandon his analytic neutrality. He is bombarded by a stream of complaints, supplications, subtle seductions, bitter accusations, and ingenious bits of blackmail from his patients.

He is also subjected to an intense pull from within his own being to ease his burden by obtaining some measure of instinctual gratification from the analytic experience to make up for the deprivation and abuse to which he has given himself up. The analyst is continually drawn to do more than analyze, and his very humanness makes it difficult for him to invariably resist all the temptations. (Silverman, 1985, pp. 176–77)

Countertransference, in this progressive but traditional perspective, may at times be inevitable, but it is essentially a contaminant, distracting and potentially dangerous. According to the implicit anal metaphor embedded in the classical concept, countertransference is something that "happens," but something that needs to be gotten under control and eliminated as much as possible.

The same irrelevance regarding the analyst's authenticity applies to some versions of the self-psychological approach. Here too the analyst is understood to be providing necessary functions—self-object functions. The whole point of listening in the "empathic mode," as it has been developed by Kohut, Schwaber, and others, is to be listening and articulating things from what is assumed to be the patient's point of view. Allowances are made for the inevitable intrusion of the analyst's point of view, but it is regarded as essentially an intrusion and contaminant, diverting the analyst from his function as a benign reflector of the patient's experience.[22]

The question of authenticity arises in perspectives on the analytic process influenced by interpersonal theory, particularly the line of interpersonal psychoanalysis shaped by Fromm. (Sullivan saw the analyst in more traditional terms, as an "expert" serving a function.) But for Fromm, the place of authenticity and inauthenticity in the analytic relationship is crucial. Fromm felt that people in our culture rarely speak truthfully and frankly to each other. The patient comes to analysis partly, or largely, in search of a more authentic response. If the analyst plays a role, subordinating her own reactions to the patient, the analysis is built on bad faith. From this perspective, analytic "neutrality" is an inhibiting fraud, and "holding," "mirroring," and other more self-consciously benign roles are forms of infantilization. What the patient requires more than anything else is some sense of his impact on another, some honest expression of what the analyst is really feeling.[23]

Good classical or self-psychological analysts pay attention to what they are feeling. What I am suggesting is that in those two models, there is one primary focus of attention—the patient's associations, the patient's experience. In the interpersonal and in some versions of the Kleinian approach, there are two primary foci. The analyst's experience, particularly passionate experience, may contain information crucial to the analysis not obtainable in any other way.

But how does the analyst know what he is feeling? If we want to locate authenticity in the analyst in his current affective state, how does the analyst who is conscientiously trying to be true and authentic, first to himself and then, when optimally useful, with the patient, decide which among his various feelings and reactions are most authentic?

There are times when a particular reaction dominates the countertransference—rage or erotic interest, for example. Feeling enraged at or aroused by a patient is similar to feeling enraged at or aroused by someone else in a different context, but not exactly the same. With a patient, there is also, no matter what else is going on, a commitment to the analytic process, to the inquiry. Outside analysis, one might feel free to pursue a fight or flirtation with a certain abandon: I will figure out what to do later when I get there. What is going on right now may be more fun or compelling. Doing analysis demands a self-reflectiveness that struggles to keep rage from becoming an unloading on the patient, to keep arousal from becoming a seduction of the patient, either through affective ambience or through "interpretations."

Some argue that one might as well just express whatever one is feeling because it becomes apparent to the patient anyway. This seems simplistic and somewhat disingenuous to me. The analyst feels many things and is constantly selecting and making choices, both in terms of what to say and also in terms of what to think about. No analysis in which the analyst simply reports on her personal experience would uphold the crucial importance of the patient's sense that the analysis is for him. (Ferenczi's experiment in "mutual analysis" foundered on these shoals.) So analysts make choices and spend a great deal more time thinking than speaking. Authenticity in the analyst has less to do with saying everything than in the genuineness of what actually is said.

Am I being less authentic restraining an angry or erotic impulse in the analytic situation and struggling to reflect upon it than I am in situations outside analysis where I might pursue impulses with relatively greater abandon? In some ways yes; in some ways no. Analytic reflection forces an attention to other features of the analyst's feelings about the patient than may be in the immediate forefront at any particular moment. Perhaps the rage or arousal is not the "truest" or most "authentic" feeling at all, but merely the one with the most intense immediate charge. Perhaps abandoning myself to the fight or arousal would entail a betrayal of myself and/or the relationship in a much more profound way.

When my older daughter was about two or so, I remember my excitement at the prospect of taking walks with her, given her new ambulatory skills and her intense interest in being outdoors. However, I soon found these walks agonizingly slow. My idea of a walk entailed brisk movement along a road or path. Her idea was quite different. The implications of this difference hit me one day when we encountered a fallen tree on the side of the road, about twenty yards from our house. The rest of the "walk" was spent exploring the fungal and insect life on, under, and around the tree. I remember my sudden realization that these walks would be no fun for me, merely a parental duty, if I held on to my idea of walks. As I was able to give that up and surrender to my daughter's rhythm and focus, a different type of experience opened up to me. Was this shift a movement from something authentic in me to something inauthentic? It is hard to say. My natural pace is quite rapid, but that rapidity could be thought of in terms of hypomanic defenses. Perhaps I became more truly authentic when I slowed up. If I had simply restrained myself out of duty, I would have experienced the walk as a compliance. But I was able to become my daughter's version of a good companion and to find in that another way for me to be that took on great personal meaning for me.

A very important counterbalance to the pursuit of the analyst's authenticity is the usefulness (sometimes) to the patient of the analyst's allowing himself to be "used" by the patient as a vehicle for self-exploration.[24] Intimacy, sexual and otherwise, involves a continual, mutual surrender. One offers oneself up to be shaped, arranged, explored, in the service of the other's self-expression. This happens all the time in analysis, sometimes deliberately in the analyst's allowing the transference to deepen in certain ways, sometimes unwittingly in the analyst's discovery that he has become a character in the patient's inner world.

Would we want to consider the process of the analyst offering herself up for use by the patient (to use Winnicott's evocative term) a form of inauthenticity, a denial and betrayal of the analyst's true self? Probably not. One of the most unique and essential dimensions of the analytic process is precisely this form of play in the transference and the countertransference, this process of forming and unforming, integration and disintegration, in which the patient is able to encounter and reclaim features of his inner world and also to imagine and invent new versions of themselves for the first time.

The exploration of the interaction between analysand and analyst and the expansion of the analysand's own inner world are not alternative routes but different facets of the same route. It is a mistake to assume that the analyst who offers himself up for the patient to shape and use is really leaving himself behind; his own familiar subjectivity has merely become part of the background. What happens most frequently (as in the interaction between me and my daughter) is that a surrender to shaping by another becomes a vehicle for discovery of a new, often unanticipated, form of authentic experience, which then enriches the interpersonal interaction.

It is important to note that no analyst is—nor should any strive to be—infinitely malleable. There are subtle but crucial borders between an openness in interaction with a patient, allowing one's experience to be shaped by him, and a squelching of the analyst's capacity for authentic participation in a fashion that destroys the possibility for constructive engagement. The analyst's knowledge of her own personal limits is crucial. If the analyst transcends those limits, guided by ideals like neutrality (Freud), empathy (Kohut), or object-usage (Winnicott), the stage is set for a masochistic experience in the countertransference and her eventual active or passive retaliation.

One important dimension of the analyst's work is a sorting through of the patient's productions, to distinguish the potentially useful from the diversionary, the analytically fruitful from the familiarly perseverative. Another central feature of the craft of psychoanalysis is a continual monitoring and sorting through of the analyst's own experiences and self-states with the patient: steering away from those that seem unproductive; entering further into those that seem important to explore; struggling to remain in those that are opaque but may become useful later on.

The relationship between reality and fantasy in the analytic relationship is extraordinarily complex. In a superficial way, the analytic relationship could be defined as unreal, in contrast to real relationships in the rest of the analyst's life. Yet the unreal dimensions of the analytic situation often serve to make possible a much deeper, personally riskier, more profound experience than is possible in "real" life. In this sense, the analytic situation is often more real, for both participants, than nonanalytic relationships. The challenge, of course, is to find a way to integrate the depths of self experience discovered in the "unreal" analytic situation into the "realities" of ordinary life. In a parallel fashion, many people use the "unreal" features of extramarital affairs in contrast to the daunting "realities" of married life to discover and develop deeply personal aspects of self. Deciding which is real and which is artificial is often very tricky. As in the relationship between analytic and extra-analytic realities, the possibility for a less fragmented experience depends on the integration of the real and the fantastic so that they potentiate rather than deplete each other.

The assumption that anger or arousal is more authentic than curiosity is a holdover from classical theory and nineteenth-century romanticism. What is so unique and invaluable about the analytic process is precisely that it demands a curiosity about one's feelings on the part of both participants and especially a curiosity about the moments when one feels a virtual lack of curiosity. The outcome is not a less authentic experience, but a pushing through to a level of experience that may be much more deeply authentic, both for the patient and for the analyst. I argued in chapter 2 that self-understanding, as well as understanding of another, is not a revelation but a construction. What is crucial in the self-understandings constructed by the analyst is the struggle toward an emotional position that also keeps going the inquiry into the patient's experience.

Authenticity for the analyst as well as for the patient is essentially ambiguous, more discernible in its absence than its presence. Critics of the classical notion of "neutrality" have been extremely useful in pointing out the manner in which a preoccupation with neutrality or objectivity can constrict the analyst's experience in an unhelpful fashion. When trying to enact the role of the analyst or trying to apply technique, one is not doing analysis.

However, the argument for a freer attitude toward the analyst's own experience is a corrective more than a guide. It points out a way the analyst can close himself off to useful information, not a set of criteria on the basis of which the analyst can decide what to do with all the information, all the reactions, all the ideas that he has. How to decide which among many potentially authentic voices will move the inquiry forward remains an extraordinarily ambiguous and complex problem.[25]

According to the Taoists, setting out to find Enlightenment is like pursuing a thief hiding in the forest by banging loudly on a drum. Setting out to find one's true self or trying to hold onto one's true self entails similar problems. The rushing fluidity of human experience through time makes authenticity essentially and necessarily ambiguous. The fascination with and pursuit of that ambiguity lies at the heart of the analytic process. Clinicians who love doing analytic work hold this fascination in common. I do not agree with Schafer (1983) that doing analysis entails a "subordination" of the analyst's personality. Certainly there is a kind of discipline involved, but, like the discipline and technique in sports or artistic expression, the form makes possible a liberating kind of experience that is hard to come by in any other way. Doing analysis, either as a patient or as an analyst, involves a struggle to reach a fully authentic experience of a particular kind that, when fully engaged, makes possible a kind of freedom and authenticity that is both rare and precious.

The analytic process, for both the analysand and the analyst, provides a deeply personal experience. What makes psychoanalysis a quintessentially personal process is not deriving individual experience from outside the social field, but its focus on the subjective meaning of any piece of mental life. Psychoanalytic theorizing will have more to contribute to our understanding of personal individuality if we can get away from a search for presocial or extrasocial roots of the core or true self and focus on what it means at any particular moment to be experiencing and using oneself more or less authentically.

6

Aggression and the Endangered Self

Whatever cultural conditioning we may do, we must remain cognizant of the fact that human beings who have been trained and conditioned to be nonviolent retain the capacity for violence; as constrained as that capacity may be in certain contexts, it can come out in others. It is subdued, reduced, dormant, yes. But it is never abolished. It is never nonexistent. It is always there.
—M. Konner, *The Tangled Wing: Biological Constraints on the Human Spirit*

It would be hard to find an issue that has generated more controversy during the history of psychoanalytic ideas than aggression. Divergent views on aggression played a major role in the split between Freud and Adler as far back as 1908; and differences in thinking about aggression play a significant role in the attitudes today toward the major contemporary psychoanalytic schools (for example, the Kleinian school and Kohut's self psychology).

Since 1908, theorizing about aggression has tended to bifurcate into two positions, depending on whether aggression is viewed as a fundamental and irreducible human instinct. That question seems to be answerable by either a yes or a no and which side one comes down on has profound consequences for theory-making. If the answer is yes, aggression in its various manifestations is seen to operate necessarily and inevitably at the center of emotional life. Sadism, hatred, the thirst for revenge—the darker passions—are regarded as a fundamental and inescapable domain of the self. Prolonged immersion and direct work on negative transference (and perhaps negative countertransference) are viewed as crucial and unavoidable realms of analytic experience.

If the answer is no, aggression is seen as reactive and defensive, lacking in primary dynamic significance. The explanatory emphasis tends to shift to the environment that provokes aggression—family pathology and early deprivation. The analytic focus similarly shifts to the affective experience that is felt to underlie or precede the aggression: for example, anxiety (Sullivan) or the experience of empathic failure and the disintegration of a cohesive self (Kohut).

In thinking about aggression, polarization, one might almost say "splitting," transcends psychoanalytic circles. Aggression has been a fundamental problem of human experience in all cultures and at all points in history. How one understands the origins of aggression determines one's positions on many of the most problematic features of life: historical, philosophical, political, and theological. How does one account for the horrifying bloodbaths that characterize human history? How does one understand the cruelties that seem to be a never-absent feature of human interactions? What are the origins of social violence? Why are good and evil so closely intertwined?

It is not just in psychoanalytic theory that we gravitate to one or the other clear solution to the problem of evil. Consider the political poles of conservatism versus liberalism. From one perspective, violent crime is a product of laxness in controls and a failure to maintain "law and order." The problem is in the individual, in whom it must be controlled. From the other perspective, violent crime is a social disease from which the individual suffers. The problem is in the environmental failures to which the individual reacts.

Clearly the question of the nature and origins of aggression is not merely an abstract or intellectual consideration. How one thinks about and experiences the roots of evil and cruelty, the darker passions, is an important part of the shaping of the personal self. In finding our own position on the origins of aggression, we are framing a view of our individual experience, establishing a version of personal history, shaping the categories and tones of inner life. Where does one place oneself within one's own life historical events? How does one understand one's own motives? explain one's own cruelties and betrayals?

In the choice of a psychoanalytic theory, no small part is played by the way in which the ideology of that theory explains one to oneself, assigning blame and innocence, responsibility and victimization, locating causes and justifications. And when it comes to issues related to aggression, explanations tend to drift to the two clear and polarized positions: We are driven by our instincts toward hatred and cruelty and life is a struggle to master and renounce those passions, or we are born innocent and some of us are made hateful through deprivation and cruelty perpetuated upon us. Perhaps it is precisely because the theoretical issues have such profound personal dynamic implications and resonances that we tend to move generally with great conviction toward one or the other solution.

For many analysts, the very identity "Freudian" embodies this central issue, pro and con. Those who choose it feel that those who do not are denying the darker, bestial side of human experience, taking the easy way out by avoiding the deeper, darker truths about human nature and motivation. Those who do not choose the identity of "Freudian" tend to feel that those who do root human difficulties in a psychological version of "original sin" rather than in the abuse, neglect, and mystification perpetuated upon children.

I propose a perspective that overcomes this traditional polarity regarding aggression, grounded in the perspective on self developed in the preceding chapters, viewing self in temporal as well as spatial terms. I believe that the impossible choice between locating aggression at the core of the self or at its periphery is anchored in a reified spatial account of the self as layered. Thinking about self in temporal terms once again provides a crucial counterpoint. But first I must trace more fully the two major lines of psychoanalytic contributions on aggression—aggression as a drive and aggression as a secondary reaction. I will be drawing a great deal from both.

AGGRESSION AS A DRIVE

Before 1920 Freud regarded the pleasure principle, along with self-preservation, as the basic motivational framework of mental life. Adler had proposed that aggression is better understood as an autonomous drive. No, Freud countered, aggression is a reaction to frustration in pleasure-seeking.

In 1920, in *Beyond the Pleasure Principle,* Freud dramatically reversed himself and adopted a view similar to Adler's, establishing aggression as a special and self-subsisting instinct arising independently from libido, from the Death Instinct, and operating "beyond the pleasure principle." (Freud did view libido and aggression as merging continually through instinctual fusion.)

When Freud established aggression as a primary drive, he attributed to it the same properties he ascribed to libido, which were built into the very definition of what he meant by "drive" (*trieb*). Freud regarded aggression as an endogenously arising, continuous pressure demanding discharge. There is a need to harm and destroy, which often finds frustrations to serve as a rationale; but if there are no causes to be found, no rationales, the need for the discharge of aggression may overrun the defensive controls that ordinarily hold it in check and aggression emerges spontaneously.

There is no clearer and more powerful depiction of Freud's notion of the aggressive drive than his sober reflections on human misery in *Civilization and Its Discontents* (1930):

> men are not gentle creatures who want to be loved, and who at the most can defend themselves if they are attacked; they are, on the contrary, creatures among whose instinctual endowments is to be reckoned a powerful share of aggressiveness. As a result, their neighbour is for them not only a potential helper or sexual object, but also someone who tempts them to satisfy their aggressiveness on him, to exploit his capacity for work without compensation, to use him sexually without his consent, to seize his possessions, to humiliate him, to cause him pain, to torture and kill him. *Homo homini lupus.* Who, in the face of all his experience of life and of history, will have the courage to dispute this assertion? As a rule this cruel aggressiveness waits for some provocation or puts itself at the service of some other purpose, whose goal might also have been reached by milder measures. In circumstances that are favourable to it, when the mental counter-forces which ordinarily inhibit it are out of action, it also manifests itself spontaneously and reveals man as a savage beast to whom consideration towards his own kind is something alien. (pp. 111–12)

Two quite different major lines of theorizing have developed out of Freud's theory of the aggressive drive. One strategy, fashioned by Hartmann, Kris, and Loewenstein, developed within Freudian ego psychology; the other strategy has flourished within Kleinian thought.

Hartmann, Kris, and Loewenstein argue for the separation of the aggressive drive from Freud's more speculative notion of a Death Instinct. Like Freud, they regard aggression as a powerful motivational force from the beginning of life, but unlike Freud, they do not think aggression begins by being directed inward in a Death Instinct. They regard aggression as directed outward, toward others, from the start.[1] Hartmann, Kris, and Loewenstein (1949) retain the central feature of Freud's approach to aggression, based on the latter's understanding of sexuality. They emphasize, as did Freud, the endogenous, spontaneous, propulsive origins of aggression, not derivable from deprivation or frustration of pleasure-seeking, but "a constant, driving power comparable to that of libido" (p. 78).

The second line of theorizing deriving from Freud's concept of an aggressive drive was developed by Melanie Klein and has led to some of the most interesting contributions to our understanding of human destructiveness. Unlike Hartmann and Kris, Klein took very seriously the idea that aggression originates in a Death Instinct. Because of the persecutory terror she felt was the consequence of that instinct, she saw aggression as central in the formation of psychic structure beginning early in life and continuing throughout.[2] For Klein, dealing with the implications and consequences of one's aggression on one's loved ones, both external and internal, is the central drama in life. Hostile destructiveness is never far from love and devotion. In fact, the very capacity to risk loving presupposes the development of a belief in one's own ability to repair the damage one continually inflicts on one's love objects, external and internal.

AGGRESSION AS A SECONDARY REACTION

The alternative strategy for theorizing about aggression, ironically dating back to Freud himself in his argument against Adler (1909, pp. 140–41) is to view it not as a primary motivation but as a derivative of or defense against other primary motivations. This basic starting point is shared by all the major non-drive theory approaches.

For Sullivan, for example, aggression operates largely as a defense against the profound helplessness generated by the experience of anxiety. For Fairbairn, aggression is a reaction to deprivation and lack of gratification of the infant's intense dependency and object-seeking. He argues that it is the "analyst's task to point out to the patient the libidinal factor that lies behind his aggression" (1952, p. 74). The word "behind" is of particular interest here because of the spatial metaphor it implies in visualizing mind and motives. Mind is seen as layered, as if in space; non-drive theorists portray aggression as a more superficial layer, nearer the surface.

The spatial metaphor is more clearly apparent in Guntrip's contributions. He characterizes aggression as a reaction, less basic, less primary, less fundamental to human nature: "the chronic aggression which has always seemed to be the hallmark of 'man' is but a defense against and a veneer over basic ego weakness" (1969, p. 129). Aggression, in Guntrip's view, is a more superficial, defensive dimension of human experience. The deeper core of the self is concerned with the regressive retreat from object-seeking and love. It is crucial, Guntrip argues, "to separate classic depression as the defensive top layer of aggression and guilt, from regression as the bottom layer of fear, flight, and infantile ego-weakness" (1969, pp. 149–50).

Kohut offers a very similar understanding of aggression as a reaction to "self-object" failure to provide requisite responses for crucial developmental needs. Under normal circumstances, the child manifests healthy assertiveness, which Kohut likens to fundamental biological units, organic molecules. Only under extreme, pathological self-object failures does healthy assertiveness break down into hostile destructiveness, much as organic molecules may be broken apart into inorganic molecules. The inorganic molecules are simpler—more primitive, so to speak—but they are not the fundamental building blocks of organic life. Rather, they are a disintegrative, pathological breakdown product. Thus, Kohut argues (and note again the spatial metaphor of depth and surface):

> I believe that man's destructiveness as a psychological phenomenon is secondary; that it arises originally as the result of the failure of the self-object environment to meet the child's need for optimal—not maximal, it should be stressed—empathic responses. Aggression . . . as a psychological phenomenon, is not elemental. . . . The deepest level to which psychoanalysis can penetrate when it traces destructiveness . . . is not reached when it has been able to uncover a destructive biological drive, is not reached when the analysand has become aware of the fact that he wants (or wanted) to kill. This awareness is but an intermediate station on the road to the psychological "bedrock": to the analysand's becoming aware of the presence of a serious narcissistic injury, an injury that threatened the cohesion of the self, especially a narcissistic injury inflicted by the self-object of childhood. (1977, pp. 116–17)

Similarly, in his important treatise *The Anatomy of Human Destructiveness,* Fromm (1973) concludes that aggression in both humans and other animals is a response to a threat to survival or vital interests: "phylogenetically programmed aggression, as it exists in animals and man, is a biologically adaptive, defensive reaction" (pp. 95–96). Fromm poked fun at the way in which Freud and other "instinctivists" have taken a reaction under very specific circumstances and made it into what they presume is a constant pressure.

> The impulse to flee plays—neurophysiologically and behaviorally—the same if not a larger role in animal behavior than the impulse to fight.
>
> Neurophysiologically, both impulses are integrated in the same way; there is no basis for saying that aggression is more "natural" than flight. Why, then, do instinctivists talk about the intensity of the innate impulses of aggression, rather than about the innate impulse for flight?
>
> If one were to translate the reasoning of the instinctivists regarding the impulse for fight to that of flight one would arrive at this kind of statement: "Man is driven by an innate impulse to flee; he may try to control this impulse by his reason, yet this control will prove to be relatively inefficient, even though some means can be found that may serve to curb the power of the 'flight instinct'" (pp. 96–97).

AGGRESSION AND THE RELATIONAL FIELD

The culture comprising psychoanalytic ideas, like most intellectual disciplines, grows in dialectical swings. Each psychoanalytic theorist since Freud is trained and comes to intellectual maturity in a professional community composed of preexisting theoretical positions, commitments, and battles. No psychoanlytic theorist builds theory just to express his own thought or to share her clinical findings. Each also selects from the by-now enormous and heterogeneous collections of psychoanalytic perspectives some particular points of reference, with the intent to expand and develop some and to contrast with and argue with others.

The most important and compelling point of reference on any major theoretical issue is Freud. As we have seen, the choice of whether to commit oneself to Freud on the problem of aggression has dominated the course of subsequent theory development. Those who do are free to grant aggression the psychodynamic centrality it seems to deserve in light of the historical significance and universality of human destructiveness. Yet these same theorists are burdened by a vision of human motivation fueled by innate, propulsive aggression, which, as I will argue, is both anachronistic and improbable. Those who have developed approaches to aggression based on the abandonment of drive theory do so in dialectical contrast to Freud; they tend to portray aggression not as spontaneous but as provoked, not as inevitable but as avoidable, and not as central but as peripheral to the development and structuralization of the self. In the concern to break with Freud on the origins of aggression, they have not dealt satisfactorily with the implications and consequences of aggression.

The bifurcation of psychoanalytic thinking on aggression between drive and non-drive theorists derives partly, like the search for the core of the self considered in the last chapter, on an account of mind in spatial terms common to both approaches. Both groups of theorists portray mind as layered: Some things are more fundamental, underneath; others are more superficial, less basic. For the drive theorist, since aggression is so fundamental in human experience, it must be at the bottom layer of mind, in a powerful and relentless drive. For the non-drive theorist, human beings are regarded as most fundamentally involved with other motives (such as attachment or self-realization). Therefore, aggression must not be foundational and is located in the upper, more superficial layers of mind. If mind is a place, aggression needs to be located somewhere, at the center, or farther out on the periphery. And where one locates aggression in the mind has enormous consequences in terms of how one organizes and prioritizes clinical data.

Consider the question of justification. Is the child's rage and aggression toward the parents an explosive, propulsive event or a reaction to fear and/or intense frustration, a betrayal of the child by the parents? Is the negative transference of the patient brought to the analytic situation pressing for expression or a reaction to intense disappointment provoked by the analyst's way of participating—a betrayal in the analytic situation?

If one believes in an aggressive drive at the core of the self, then intense aggression (toward parents and the analyst) is assumed to be not justified, and really understanding and accepting its nonjustification is the crucial insight that releases patients from infantile conflicts and makes for an emotionally richer life. Accepting the patient's justifications is a collusion with the patient's disclaimers of his own inherent aggressiveness.

If one does not regard aggression as a drive but as a reaction to frustration and disappointment, the aggression itself is not the crucial analytic focus. The aggression is a reaction to the threat to something more central, more basic. The aggression is justified, and the attention shifts to the traumatizing conditions that are understood to precede and underlie it. The patient's understanding of these more fundamental experiences—the hurt, the anxieties, the longing—is what releases her from the need to react to disappointment and betrayal aggressively, making possible a richer emotional life.[3]

Here I present an alternative approach to the problem of aggression that struggles to avoid the customary two-sided slippery slopes of the positions that have shaped themselves around the question: Is there an aggressive drive, yes or no? My approach is consistent with those who have abandoned the belief in an aggressive drive when it comes to thinking about the origins of aggression, but much closer to those who have maintained the belief in an aggressive drive when it comes to thinking about the universality, depth, and dynamic centrality of aggression. Once again, thinking about self in temporal as well as spatial terms is crucial.

The term aggression has been used to cover the whole range from assertiveness on one end to hostile destructiveness on the other, and in some theoretical systems this may make sense. What follows, however, is a discussion of hostile destructiveness, not assertiveness, which I believe is something quite different. For Freud, the whole continuum derives from the same source—benign assertiveness is a derivative of more primitive aggression, in the same way that love is an aim-inhibited form of sexual wishes. For Kohut, the whole continuum also derives from the same source, but the other way around. When healthy assertiveness is blocked, hostile destructiveness emerges as a deterioration product.

I believe that assertion and destructiveness are distinctly different experiences: Assertion derives from a joyful sense of living and engagement; destructiveness derives from an endangered sense of personal threat and retaliation. Sometimes they are combined, when self-assertion takes place in a context experienced as combative and hostile. But they are distinctly different experiences. I also believe that a different physiology accompanies these two different psychological states; they feel different and lend themselves to distinctly different, even though closely related, clusters of meaning.[4]

Let us begin by reconsidering the larger context in which Freud developed his concept of instinctual drive.

Freud's application of the Darwinian revolution to psychology is one of the most pervasive of his multifaceted contributions (Sulloway, 1983). Darwin locates humans in a broad evolution from lower and more primitive species. What are the implications of this vision for thinking about the human mind? The structural model is a striking microcosmic replica of Darwin's theory of the origin of species. Mind is layered according to its phylogenetic history; more primitive motives and impulses of the "id," the "seething cauldron," the "savage beast" are overlaid and tamed, regulated and channeled, by "higher," more civilized and social imperatives and compromises of the ego and superego. Libido constitutes our link to our animal past. After 1920, aggression became a second link.

I have argued elsewhere (Mitchell, 1988) that the metapsychological dimension of Freud's theory of sexuality has essentially been superseded. In contrast to his portrayal of drives as continual, endogenous internal pressures, the evoking stimulus is now understood to play a crucial role in both animal and human sexuality. Sexuality, which is a powerful biological and physiological force, emerges inevitably within a relational context, an object world. The evocation of the physiological response, the manner in which the response is experienced, and the form in which it is remembered—these are all shaped by the interpersonal context within which the sexual response arises and takes on psychological meaning.

In this view, sexuality is most usefully regarded not as a push from within (although it is often experienced in just that way) but as a response within a relational field to an object, either external or internal. This does not make sexuality less biological, or minimize its physiological power. Rather, it posits a different understanding of how the biology of sexuality works. Sexuality is a powerful physiological response, biologically mandated and prewired, which emerges within the mutually regulatory, intersubjective, or relational contexts that constitute the medium within which mind develops and operates.

Many of the authors who have rejected the belief in an aggressive drive—including Guntrip, Sullivan, Kohut, and Fromm—have referred to the notion drawn from classic motivation theory of "fight/flight" behavior in response to danger and threat. This kind of approach is also consistent with the major trends in contemporary ethology, where (apart from Konrad Lorenz) aggression tends to be understood not as a spontaneously arising endogenous stimulus but as a reaction to specific stimuli. As the ethologist Robert Hinde (1977) puts it, "each aggressive act lies in a nexis of events that precede and follow it" (p. 5). Those acts, Hinde argues, have "eliciting factors" and "predisposing factors."

What happens if we think about aggression, like sexuality, not as a push from within but as a response to others, biologically mediated and prewired, within a relational context? Then the question of whether there is an aggressive drive or not is replaced by questions concerning the conditions that tend to elicit aggressive responses and the nature and variation of those responses.

Viewing aggression in this way preserves, in a different manner from drive theory, an emphasis on the importance of what the individual brings to the interpersonal field. Anyone who has spent any time around babies knows they are very different from each other, from very early on. There is by now compelling evidence that temperamental differences are present from birth and hold up over time. One of the most important concepts emerging repeatedly from recent infancy and childhood research is the importance of "fit" between the baby's natural rhythms and thresholds and those of the caregiver. All this suggests that whether and in what way a baby feels endangered is likely to vary greatly from baby to baby. All babies feel uncomfortable and insecure some of the time, but there are strikingly different thresholds, from easily ruffled and irritable on the one extreme to centered and peaceful on the other. The response to discomfort and/or frustration also varies greatly from baby to baby, covering a wide range from fussing, to listlessness, to intense rage.

Thus, to characterize aggression as a response does not minimize its biological basis; rather, the biology of aggression is understood to operate not as a drive but as an individually constituted, prewired potential that is evoked by circumstances perceived subjectively as threatening or endangering.[5]

The often-cited observational data on aggression in children published by Henri Parens (1979) bear directly on the question of whether aggression operates as a propulsive force or as a reaction to the experience of danger. Parens spent a great deal of time observing children and looking for evidence of an aggressive drive. He concluded that the capacity to express aggression is a biological given: "the normal-enough neonate is born with a capacity to experience and express rage . . . born with a ready-to-function organization of rage-experience-discharge, which is not acquired" (p. 107). However, this apparatus does not discharge spontaneously from endogenous pressure. Rather, Parens argues, "a unique condition seemed required for rage to appear: *the internally-felt experience of excessive, sufficient unpleasure*" (p. 108). Although he clearly very much wanted to be able to characterize it as a drive, Parens found aggression to be reactive rather than propulsive.

Two other results of Parens's studies are important to note. First, although aggression operates as a reaction to unpleasure, it seems to be universal in all children. Parens was impressed both by "its early appearance and . . . its overriding unavoidability. It appears even in what seems to be excellent child-endowment and child-object circumstances" (p. 106). Although aggression emerges as a reaction to danger and threat, all babies at times seem to feel endangered and threatened.

Second, Parens considered the question of the goal of aggressive behavior. Does aggression operate as Freud assumes sexuality operates, toward a goal of discharging aggressive energy? No. Parens's observations led him to believe that the goal of aggression is the elimination of the unpleasure that has precipitated it. If the noxious situation is altered, the aggression stops immediately.[6]

According to Parens's observations, only after prolonged experience of aggression generated by chronic unpleasure does aggression sometimes become a goal in itself, resulting in sadism. Therefore, he concludes, aggression may "appear [to be] an instinctual drive, though it is not, since no absolute vegetative generation of hostility exists which must be discharged" (p. 6).

This way of thinking about aggression might be considered in connection with the different kinds of threats and dangers in infancy and early childhood that have been described in various psychoanalytic (and nonpsychoanalytic) developmental theories: separation (John Bowlby), breaks in attunement (Daniel Stern), spiraling physiological need (Freud), parental anxiety (Sullivan), impingement (Winnicott), being interrupted or interfered with (Jerome Kagan), and so on. All these inevitable features of infantile experience are likely to be experienced as endangering; all are likely to generate aggression.

The universality of some experiences of endangerment in infancy and early childhood leads to the inevitable dynamic centrality of aggression. The infant exists in a state of great dependency; even with the best care, there are inevitable periods of distress, helplessness, and longing. How does the infant understand why this is happening? Racker (1968), in a neo-Kleinian account of "paranoid anxiety," reasons that the baby must feel that the good breast is not there because it is being withheld, that the good breast wants the baby to suffer, because if it did not, it would be always available. Thus, the baby feels persecuted (not, as Klein saw it, through projection of his own aggression), but because this is the most natural way for him to construe his situation. His own aggression is then a subsequent response to the feeling of persecution and endangerment.[7]

The conclusion that one's suffering must be intended by another is a recurrent feature not only of infantile but of adult reasoning. The patient feels that the analyst could be more helpful and forthcoming if she really cared. The lover feels his own sense of hurt and neglect are sure signs of faltering love or uncaring on the part of the beloved. The victim, as we might well characterize it, of a run of bad luck feels "cursed," looking up to the skies, like Job, and demanding to know "Why me?" For all of us occasionally, and for many people chronically, life itself is "cruel," and that very characterization personifies an agent responsible for our experience. We feel treated badly, done to, and are angry in response.

What about people who constantly seem to be looking for a fight and can generate great quantities of rage with seemingly little or no provocation? Are not such people walking evidence of an endogenously arising, propulsive drive? What needs to be considered in such cases is the climate within the internal object world of such individuals, which may very well generate a chronic sense of threat and danger, both within and, through projection and selective attention, from without. With such people, the aggression and sadism have developed way beyond their points of origin into a complex version of the self, but it is a version of the self that is embedded in and sustained by an enduring sense of internal and external danger.

It is important to note that endangerment is a subjective experience, unrelated to what an external observer might evaluate as degrees of danger. And endangerment does not concern just the threat of physical harm but a subjective sense of endangerment to the self as well. Threats to the integrity of the self, as subjectively defined, tend to generate powerful, deeply aggressive reactions. In fact, the pursuit of revenge generated by a need to redress past insults or humiliations often propels people into situations that are physically very dangerous. Much of the political aggression and violence in the world today is connected with nationalistic and ethnic identifications that are rooted in a collective sense of endangerment and past humiliations.

AGGRESSION AND THE BODY

Aggression is an extremely powerful, universally wired (although individually varied), biological response to the subjective experience of endangerment and being treated cruelly. (It is unnecessary to assume actual and/or intentional mistreatment, although many children are actually and/or intentionally mistreated.) Because of the universality of the subjective experience of endangerment, rage and destructiveness are powerful experiences for all of us, playing a crucial role in the shaping and vitalization of the self.

Today the more interesting question for psychoanalytic theorists is not whether there is an aggressive drive or not, but the nature of human needs and possibilities for relative security and normative responses to insecurity. How secure is the environment created by "good-enough" parents? What is the normal range of narcissistic injury and threat? What is the range of fight/flight reactions to such threats? What internal residues do the original threats leave behind in enduring psychic structures?

Consider this vivid description of aggression in infancy by Joan Riviere:

> The baby's typical response, say to acute hunger, is a reaction in which the whole body is involved: screaming, twitching, twisting, kicking, convulsive breathing, evacuations—all evident signs of overwhelming anxiety. Analytic evidence shows without any doubt that this reaction to the accumulated tension represents and is felt to be an *aggressive* discharge, as we should in any case imagine. If this reaction brings the required satisfaction, narcissistic phantasy can resume its sway. But if the desired breast is not forthcoming and the baby's aggression develops to the limit of its bodily capacities, this discharge, which automatically follows upon a painful sensation, itself produces unpleasure in the highest degree. The child is overwhelmed by choking and suffocating; its eyes are blinded with tears, its ears deafened, its throat sore; its bowels gripe, its evacuations burn it. The aggressive anxiety-reaction is far too strong a weapon in the hands of such a weak ego; it has become uncontrollable and is threatening to destroy its owner. (1952, p. 44)

In this evocative description of the infant's rage, written in a Kleinian mode, the rage is seen not as a propulsive force but as a response to a perceived sense of threat and danger, a response that in itself becomes dangerous, problematic, and dynamically central. If feelings are not substances and motives are not layered on top of one another from surface to depth, aggression may be precipitated by other feelings and yet still be a powerful, fundamental, central constituent of emotional life. To regard aggression as a reaction does not necessarily minimize its motivational or structural primacy.[8]

One of the most persuasive arguments of those theorists and clinicians who still find classical drive theory useful is the centrality it gives to sex and aggression. Drive theory explains, in a direct and simple fashion, why patients' lives, in both their actions in the external world and in the private fantasies of their internal worlds, so often are dominated by conflicts involving sex and aggression. Non-drive theories sometimes seem convoluted, contrived, and pallid in their efforts at demonstrating that what look like primitive sexual impulses or violent destructive fantasies are really expressions of something else, such as object-seeking or assertion. (On the other hand, drive-theory accounts become convoluted and contrived when they claim that phenomena like attachment and assertion are really derivatives of raw sexual and aggressive impulses.)

In *Relational Concepts in Psychoanalysis* (Mitchell, 1988) I argued that sexuality is central and important in human experience because it is a powerful vehicle for establishing and maintaining relational dynamics. The power of sexuality derives very directly from its sheer physicality, which enables sexual arousal to preempt other concerns, generate an enormous sense of urgency, and provide powerful, transformative experiences.

The same is true of aggression. Non-drive theorists generally do not take into account how exciting, how stimulating aggression can be. Aggression is a psychological experience embedded in and accompanied by a physiological surge. As the passage from Riviere just quoted suggests, the body aspect of the experience is very important. Intense anger is arresting and preemptive. When unintegrated, it can shatter and diffuse other concerns and intentions, generating mental disorganization. When integrated, it can generate and energize other motives and actions. Aggression, like sexuality, often provides the juice that potentiates and embellishes experience.[9]

The physiological charge that accompanies intense aggression often plays an important role in the way in which aggression serves as a vehicle for identification. It is precisely because aggression generates hormonal surges that alter experience, changing states of mind, that it often facilitates identificatory ties to significant others. This is most obvious in men, where identifications mediated through aggression serve as a dimension of what is now popularly referred to as "male bonding."

Recall Robert's crucial, hidden identification with his father, transformed into a desperate search for a man who would be able to introduce him to his own manhood. In Robert's volcano dream, he located his own rage far away from himself, across a vast plain. He had not been able to find a way to draw on that experience, that energy, without threatening his very sense of existence. His own rage was identified with his father's family-smashing defiance, and it was only in analysis that Robert began to find a way to lend structure to those feelings, to draw them together with his loving feelings and his ongoing sense of self.

None of this requires an antiquated view of aggression as an autonomous, relentless endogenous force. By redefining drive as a psycho-physiological reaction in a relational context rather than an extrapsychological push deriving from the body, it is possible to retain the body-based centrality of aggression without the anachronistic drive metapsychology.

The bodily states accompanying aggression, in which one's sense of self is transformed by altered physiology ("I don't know what came over me"), often make aggressive, destructive versions of self difficult to integrate and contain alongside of other versions of self. This is particularly difficult for women in our culture, where acceptable levels of aggression are so closely tied to gender stereotypes. Where aggressive men are considered "macho," a term reflecting considerable ambivalence, aggressive women are considered "bitchy," a thoroughly negative designation. Women who are aggressive toward men also are frequently called "castrating," which reflects implicit assumptions about who is allowed what versions of self. It is as if such a woman, by acting aggressively, is taking away something, something very important, that belongs to men, that makes a man a man. For men, on the other hand, passive and yielding versions of self are often extremely dangerous, because gender identity as a male is so often tied to aggression and the powerful surges of aggressive states of mind.

AGGRESSION IN A RELATIONAL CONTEXT: JUSTIFICATION RECONSIDERED

Regarding aggression as a biologically based response to subjectively perceived endangerment allows us to keep what is most helpful about the two polarized traditional approaches to aggression.[10] From the drive theory side comes the notion that aggression is biologically based, physiologically powerful, and universal, playing an inevitable and central dynamic role in the generation of experience and the shaping of the self. From the non-drive theory side comes the notion that aggression is a response to endangerment within a personally designed subjective world, not a prepsychological push looking for a reason.

Aggression in childhood and in the analytic situation is always both justified and unjustified. Because it is a response, not a push, aggression is always subjectively justified in that it always has reasons, meanings related to the perception of threat or danger. These are not post-hoc rationales for discharge; they are the actual triggers for the aggressive response. If there is aggression, there is, by definition, threat. (The development of this principle has been one of the most important contributions of Kohut; it was anticipated by Sullivan [for example, 1956, pp. 95–98].)

Yet because the response to endangerment is a prewired, individually styled one, arising in the context of a subjectively constructed world, aggression is never simply reducible to its external causes. There is always more to say; acknowledging the subjective perception of an empathic failure, for example, is not enough. The reasons never fully explain or account for the response, which can be fully understood only in the context of an analytic inquiry into the structure of the analysand's subjectivity: the personal world, both external and internal, in which the analysand lives and reacts, lovingly and aggressively. Chronic aggression is continually regenerated in the context of ongoing commitments to internal object relations and familiar patterns of integrating interpersonal relations.

We all expect to find in new situations what we have experienced in the past and what we carry around internally. But even the most regressed schizophrenic is not wholly out of touch with actuality. We all selectively find and sometimes induce the patterns we anticipate, and although they may be highly selective, our interpretations of these situations are always compelling and plausible, at least to us (Gill, 1982).

For many patients—perhaps for all in some way—the analytic situation is reasonably construed as extremely dangerous and threatening to the integrity of the self. No matter how neutral or empathic the analyst is trying to be, there is always ample evidence of danger, including, perhaps, the analyst's need to be regarded as neutral and/or empathic.[11] To regard aggression as a drive (in Freud's and Kernberg's sense) and therefore, by definition, as distorting and unjustified, demands wrenching it from its psychological context of endangerment, forcing either a compliance to or defiance of the analyst's interpretations, generally both.

On the other hand, there are people for whom aggression has become a way of life, whose sense of self and connection with others is vitalized through hatred. Analysands come to the analytic situation not only with good intentions but also with bad and destructive ones. The latter always feel subjectively necessary and may be plausibly justified; yet to regard that aggression as simply a defense against frustration of more fundamental, benign motives may draw the patient away from some of the deep roots of her being. Neglecting the central place of aggression within human motivation and psychic structure may engender a splitting of both internal world and external relationships into the "sensitive" (including the more conscious aspects of self in relation to the analyst) and the villainous (generally including the more unconscious aspects of the self in relation to dissociated identifications with the parents).[12]

ATTACKS AGAINST THE SELF: VICTIM AND EXECUTIONER

George, a moderately successful salesman in his mid-forties and the father of two young sons, had been in a series of nonanalytic therapies, none of which had relieved him of his deep self-hatred and profound doubts about his own value as a person. He began treatment by describing a sense of inner weakness, a feeling that he had long ago withdrawn from the real world; his considerable skills and successes were false contrivances, a mimicking of the strong mentors he attached himself to. He would attack himself mercilessly for his incompetencies and ignorance and continually express a plaintive lament of "too late" regarding any real possibility for change. George was a broken spirit, "damaged goods," thoroughly and irreversibly.

His father was a passive man, very much in the shadows in the home. His mother was very effective, intimidating, and explosive; she felt she could accomplish anything, loved to fight, and took care of her children in a fiercely protective fashion. One prototypical memory concerned his ride on a roller coaster when he was quite small. George had gone on the ride with his older brother, but as soon as the roller coaster picked up speed, he became quite scared, probably like everyone else on a roller coaster for the first time. His mother, down on the ground, perceived his fear and, to the great amazement of all, managed, through her great insistence and persuasiveness, to get the operator to stop the roller coaster and bring her boy back to the ground slowly and carefully. This feat, roughly equivalent to stopping the earth's rotation, left him feeling both humiliated and profoundly taken care of.

My initial experience in the countertransference was an uncomfortable feeling that I was being called upon to witness his self-flagellation. Any effort to intervene in his systematic atacks on himself, to protect him from himself, to call for mercy, were totally ineffective. We realized that my position was a re-creation of his own early experiences as more or less helpless witness to his mother's attacks on both his father and his older brother, but that realization did not seem to change anything. George would criticize himself mercilessly, and any attempt I made to intervene on his behalf, to plead for greater generosity or tolerance for himself, were basically regarded as indications of misguided benevolence or lack of understanding. At those points, the aggression and contempt implicit in his attitude toward me became quite explicit. So I gave up and learned to tolerate the helplessness and sadism generated in the countertransference. He felt that although nothing was changing and probably nothing could, we were dealing with his pain at a deeper level than had been possible in any of his previous treatments.

Certain things became clear about his aggression toward himself. The original model for this critical rage and unyielding perfectionism was his mother. George had felt abjectly dependent upon her protection, despite the fact that it made him feel perpetually worthless. I pointed out that her protection seemed to operate like the "protection" sold in extortion by the Mafia—you pay them to protect you from them. He felt greatly endangered by his mother and her intimidating, critical strength and also that his only safety lay in surrendering to her care.

In his current life, George would seek out mentors to apprentice himself to. They would give advice, which he would use in a self-deprecating fashion, desperately needing the guidance but berating himself for never knowing what to do on his own. I began to become interested in some of these exchanges. I pointed out that often the advice he would get from his curent mentor was inconsistent with previous declarations, so that there was no way for him ever to really learn to do anything on his own. The solution kept changing. It became clear that the content of the solution was irrelevant. What was important was the certainty with which the advice was given; it was the deep conviction in the other person that made him feel safe. George then lapsed into an extended criticism of himself for his spineless, wishy-washy ways: He is a jerk who has never felt certain about anything.

I noted, somewhat admiringly, that there was one thing he had felt very certain about for a long time—that he was a loser. I had begun to feel genuinely impressed with his high standards and his dedication to them, against which his status as a loser was determined. That intrigued him very much and served as a point of departure for both of us to become much more interested in and identified with the version of him that criticized, berated, and punished himself rather than the version of him that was the damaged victim of those attacks. Interestingly, toward the end of that session he lapsed into an extended silence, which he later described as an extremely peaceful state in which he was listening to the birds outside my window and just enjoying being, an experience he allowed himself very rarely. The tone of subsequent sessions began to shift slowly; he started to bring in different kinds of experiences, including moments of pleasure, pride in some of his accomplishments, assertion and anger used effectively against others, including me.

The considerable rage generated in this man's childhood was tightly organized around his identification with his mother, who loomed larger than life as both his endangerer and his protector. The only safe forum for his aggression was his self-directed attacks. George recognized himself only as the victim of those attacks, not the tormentor. My counter-transferential shift from identifying with him as victim to identifying with him as tormentor seemed to open up the possibility for him to relax his self-attacks, to start to claim his aggression, his own certainty, his own perfectionism, and, eventually, his own prideful effectiveness.

At the heart of the resolution of each analysis is an individually crafted or, considering the role of the analyst, jointly coauthored movement beyond either/or solutions to the problem of justification. The analysand is more able fully to identify with and experience as justified his aggression and destructiveness. At the same time, the analysand is able to appreciate his reactions as an individually styled, creative adaptation to a limiting and limited set of circumstances. He now has greater resources, broader options, the possibility of more constructive solutions.

AGGRESSION AND THE SELF

What is the place of aggression within the development of personality in general? One might think of aggression as a relatively ad hoc, transitory reaction, similar to a discharge, which serves to reestablish a threatened self whose equilibrium has been undermined by narcissistic injury and threat. (Kohut took this position in his important 1972 paper on narcissistic rage and revenge. He argued that it is more useful to address aggression indirectly, rather than directly, by focusing on the narcissistic injury that disturbs the equilibrium of the self, which the aggression functions to shore up.) This view posits an essentially singular, coherent if brittle self, with aggression as a bolstering device.

I find it more compelling to think of aggression not as bolstering a singular, essentially nonaggressive self but as a central organizing component among multiple self-organizations. In this view, all of us experience enough danger and threat in childhood, regardless of the balance of health or pathology in our caregivers, to have experienced at least a fair amount of destructive aggression. It is universal to hate, contemplate revenge against, and want to destroy those very caregivers we also love. Therefore, multiple self-organizations develop, in different relationships with different significant others, and with different dimensions of the same significant other. It is normative for these different self-organizations to remain somewhat discrete from and in inevitable conflict with each other.

All patients (and all analysts as well) are likely to experience, either consciously or unconsciously, one or more versions of themselves as quite destructive, sadistic, and vengeful. The aggression operates not only as a temporary equilibriating device but as a version of the patient with its own history, worldview, values, and interests. One important task of the analysis is to create an atmosphere in which that version of self can come to life, become known, so that the patient can become better able to contain and to be reconciled with various versions of the self, including destructive versions. From this perspective, one cannot simply work on or through aggression indirectly (as Kohut suggests), because in so doing, one bypasses a full immersion in and conscious processing of an important domain of self experience.

Is it desirable that hostile aggression be more or less eliminated at the end of a successful analysis? Both drive and non-drive theorists tend to overlook the constructive, arousing, enlivening features of hostility: Drive theorists regard aggression as something to be renounced and controlled; non-drive theorists think aggression fades as the threat to the self is diminished.

In my view, each of us maintains destructive versions of self. Endangerment is an unalterable and perpetual feature of human existence. Destructive versions of self are not, at the end of analysis, subsumed by a more loving version. They remain intact, with their own physicality, their own developmental history, their own worldview. Arriving at a sense that "I am a basically loving person who sometimes, atypically, gets angry and hateful when threatened" is not an ideal ending of an analysis. Such an ending leaves out too much and smooths over a great deal that is potentially vitalizing and enriching in aggressive experience. A more ideal ending involves a sense that "I exist in different states of mind at different times, some loving, some hateful." A more meaningful sense of continuity and integrity of experience over time entails not a tucking in or concealment of aggression into a preferred, loving view of self but an increased ability to recognize, hold, and work through aggressive states. What changes is one's ability to contain destructive states of mind and to recognize them as one among many expressions of a distinctively subjective and potentially constructive personal experience.[13]

In a deeply analytic experience, analysands learn to appreciate the destructiveness that is so central to the experience of self and the always-present underside to the capacity to love. Only by embracing one's destructiveness can one transcend it through forgiveness and reparation toward real others, internal objects, and ultimately, the self. The drive models of aggression have contributed to our understanding of the profound signficance of destructiveness in human motivation and its centrality in the shaping of the self. The non-drive models of aggression have contributed to our understanding of the subjective context within which rage and destructiveness arise. Good analysts of any persuasion probably work in both realms and generally regard their theory as adequately comprehensive. Yet in my view, the polarization around the concept of an aggressive drive has precluded the development of a perspective that grants aggression the centrality it needs while placing it in its original context of an endangered self, which makes possible its fully analytic resolution.

III

THE ANALYTIC
RELATIONSHIP

7

Wishes, Needs, and Interpersonal Negotiations

You can't always get what you want,
But if you try sometimes,
You might find,
You get what you need
        —Rolling Stones, "You Can't Always Get What You Want"

[Patients] try to find speech to fill the silence that's hurting them.
They try to fit empty, feeble, wild, and always inadequate words to
the sensations and passions they imagine they experience, but that in
fact exist only when they are named.

        —Julia Kristeva, *The Samurai*

As the world around psychoanalysis has changed, psychoanalytic theorists have attempted to modify Freud's model to keep pace. The most
important shifts in the psychoanalytic literature over the past several
decades, shifts in both theory and metatheory, can all be seen as reflecting these larger intellectual and social currents: from id psychology to
ego psychology, from drive to relational theories, from one-person to
two-person psychologies, from oedipal to preoedipal concerns, from
historical reconstruction to current experience, from causal explanation
in Freud's nineteenth-century positivism to "understanding" in a contemporary hermeneutic perspective. Although we can arrange these various movements in many different ways, taken together they reflect a
fundamental shift from Freud's vision.

Theory of technique has been the domain of psychoanalysis that has been most resistant to change. That is because theory of technique is so important as a guide to everyday clinical practice. Classical theory of technique provides an answer to virtually every clinical problem or theoretical question—very comforting in a profession as intellectually challenging, emotionally draining, and ethically harrowing as psychoanalysis. This is partly why, as Robert Wallerstein (1988) has argued, Freud has been as dominant a presence among us since his death as he was before it. Wallerstein points to our inability to mourn Freud properly, and I think this failure has contributed to our slowness in realizing that many of the solutions of classical theory are derived from anachronistic premises that do not work in a more contemporary theoretical and clinical context.

In this chapter I explore a single but extremely important clinical problem: Should the analyst gratify or not gratify desires and requests by the patient that transcend or alter what is generally considered to be the analytic "frame"? In Part I we explored the question of the patient's need and the analyst's knowledge in more abstract and general terms. Here we will consider what actually happens when the patient expresses needs that are not congruent with the typical format of analytic practice.

This problem, which has arisen frequently in my own clinical work of recent years and in the work I have supervised, involves complex distinctions and judgments. The issues go to the heart of the nature of the analytic relationship. An exploration of how contemporary analysts struggle with these issues highlights the distance psychoanalysis has come from the vision of its founder and points to the importance of turning Freud, to borrow Loewald's (1960, p. 249) wonderful distinction, from an improperly buried ghost who haunts us to a beloved and revered ancestor.

TO GRATIFY OR NOT TO GRATIFY

Within the classical psychoanalytic model, the analytic relationship is essentially frustrating, and therein lies its leverage for meaningful change. The regressive invitation of the "fundamental rule" of free association, the uncovering action of the analyst's interpretive activity, the anonymity of the analyst's presence, all arouse and intensify the deep desires, derivative of infantile sexual and aggressive life, that have silently shaped and dominated the analysand's character and fate. The analytic situation stirs up these impulses in their purest, starkest form and, by not gratifying them, forces their emergence into consciousness, their articulation and their eventual renunciation. The analyst's role in this model of the analytic process is clear: Do not gratify. Any misguided efforts to soften the rigors and abstinence of the analytic experience is quite irresponsible and robs the analysand of the chance to more fully free himself from a seductive embeddedness within infantile fantasies and illusions.

That injunction is a central and important feature of our inheritance from classical theory; it helps shape the experience of anyone doing analysis today. No matter what other ideas one has about the analyst's role, I think all analysts have at least a twinge of uneasiness from our "classical superego" when doing anything, even when interpreting, that may be gratifying to an analysand: certainly when answering a question, letting someone use the phone, borrow a magazine, schedule an extra session, and so on.

However, there have been two major problems with the model of the analytic relationship as essentially frustrating. First, it does not work with a large segment of the patient population. Second, the metapsychology of drive, which provided its rationale, is no longer a compelling, certainly not an exclusive, explanatory framework for most of us.

The interest in what has been termed the "widening scope" of analysis over the past several decades has been concerned with the first of these problems, leading to efforts to broaden the process to include the large number of patients, perhaps the majority, who are not able, or cannot afford, or perhaps just do not want to accept the rules of the classical analytic setup. Either the analyst modifies his approach and plays it at least partly his way, or the patient finds someone else in the infinite population of therapy vendors who will. Some analysts choose to preserve the purity of their practice and work only with patients, generally other mental health practitioners (or else the very wealthy), who will play it the traditional way—four times a week, the couch, free association and interpretation. But that is not feasible for most practitioners. Even if it were, it would be hard to avoid a sense of bad faith, that one is preserving one's purity at the price of turning away people seeking help.[1] So most of us, in one way or another, try at times to bend the treatment to the person. Is this a fateful corruption of the purity of the analytic frame? I believe it most commonly entails a responsible and realistic effort to find a way to engage the patient, to reach him, to make him feel connected enough, secure enough, to participate in an analytic inquiry into his experience and difficulties in living. This effort generally requires the analyst to depart from her role as a stimulator yet frustrator of patient's desires and places her face to face, so to speak, with the classical superego and its injunction, "Do not gratify."

Recent theoretical developments come to our rescue at this point. The pure analytic experience, in all its frustrating abstinence, is possible, according to many contemporary theorists, only with patients who possess an intact ego. Patients with less than healthy egos are suffering from deficits, developmental arrests, and the gratifications they seek must not be understood in the same way Freud thought of instinctual wishes. Winnicott (1954) puts it most clearly. The desires of the more disturbed patient represent "ego needs," not instinctual wishes. Unlike the latter, they must be met and, to one extent or another, gratified, before anything else can happen.[2] It is not just a question of keeping patients in treatment, but of providing them with what they can truly use. With more disturbed patients, the rule of abstinence is waived, and gratification is permissible. The more ominous the diagnosis, the less ascetic the experience.

With these developments in theory and clinical practice, diagnosis has become quite central. Michael Balint (1968) makes the distinction between "malignant regression" and "benign regression." A patient insists on a particular set of conditions: The analyst must not speak, must schedule extra sessions, must be available between sessions, and so on. Sometimes granting these wishes can be disastrous—the patient simply escalates demands with greater intensity. Sometimes granting these wishes can be highly beneficial—the treatment seems more profoundly engaged than before, and things begin to move. In the former case, Balint suggests, the demand derives from an instinctual wish, and gratifying any instinctual wish is by definition calamitous. In the latter case, the demand derives from an ego need, an effort to heal the "basic fault," and meeting the demand is the only way to move beyond a therapeutic impasse. How does one know whether gratification is likely to precipitate malignant or benign regression? It is not easy. Clearly the analyst's choice of whether to consider the patient's desire a wish or a need is complex, often ambiguous, and itself determinative of subsequent clinical events (Meyerson, 1981). It is, in the terms we considered in chapter 2, a construction, not simple discernment of something that is clearly there, already formed.

WISH VERSUS NEED RECONSIDERED

The problem with the need/wish distinction is that it retains the purely intrapsychic framework of classical theory. Needs and wishes are considered different motivational states, which the analyst is supposed to be able to discern.[3] In my experience, as in Balint's, it is often impossible to know beforehand what will happen. But to decide by outcome that if it worked it was an ego need and if it precipitated more numerous and strident demands it was an instinctual wish seems unsatisfactory.

We get further with this question if we shift the focus from a purely intrapsychic to a more relational perspective and consider the process by which the analyst decides whether to meet the patient's demand or not. Hoffman (1987a) has described the complexity of these interactions:

> a patient's desires generally involve a complex, shifting hierarchical arrangement of needs and wishes. . . . it is virtually impossible to formulate an assessment of their relative weights and positions in that instant when the participant analyst or therapist is called upon to respond. After all, the analyst's actions (whether interpretations or other kinds of responses) are themselves embedded in and even partially constituting of this perpetually fluctuating arrangement of desires. Thinking it over is a response too, of course, which can be plausibly interpreted by the patient in various ways. The interaction within the session is continuous; there are no "time-outs." (p. 212)

Decisions about how to respond to the patient's desires are made essentially in the countertransference (broadly conceived), in an intuitive reaction to the patient's requests—sometimes it feels right and sometimes it does not. If it feels right, it is likely to be diagnosed as an ego need; if it does not feel right, it is likely to be diagnosed as an instinctual demand.

What determines whether it feels right or not? This is a very complicated question, since decisions like these are not generally made simply on impulse but within a continual process of ongoing reflection. By locating this judgment within the analyst's subjective experience rather than in an illusory objective and detached discrimination of something in the patient, I do not at all mean to suggest that such choices are (or ought to be) made in a flip, casual, or arbitrary manner. Rather, as my argument will make clear, I regard these choices as operating in a meaningful and rational fashion, but within the relational field between the patient and analyst. The analyst's experience of the patient's desire is codetermined by the interaction of the range of potentials that compose the patient's repertoire, on the one hand, and the range of constructive identifications that are available to the analyst at any given time, on the other.

There are patients who portray themselves in great pain, requiring various "extraanalytic" responses on the part of the analyst. Whether the analyst feels like meeting the patient's need or not is sometimes, I believe, a useful indicator of the affective context in the patient out of which the need arises. Can the analyst feel the patient's pain? Is he moved by the anguish? the urgency? Or is there some sense of contrivance, lots of noise and smoke, where the effect intended seems more salient than the urgency of the need itself? Does the request seem deeply anchored in whatever hope the patient has about the process? Does a denial of the request seem likely to plunge the patient into dread and despair? There are times when subtle differences in countertransferential responses enables the analyst to make useful distinctions between an utter helplessness due to massive deprivation and inexperience and a dramatic helplessness, learned as a gambit to elicit a certain kind of rescuing operation. To the latter patient, it can be powerfully reassuring to have the gambit for rescue declined by the analyst.

The analyst might often have the impulse to meet the patient's request or demand but refrain from doing so because she does not consider it to be in the patient's best interest. It might be easier or more pleasurable for the analyst, but there is a concern about undercutting the patient's growth. There is, for example, a danger of infantalizing the patient by leading her away from a struggle with inevitably conflictual desires by portraying her to herself as excessively needy (Meyerson, 1981).

Maintaining the analytic "frame" can mean very different things to different analysands. Consider even basic features of the analytic setting, such as remaining in one posture, either lying or sitting. Some patients experience an impulse to move around as a kind of manic distraction. Being urged to contain the anxiety by not moving may be a highly constructive intervention, which declines a seductive and collusive gambit that would enable the patient to distract himself from potentially growth-facilitating experience. On the other hand, for one patient, whose mother used to insist on her remaining silently in bed after being put to sleep so that the mother could have her "own time," never violated by the child's needs, remaining immobile was a terrifying repetition of her masochistic tie to her mother. The analyst's encouragement of her moving freely around the office, inspecting and asking about things, moved the treatment forward. (Of course, this encouragement itself also had meanings to the analysand related to her resistance to an awareness of her experience of the analyst as demanding and sadistic; these meanings themselves necessarily became a part of the inquiry.)

The patient's acceptance of the traditional structure of the analytic situation and the patient's efforts to transgress those structures can both carry many different meanings that can have very different kinds of impact on the analyst. In some circumstances, the patient's acceptance and/or testing of the frame may evoke an idiosyncratic reaction in the analyst, countertransference in the classical sense. But variations in countertransference impact often carry important information about the meaning to the patient; the analyst's experience of the analysand's desire is an important indicator of the nature of that desire, its developmental resonances, its defensive properties, its interpersonal functions.

THE ANALYST'S PARTICIPATION

Is the difference with which the analysand's desires register in the countertransference reflective only of differences in the nature of the desire in the patient? I do not think so. It is also codetermined (constructed) by the analyst's own character, values, and interests; there is a generally neglected, personal dimension of the analyst's response.

Consider the parent sitting at the breakfast table with a one-year-old who, from the elevated perch of her high chair, utters some mumbled sounds that are close enough to "more juice" to be recognizable. This experience is extraordinary for both people. The parent is likely to spend many months serving as the willing executor of the infant's demands. Why? In better circumstances, what takes place is a passionate identificatory process. There is something incredibly wonderful about the baby's discovery of language, of generating an impact on her environment, of actively and deliberately shaping her own experience. This is thrilling to parents because in their surrender to the child's agency, they identify with the freshness of the child's sense of power, impact, creativity. This description might be considered to be an example of Winnicott's (1956a) concept of "primary maternal preoccupation" (which should be extended to "primary parental preoccupation") in which there is evoked a willing suspension of the parents' personal interests that deeply enriches and extends their experience in a way no other experience probably could.

Shift to the same scene a year later. The two-year-old is still demanding more juice, but the parent's response is a bit more sluggish. The father has done this thousands of times already, and other things compete for his attention. It is less thrilling. He finds himself considering ways in which the child might get her own juice, or ask for it by using "magic words" like "please," which are clearly meaningless to the child but make the demand seem less imperious and soothe the parent's fleeting but horrifying vision of spending the rest of his life a functionary in the court of a Napoleonic two-year-old.

What has changed, the demand or the response? Probably both. Perhaps the two-year-old is more imperious in intent because of her more advanced development, the more clearly perceived threat of separation, autonomy issues, her increasing awareness of her diminutive status in the world outside the family, and so on. But something has changed in the parent as well. The thrill for the parent fades over time; what was originally fresh becomes staler, although a similar identification and passionate participation is reborn over and over in connection with other skills and new experiences together.[4]

The parent of the older child, like the analyst of the patient to whom he is less inclined to adapt, decides the child is now expressing a "wish" rather than a "need." This denotes something the child can certainly do for herself or do without. I am not sure whether it is only in the very skewed sample of children of New York City analysts that one frequently hears the child counter the parent's diagnosis of conflictual wish, often in regard to a desired object in a toy store, with their own developmental arrest diagnosis embedded in the claim "But I neeeeed this."

What I am describing is best understood not only as a transformation of motivational states in the child but as a transition of modes of interaction in a relationship. This transition can be disastrous when the original adaptation on the parent's part is done through a sense of obligation or an intellectual determination of the child's "needs." In such cases the subsequent reclaiming of the parent's needs and interests is accomplished with deep resentment and often sadistic retaliation for the previous masochistic surrender. Yet even under the best of circumstances, the negotiations between parents and children over desires and adaptations are complex, last a lifetime, and are inevitably conflictual. I regard the position sometimes found in the psychoanalytic literature suggesting that sensitive parents can make the frustrations of childhood less conflictual and generally joyful as a kind of grandparents' theory. On occasional visits it can seem as if gratification or sympathetic understanding of disappointments is the simple answer; actually living together, however, requires continual negotiation.

Viewing the definition of the desires and requests of children as established through negotiation does not in any way deny or minimize the developmental maturation of capacities and vulnerabilities over the course of childhood. Clearly, a great deal changes in the child over time. But how those changes are to be viewed, what the child is ready for and can handle, what the child needs protection from: These are codetermined by the changes in the child and the participation of the adult who is helping that child shape her experience in the world.[5]

Let us return to the analytic dyad. I have suggested that some desires emerging either explicitly or implicitly in the analytic situation have an intense sense of freshness about them, which contributes to inducing a cautious willingness on the part of the analyst to go along. One has the sense that here is someone who has never had the kind of experiences many others take for granted: really being listened to quietly and attentively, having one's needs granted priority, even one's whims indulged, having one's curiosity welcomed, one's intellectual interest respected, and so on. I suspect that in these situations most of us are inclined to bend the conventional analytic frame, often with good results. There is a sense of something happening for the analysand that has never happened before, a use of capacities, an opening up of a dimension of the self, a kind of connection never thought possible. As with the parent of the one-year-old, there is something very exciting for both participants about that experience. I do not mean to imply that analytic change can come solely from inviting or following the participation into a new kind of experience without an understanding of the conflicts and inhibitions that have prevented the patient from having such experiences independent of the analyst. But analytic change is sometimes greatly advanced when the analyst is willing and able to accompany the inquiry and analysis with a form of participation shaped by the patient's newly emerging desires. Of course something that feels fresh at first, as with our developmental analog, can grow stale over time and require renegotiation.

Other kinds of situations seem to me quite different, where the patient's desires emerge, often right at the beginning of treatment, in a form that feels less fresh than coercive. These are the rules: You have to be available to me in such-and-such a way, speak to me in such-and-such a fashion, and so on. What is this? A need? A wish? Such patients have often had many analysts who have responded, in one way or another, by refusing to accommodate themselves, reasoning that the patient does not really need what he wants. The patient, not suprisingly, usually does not stay long. The patient's hopes for the treatment are pinned on these desires, which the patient deeply believes he needs. What the analyst thinks she knows is irrelevant. Sometimes a skillful analyst can decline to provide what the patient wants and explain it in such a way, or find something else to offer, that intrigues the patient enough to hold his interest, at least for a while. Now there is a chance for something different to happen. Sometimes a frank, nondefensive, genuinely curious disclosure of the analyst's experience of the patient's demands can stimulate the latter's own curiosity.

But such patients may find an analyst willing to go along for a considerable period of time. I have heard of several situations in which the analyst was a candidate in analytic training when treatment was engaged and was able to commit herself to a way of working at that time that she would not be able to continue later. These candidate analysts were younger, full of therapeutic zeal, had more time on their hands and less family life, fewer referrals, and so on. All these factors contribute to the kind of relationship we are interested in participating in, which is then often transformed, through psychoanalytic theory, into a diagnostic formulation about what a patient really needs or does not need.

What happens in these analytic dyads? As Balint says, sometimes it does not work, sometimes it does. Sometimes the patient finds a way to feel betrayed, even after many years of faithful service on the analyst's part, and the treatment becomes one more in a series of proofs of the futility of hope. Sometimes nothing much seems to change, and the analyst feels either masochistically martyred or reconciled to an extended kind of maintenance function. However, sometimes very dramatic progress takes place, often after a long period of stasis. It is as if there is an extended testing period, perhaps lasting years, in which an analyst's willingness to accommodate to a patient's wishes and demands passes some critical point. On the other side of that crucial test the patient can risk participating in some other way without anticipating certain self-betrayal or disintegration.

The analyst's genuine attitude toward the patient's requests/demands is often more important than the content of the response itself. Let us assume an analyst feels unable or unwilling to meet the request. There is a world of difference between declining in a way that shames the patient for wanting something (diagnosed as infantile) that she should not want and declining in a way that acknowledges the potential legitimacy of the request. Sometimes simply acknowledging that although this analyst is unwilling to engage in the treatment in a particular way, and that the patient may find an analyst who would, provides the patient with enough self-respect and room to negotiate another form of engagement.

On the other hand, the patient's request also can be adapted to in different ways. An analyst's knowing assumption that she is giving a patient enough rope to hang himself is quite different from an authentic willingness to try something that might not fit into her customary way of working.

Adult analysands often experience their current desires as simple replacements or reparations for what they did not get as children. They can never be simply that. Childhood trauma is always transformed in adulthood in one fashion or another. Pain, passively experienced, is regularly transformed into angry revenge; aching longing, chronically endured, is regularly transformed into fantasies of magical rescue. It is a central task of analysis to help the patient sort out genuine need from vengeance, possible help from fantastic solutions.[6]

Recall Robert's fantastic notions of initiation into manhood, potency, and male camaraderie. In some respects, only as the illusory features of these wishes were integrated and understood did it become possible for him to get more of what he really needed from his experiences, including an internalization of his relationship with his male analyst.

Fairy tales contain a recurrent theme concerning the unfortunate consequences of obtaining one's heart's desire. (Catherine Bateson, 1987, has captured this principle succinctly in the title of her essay, "The Revenge of the Good Fairy.") Think of poor King Midas! Yet it is not easy truly to discard lifelong wishes without first having them gratified. One of the greatest advantages of the analyst sometimes adapting to the patient's wishes/demands is that doing so is often the most effective way for the patient to learn that what he always thought he wanted is not necessarily what he now needs.

When I was a child, the good fairy regularly appeared on my block in the form of the Good Humor truck. I always thought of Good Humor ice cream pops as the most wonderful possible treat. Even as an adult, after I had long become a connoisseur of Häagen-Daz and other ice cream wonders of the modern age, I always secretly felt, without quite articulating it to myself, that Good Humor was superior and constituted one among many features of my childhood lost forever. It was quite a shock when Good Humor made a comeback and I noticed it as a possibility within my world once again. What a surprise to find that it did not compare with the ice cream I was regularly eating. The granting of my wish made possible a working through of my childhood longing in a much more effective and powerful a fashion than the sad, renunciatory denial of my wish ever could.

Similarly, the principle of "abstinence" enshrined in classical theory of technique is probably one of the most effective ways to ensure that some patients never work through childhood longings. The longing is ostensibly given up through a process of rational conversion (subjecting the unconscious wish to "secondary process"), but there is a sad, wistful quality to this disciplined "maturity" and abstinence. The analyst's willingness to try out the patient's solution, when possible, can open up another very different kind of experience. There is a world of difference between "knowing" that my memories of Good Humor must be colored by retrospective elaboration and having the opportunity to live Good Humor once again in the context of my currently expanded world of resources and options. (There is, of course, the possibility, which several of my friends insist on, that they just don't make Good Humor like they used to.)

FITS AND MISFITS

Consider two illustrations of the idiosyncrasies and timing of fits and misfits between patient and analyst. Many years ago I briefly saw a young man who maintained a humdrum public life as a civil service employee and a secret life as a writer of poetry and essays read by virtually nobody. He was extremely bright and thoughtful and also extremely grandiose and contemptuous of everyone. He had come from a family seemingly impervious to his talents: Indeed his entire subjective experience was invisible to those around him, and his inner life seemed to have gone underground quietly and pervasively. He was very conflicted about beginning treatment and soon after starting began to produce long treatises on his views of the analytic process as an adjunct to our actual meetings.

I have had patients who delivered all sorts of written or recorded material to me with whom it was possible to discuss the meaning of the communication in the sessions. Often the simple act of accepting and holding the material had powerful symbolic significance, which has allowed the treatment to move forward. But that was not enough with this patient: I had to read everything, on my own time, and we had to talk about it. These conditions were a prerequisite for his participation; whether a need or a desire, they were nonnegotiable.

He came to me when I was enormously overcommitted and had very little time. Although I was intrigued by his brilliance and thought the dialogue might be fun for me and helpful for him (which I told him), I decided to decline this unusual contract. Of course, I offered many interpretations about the possible meanings of his demand with regard to his concern about my abilities to understand and/or care about him. He quit anyway. Is this patient unanalyzable? He certainly was by me at that point in time. But what if I had gone along? How long would it have been necessary for me to break with my normal way of working to demonstrate my interest and concern, my willingness to step outside my own framework to find him? Could someone else have found another way to seize his interest? These are, of course, unanswerable questions.

Another patient spent a good part of a year and a half lecturing me on the ecological crisis. He was an extremely talented, egocentric, quirky entrepreneur, who entered treatment because those around him had finally persuaded him to realize that he was a very difficult person to bear. He was controlling, highly disdainful, and mocking of everyone else, and often bitterly nasty. He was a first-generation American, from a very wealthy South American family, organized around the money and philosophy of life of a grandfather/patriarch. Most of the other grandchildren remained in the grandfather's city and had been slotted into the family business and the "good life" that it generated. When the patient was six years old, his mother, the only daughter of the patriarch, discovered that her husband, a fortune hunter and ne'er-do-well, had been conducting an adulterous affair. She secretly consulted her father and the family lawyer, waited until her husband's next business trip, and then emptied the safety deposit boxes and changed the locks on the doors. My patient's father was replaced in due course by a new stepfather, much more respectable in every way.

The boy became an underachiever, borderline delinquent, drug user, powerfully identified with his exiled father. In his late teens, he discovered that his father had been cheating on him too, stealing money from a trust for the grandchildren that had been set up by the grandfather. He eventually grew up to be a young man of sharp contrasts: a businessman like the grandfather, but not in the family business; driven to succeed, but socially and interpersonally fond of being "bad" and shocking; a blend of intense idealism in his business goals and ethics combined with a profound cynicism about the workings of the world.

In the sessions, he would frequently launch into a deeply felt monologue on the precarious ecological condition of our planet. It did not matter too much how I responded—in fact, no response was required other than attentiveness. If I found some way to bridge his discourse to whatever dynamic issues we were pursuing, he might agree or disagree with the connection and then continue. I began to think of this material in terms of his early life. The authorities, the holders of the public trust, are not doing their jobs—they are concerned only with their own immediate greed and gratification and not with protecting the environment in which future generations will live. Consequently, insidious contamination, almost unnoticed, is spoiling our world and threatening our very psychological survival. My patient feels he needs to focus constantly on this situation so as not to be totally surprised by the collapse of his world as it collapsed when he was a child. He has also projected many of his own feelings about these experiences, which he fears will contaminate his own internal world, into the external world in an effort to control them.

I was rather pleased with these formulations; he was less impressed, basically said "So what?" and continued as before. I was not to be put off so lightly and pursued the point in various ways. I argued that as long as he dealt with the trauma of his childhood in symbolic form, which allowed a fantasy of omnipotent control, he would be trapped by his past; I pointed to his need to control me so as not to be surprised or disappointed by me; I called his attention to how little he felt he could ask for or get from me, and so on. He listened to all of this, often while picking his nose, found it mildly interesting, and eventually went on.

The environmental monologues were quite fascinating—certainly to him and usually to me as well. Although I am very interested in politics, I rarely make the time to read in that area; he was very creatively reading and assimilating a lot of material that was of great interest to me. Further, I shared his basic political outlook and sense of the motives of political leaders, so that I often—not always, but a good part of the time—felt myself an avid listener. Over the course of the first year and a half of treatment, I went through many different speculations about what was going on. Perhaps I was exploiting him and should terminate the work; perhaps I should give him an ultimatum on how he was using the time, demeaning the value of our sessions and my potential contribution. Every now and then I would think of a new interpretation, or a new way to put an old interpretation; or, when I become very impatient or guilty, I would restate an old interpretation in its original form.

Eventually the discourses grew shorter and less frequent, the work deepened, and we became more truly analytically engaged. It seems that there was something in the fit between what he wanted and what I was able to offer that made that possible. Of course, it is impossible to know what was most important: time itself, my genuine interest and appreciation of his creativity, his experience of being able to control me and our interaction as he felt controlled by the grandfather and his world, my not kicking him out and changing the locks on the door, my implicit and sometimes explicit acknowledgment of how terrified he was of contamination and collapse, my not simply surrendering to his control but trying over and over to expand what we did together. Although I suspect all this was important, I would give considerable weight to the way in which the fit between us enabled me to stay with him and enjoy him while he was not doing what he was "supposed" to be doing.

In discussing certain types of very grandiose, narcissistic patients, Philip Bromberg (1983) notes that, "As long as interpretations, no matter how tactfully administered, are directed towards the patient's transference resistance, the patient will process the experience as though the analyst were another version of a self-interested, narcissistic parental figure who is more interested in getting the patient to meet his own needs than in helping the patient" (1983, pp. 368–69). The analyst has his own ideas about the work of analysis and what it requires. The patient who is protecting a brittle sense of self is likely to experience the analyst's project as just another version of a denial of the patient's own needs.

This point has wider applicability than just with very narcissistic patients. With more resilient patients, what has been called the analytic "frame" is more tolerable. They can surrender themselves to the structure and strictures of the analytic situation and get a great deal from it. Analyzability is often defined precisely in terms of this capacity. Yet it has always intrigued me to hear what kinds of things people remember and consider to have been crucial about their analyses. Sometimes interpretations are recalled, but more often it is situations in which the analyst stepped outside the role of the analyst to express caring, to help out, often in a minor but important way, where the genuineness of the analyst's concern for the patient is revealed. One cannot create this effect in a conscious, intentional way, trying to convince the patient that one cares, because then it is a different sort of interpersonal event. When this becomes the analyst's project, it has a different meaning for the patient, particularly one who is protecting an endangered sense of self against the well-intentioned intrusions of others.

The incidents that are genuinely helpful are often subtle transactions—embedded in the daily work itself—in which the analyst recalls some insignificant detail of their first meeting many years before or an image from a dream told long ago. The recall suggests how important this relationship has been not just to the patient but to the analyst as well, and how deeply the analyst has grasped and can conjure up the nuances and textures of the imagery that makes up the patient's world. The power of these kinds of experiences derives from the fact that they take place within the context of the analytic situation and the analyst's role in doing the analytic work, the inquiry into the patient's experience. These are not necessarily situations in which the patient wants something—they express neither need nor desire; nor are they situations in which the analyst is trying to give something or convey something, in a self-conscious effort to be caring or understanding. But they are situations in which the patient receives something beyond the analyst's professional participation in the work that helps make the work more deeply meaningful.

THE BREAKING OF THE FRAME: FERENCZI'S LESSON

The Clinical Diary of Sandor Ferenczi (1988) is the most detailed and poignant account available of the struggle of an analyst to try to sort out the wishes and needs of his patients and the way that this struggle touches the hopes and dreads of both participants. Unlike Freud, whose deepest passions were research and theory-building, Ferenczi desperately wanted to help his patients. He became known for treating the most difficult cases, those with whom other analysts had failed. And in the months before his untimely death, he was absorbed in painful reflections on the limits of the therapeutic powers of analysis and involved in radical technical experiments aimed at expanding analytic effectiveness.

Ferenczi was an extremely original thinker and anticipated, in the early 1930s, many of the most important analytic concepts of the past two or three decades.[7] Most striking of all, he anticipated the necessity for analysts to reflect on and explore their own personal feelings and struggles in the work with patients. This led him to experiment with "mutual analysis," in which patient and analyst take turns analyzing each other. This was clearly going too far. But a consideration of Ferenczi's struggles is instructive in our current efforts to sort out wishes and needs in the analytic relationship.

The logic that led Ferenczi to "mutual analysis" proceeded in a natural and inexorable fashion. He was struggling to help very disturbed patients who had been victims of extraordinarily cruel and perverse sexual abuse as children. As they gave themselves over to free association, Ferenczi found they were prone to slip into a hypnoticlike trance, in which fragments of the childhood scenes of violence and rape would emerge in intense and seemingly cathartic outbursts. It was not easy to induce the patient to enter such states; there was considerable resistance.

One patient, R.N., relentlessly pushed and challenged Ferenczi. She sensed his own discomfort with the material that emerged. His inhibitions, which she felt as palpable presences in the work, made it difficult for her to feel safe enough to give herself over to her own reconnaissance. She needed to understand his reactions to her and their roots in his own childhood in order to feel safe.

How was Ferenczi to respond to her demands? Analysis as traditionally practiced, Ferenczi came to feel, was shot through with hypocrisy. The analyst claims to have only professional attitudes toward the patient; in fact, the analyst has all sorts of "emotions such as annoyance, unpleasure, fatigue, 'to hell with it,' finally also libidinal and play fantasies" (p. 11). R.N. was certainly right about Ferenczi's own resistance to the emergence of her memories. The denial of the analyst's real personal involvement in the patient's struggles is equivalent, Ferenczi began to feel, to the original trauma, in which the seducer/parent stimulates and provokes the child, but then lies and denies the reality of his or her participation in the abuse.

R.N. pushed Ferenczi further. It is not enough to admit to feelings of anxiety, antipathy, resistance. What are the roots of these feelings? Why can Ferenczi not provide the strong and consistent emotional presence R.N. felt she needed to be cured? Does the patient not have a right to know in some detail of the analyst's blind spots and failings so as not to be surprised and victimized by them? The relentlessness in R.N.'s expectations of Ferenczi was matched by Ferenczi's own relentless self-scrutiny. He and R.N. both shared the hope that she might finally find a parental figure, in the analyst, who could make her whole. He and R.N. both shared the dread that his shortcomings, his personal conflicts and inhibitions, would destroy all hope for her recovery. Ferenczi became more and more impressed with the parallels between the original abuse and the abuse reenacted in the analytic situation by the analyst himself:

> the time will come when he will have to repeat with his own hands the act of murder previously perpetrated against the patient. In contrast to the original murder, however, he is not allowed to deny his guilt; analytic guilt consists of the doctor not being able to offer full maternal care, goodness, self-sacrifice; and consequently he again exposes the people under his care, who just barely managed to save themselves before, to the same danger, by not providing adequate help. (pp. 52–53)

Ferenczi is clearly anguished by what he takes to be his failures and inadequacies. The analyst's own hopes to help the patient are dashed upon the debris of his own neurotic difficulties. But Ferenczi finds a renewed hope, perhaps a more realistic one, in the acknowledgment of shortcomings of the analytic method and his own failures as analytic instrument:

> there is nevertheless a difference between our honesty and the hypocritical silence of parents. This and our goodwill must be counted in our favor. This is why I do not give up hope and why I count on the return of trust in spite of all the disillusionment. If we suceed in refocusing the traumatic accent, as is justified, from the present to the infantile, there will be sufficient positive elements left over to lead the relationship away from a breach in the direction of reconciliation and understanding. (p. 53)

At other points, Ferenczi places the therapeutic action not in the recovery and working through of the childhood traumas but in the mutual forgiveness between patient and analyst in the present.

> We believe in their innocence, we love them as beings enticed into maturity against their will, and it is our aim that they should accept our compassion and understanding, admittedly an incomplete fulfillment of their hopes, for the time being, until life offers them something better.
>
> A last, not unimportant, factor is the humble admission, in front of the patient, of one's own weaknesses and traumatic experiences and disillusionments, which abolishes completely that distancing by inferiority which would otherwise be maintained. . . . then the tears of doctor and of patient mingle in a sublimated communion, which perhaps finds its analogy only in the mother-child relationship. And this is the healing agent, which, like a kind of glue, binds together permanently the intellectually assembled fragments, surrounding even the personality thus repaired with a new aura of vitality and optimism. (p. 65)

In his anguished clinical journal Ferenczi goes back and forth on the questions: How far must he go, can he go, in his efforts to help the patient? Can the patient forgive him for failing to meet her hopes and expectations? Can he forgive himself? One feels, poignantly, that Ferenczi's life ended before he was able to resolve these questions in any satisfying way. (The last entry in the journal ends with: "There must be punishment. [Contrition.]") (p. 215).

From our vantage point sixty years later, it is very, very easy to second-guess and criticize Ferenczi. We have come to understand over those decades a great deal about clinical psychoanalysis that was not available to him. By today's standards he was virtually unanalyzed (apart from sporadic months here and there with Freud). Because of his battles with Freud on theory and technique, he was working virtually without colleagues. But it is precisely because Ferenczi operated in isolation that his lesson is so powerful for us today who must inevitably struggle with the same kinds of issues; the problems expanded to dramatic proportions in the vacuum he was working in.

What did Ferenczi fail to grasp? Although he identified the "terrorism of suffering" (p. 47) that these patients exercise, he did not fully appreciate how much the tables had been turned. The abuse inflicted upon them in childhood was now inflicted by them as it was reenacted in the analytic relationship.[8] Ferenczi failed to see that the problem was not only one of egalitarianism but also of boundaries. In childhood, their personal experience, their needs had been crushed; in analysis, their needs seemed overwhelming and undeniable. Ferenczi, with his own deep guilt and desperate need to help, could find no ground to resist R.N.'s demands; he could only surrender and ask for forgiveness.

Today Ferenczi would have many more options. We have come a long way in thinking about the interplay between past and present and the reenactment of childhood issues in the analytic relationship. We have come to realize that no matter how egalitarian and mutual we may strive to make that relationship, the analyst and patient have different roles and their participation is always necessarily and inevitably asymmetrical.[9] We have come to realize that the analyst's failure to fulfill a patient's hopes and longings does not necessarily reflect a personal failure on the part of the analyst but often reflects the irreversibility of the past.[10]

What is most useful for our purposes in Ferenczi's struggle with these issues is his stark and dramatic depiction of the crisis of hope and dread at the heart of the analytic impasse. The patient comes to doubt the utility of the analyst's ordinary participation. The patient wants more: more contact, more information, more reassurance. The efficacy of the analyst's interpretive function itself is being questioned. The patient is likely to experience this crisis as one in which the analyst is required to reveal what is most important to the analyst himself. What is more important to the analyst, his role, his understanding, his privacy, or the patient?

FLEXIBILITY OR STANDING FIRM?

There are two clear schools of thought on the handling of these kinds of crisis. Ferenczi represents one end of the continuum, and his bold and torturous experiments with mutual analysis illustrate its limitations. When the crunch comes, Ferenczi felt, the human relationship with the patient must outweigh the professional requirements of the role. To insist on analyzing as usual, a rigid adherence to the formal analytic role, is to betray the patient and perpetuate the illegitimate and hypocritical power that adults ordinarily wield over children.

On the other end of the continuum we find the frequent argument enjoining the analyst to "stand firm" in her analytic role. The deepest benefit the analyst can provide for the patient is through good interpretations, precisely through her ordinary analytic function. For some analysts, this technical position is linked to the belief that on the deepest unconscious level, the analyst and her good interpretations represent the hoped-for, longed-for "good breast." The patient's demands for something else are fueled by destructive attacks on the analytic function (good breast). To cave in, to bend, to do anything other than be a good analyst is to join the patient's despair, to collude in his destruction of the analytic function (the good breast). The most caring response, not only on a professional level but on a human one as well, is to hold firm.[11]

It is apparent that one person's "firmness" is another's rigidity, and that one person's flexibility is another's "caving in." Both firmness and flexibility are important and should be among the considerations of any clinician struggling with these situations. But I do not believe either of these positions provides a terribly reliable or helpful guide.

The problem with the principle of standing firm is the assumption that it must mean to the patient what the analyst wants it to mean. Sometimes it does, and the patient feels encouraged by the analyst's ability to set limits, stand by his faith in the analytic process, resist allowing himself to be seduced into dangerous departures.[12]

However, while the analyst thinks she is standing firm, the patient may feel he is being brutalized in a very familiar fashion. Many patients are lost because they feel utterly abandoned or betrayed by analysts who think they are maintaining the purity of the analytic frame. The frame is preserved; the operation is a success; but the patient leaves, climbing off the operating table in the middle of the procedure. It is not enough to say that such a patient was simply unsuitable for analysis. Some patients who have had great difficulty recovering from experiences like these are able to find a treatment more tolerable for them that becomes deeply analytic.

Simply being as accommodating as possible, telling the patient everything she might want to know, also is not the answer. Ferenczi's experiment with mutual analysis failed; it had to fail. The very nature of the analytic process necessitates that the analyst fails to meet all the patient's desires. The asymmetry of the analytic relationship is painful, inevitably for the analysand, often for the analyst. Ferenczi did not realize that this was not a result of his own personal failings but the structure of the analytic relationship itself. To meet every demand, to disclose everything, is ultimately both impossible and dishonest. Lawrence Friedman (1988) has put the dilemma succinctly:

> Arguments for greater therapy frankness must reckon with the significance of both mysteriousness and openness as *intentions*. The *attempt* to conceal something that one would ordinarily reveal has consequences apart from, and far more important than, what is concealed. Conversely, if the therapist is frank about himself he is choosing to make the odd relationship seem more like an expectable relationship, and that conceals something about the therapist that concealment would reveal, namely his peculiar role. (p. 440)

In my view, what is most important is not what the analyst does, as long as he struggles to do what seems, at the moment, to be the right thing; what is most important is the way in which analyst and analysand come to understand what has happened. What is most crucial is that, whatever the analyst does, whether acting flexibly or standing firm, he does it with considerable self-reflection, an openness to question and reconsider, and, most important, with the patient's best interests at heart. If the patient and analyst together find a way to construe the event constructively, as an opportunity, the process opens up and is enriched. If both end up experiencing the event as the defeat of either the patient or the analyst, the process closes off and an opportunity is lost.

If the analyst holds firm and can show the patient persuasively that holding firm represents a refusal to be defeated by the patient's despair or desperation, that holding firm represents the analyst's faith in the analytic process as the most profound offer of help to the patient, then this act of maintaining the frame facilitates the process. If the analyst holds firm, but the patient experiences the analyst as hiding behind the frame, as more concerned with self-protection or correct technique than the patient's welfare, then this act of maintaining the frame subverts the process and fails the patient.

If the analyst departs from the frame and can show the patient persuasively that the departure represents a willingness to take reasonable risks in unfamiliar waters and a faith in the durability of their analytic alliance to weather all eventualities, then departing from the frame facilitates the process. If the analyst departs from the frame but the patient experiences the departure as an act of submission or desperation, then departing from the frame subverts the process and fails the patient.[13]

In short, the process itself is more important than the decision arrived at. And the process does not end at the point at which the analyst makes a decision with regard to the analysand's request. As we noted in chapter 2, the analyst may not always be in a position to understand a great deal of why she is doing what she is doing when she is doing it. Often only later on does the analyst become aware that she has been "standing firm" partly out of fear or as a way of enacting revenge, or that she has been being accommodating partly out of intimidation or as a way of being passive-aggressive. Thus, a crucial dimension of making constructive analytic use of these situations is an openness to a continual reevaluation of their meanings over time.

NEGOTIATIONS AND THE ANALYTIC RELATIONSHIP

Viewed within a relational framework, the patient's desires are never simply in the patient, with an intrinsic nature and meaning, necessarily to be gratified or frustrated. Rather, they are always desires for something particular from someone particular, and therefore are embedded in a dyadic field in which two people are able either to find and connect with each other or to deflect and miss each other. It may be that each analytic dyad develops its own distinctive rules, that what needs to happen in one relationship might be dealt with in an equally constructive but very different way in another. What is most crucial is neither gratification nor frustration, but the process of negotiation itself,[14] in which the analyst finds his own particular way to confirm and participate in the patient's subjective experience yet, over time, establishes his own presence and perspective in a way that the patient can find enriching rather than demolishing.

One of the most important areas in which needs, desires, and wants are negotiated between patient and analyst is in the area of money. Here, especially, the distinction between need and desire becomes fuzzy, and the process itself is often much more important than the result arrived at.

Should we regard the analyst's wanting to be paid his full fee as a need or a wish? Speaking for myself, sometimes it feels more like one than the other. There are times when I feel I could offer a particular hour for less and times I do not feel I can. One factor is my own financial situation and stress at the time; another factor is the potential analysand. At times I am willing to reduce my fee for one particular patient and not another. It feels very different depending on the person, and I have learned by experience to respect these feelings if I do not want to come to resent the patient later on. Aron (1989) has noted how difficult it often is for analysts (whose genuine wishes to help alleviate human conflict and pain may have brought them into the field) to acknowledge their own needs and/or desires for money. One often hears the argument that it is important for the patient to pay a high fee for the treatment to feel important. Once again, this seems to me to be using a diagnostic evaluation to justify the form in which the analyst feels like engaging the patient. Consider the following example of the complexities of money issues in the interpersonal mix between analyst and analysand.

Shortly after Roger, a young architectural student, began treatment on a twice-a-week basis, he brought up the possibility of a third session, which seemed desirable to both of us, although he felt it was out of reach in terms of his finances. He asked about the possibility of my reducing the fee somewhat. We agreed that if he came three times a week, I would reduce the fee for all three sessions by five dollars, and this served as the financial basis for our work for six years. There were many constructive developments in several areas of his life over this time, one of which involved his borrowing a considerable amount of money to serve as an investment that seemed to both of us to be very consistent with his growth as a person. The loan, however, put him under considerable financial stress, and we began to consider the pros and cons of his cutting back to two sessions on an interim basis. This step seemed to be the most desirable course of action, and as he was considering the details of his finances during these discussions, Roger asked whether I would raise the fee five dollars, back to the original level prior to his expanding to three times per week. Since I was impressed with his financial distress and since the money, at that moment, did not seem important to my finances, I said no, I wouldn't raise the fee.

We reduced the number of sessions to twice weekly, and important work was done for several months. Then the patient had the following dream, which brought the fee issue back:

I was in a restaurant. The waiter was trying to put something into the pocket of my jacket, but the pocket was sewn shut. I didn't want whatever he was giving me. Maybe it was packets of sugar. [The patient is very scrupulous about diet and considers sugar a form of poison.] I kept saying "No, I don't want it—cut it out." He was oversolicitous and invasive. Finally I told him he could forget about the tip which I had already left on the table. He grabbed for it, but I reached it first. I threw it on the floor. It felt important to let him know that what he was doing was inappropriate. Making him scramble for the tip was forcing an indignity on him for what he had forced on me.

In his associations to the dream Roger recalled several scenes from his childhood involving "sweet" moments between himself and his father, returning home from work with special presents for him, both of them overjoyed at seeing each other again.

We had spent a good deal of time trying to disentangle his complex experience of his father, who had been a loving man, very involved with his only son, yet whose impact was experienced as somehow crippling. The father had taken a great interest in his homework, for example. The boy would ask him to go over writing assignments. When he awoke the next morning, his father, a professional writer, would have completely rewritten the piece. This brought the boy great accolades at school but for work that was not really his. He had memories of his father carrying him around on his shoulders until he was five years old. (Since my own efforts to carry my children on my shoulders until they were three or so had resulted in quite a few hours with a chiropractor, I was skeptical of these memories and considered them likely screen memories.) As he grew older, his father was always more than happy to see and spend time with him, but somehow never seemed really interested in his son's own experience, his own life and interests. As Roger grew to manhood, his father was constantly trying to give him money, both larger amounts and also subway tokens, which he would try to smuggle into his son's pockets when he was not looking. The son sometimes refused his aid, sometimes accepted it. He sensed that to finally and definitively turn down his father's money would have been to somehow shatter their relationship; his saintly father would never be able to understand, and there would not be much else between them.

This whole interaction between son and father took place in secret from the mother, who often felt excluded from their intimacy. Roger experienced her as an intense, ungiving, stern, and paranoid woman who constantly berated her husband and felt he was pandering to their son, buying his love in various ways. About two years into the treatment the father died. The mother discovered that he had been giving some of their money to the son, which enraged her. What was more remarkable, however, and a surprise to the son, was that the father had been in precarious financial straits himself; his help to his son had been at the expense of his own financial security.

The relevance of the dream to the underside of his relationship to his father was clear; although it would have been tempting to stay with the past, what seemed more important now was its relevance to his feelings about him and me. The lowered fee felt to him like his father's tokens, in some way meaningless yet a powerful, two-sided symbolic statement both about my protectiveness toward him and my efforts to cripple him with my kindness. A major theme in the transference had been his tendency to split his experience of me; there had been a largely idealized, somewhat formal image of me as helpful, successful, somewhat gurulike as well as various circumscribed, split-off images of me as ruthless, sleazy, teetering on the edge of decompensation. He felt a powerful need to "keep things sweet here." It became clear that the reduced fee had been laden with meaning for him all along. It had made him feel special and cared for yet also reduced and infantalized.

One interesting feature of the themes that developed from this dream was that Roger had completely forgotten our recent discussion of the fee. He remembered our original arrangements but felt completely in the dark about whether I would raise the fee again now that he had cut back to twice a week. One fantasy was that I would deal with him as his mother did, totally unsympathetic about his plight, sternly depriving him of any help. The other fantasy was that I would deal with him as had his father, forcing my token help on him in a way that undermined his autonomy and dignity.

He now felt much more solid and substantial as a person and was clearly more financially responsible than when he began treatment. His repression of our recent conversation in which I was willing to maintain the lowered fee seemed to reflect his sharply conflicted ambivalence about how he wanted our relationship to be now. On the one hand, for me to raise the fee the token amount at a time when he felt the difference in money would make things much harder for him seemed harsh and ungiving, very much like his mother. On the other hand, keeping the fee reduction maintained him in his crippled yet protected status, which he both wanted and did not want. We also explored his fantasies about my motives. Perhaps I was not so financially solvent myself, but somehow felt it more important to maintain my generous posture toward him than take care of myself. That was both comforting and very frightening. How real or postured was my protective care?

My own experience during these sessions fluctuated back and forth between various positions and versions of myself. I began to wonder why I had been so quick to tell him I would not raise the fee. How invested was I in being his saintly protector? Was it at my own expense? Did I really not need the extra money? Surely aspirations to sainthood do not lie outside my range of ambitions. Yet as we explored some of these considerations and as my sense of the relational configuration we had established began to drift in that direction, he shifted perspectives and spoke of a fear of the "other shoe dropping." Roger's openness in discussing his ambivalence would lead me to unilaterally raise his fee, just at a time when he could least afford it. Perhaps this was a masochistic gambit of surrender to me as to the sadistic, ungiving mother, demanding of him more than he could deliver. And there was something about the extended discussions of my sabotaging "saintliness," sought after by him yet not particularly helpful for him and meddling and self-defeating for me, that evoked a different version of myself, tempting me to instantly double his fee, as a punitive and magical solution to our dilemma. We seemed trapped in the closed world of these two relational configurations in which he was either cruelly deprived or lovingly crippled. This was, in my view, precisely the sort of trap in which we needed to be caught. (See Mitchell, 1988.) If I had declined to lower the fee at either point in the treatment, we would have merely entered the trap in a different fashion.

In these negotiations I have sometimes found it useful to envision how the analysand might proceed as the other party in the negotiation if he were operating as a less conflicted, more responsible agent for himself. He could not imagine and also did not want to be able to imagine what it would feel like to experience himself as essentially self-reliant and substantial, yet also asking for reasonable help in a temporarily stressful situation. We clarified his passive surrender to me, assuming a helplessness in the face of the way I defined our interaction and construed his needs and desires. We began to distinguish between what seemed to be his psychological readiness to pay the full fee and his current financial resources, which made that difficult. Perhaps there was a way for us to acknowledge both and thereby work our way out of the trap we had created. The collaborative, interpretive delineation of the impasse itself began, over time, to provide a way out, an alternative way for us to engage each other that broadened the confining grasp of the old relational configurations.

The analytic process employs interpretations to enable the analysand to overcome experiential constrictions. Rather than being one in a linear sequence of developmental tasks, the negotiation between one's own desires and those of others is a lifelong struggle. The analyst's expertise resides in developing and drawing the patient into a collaborative inquiry that allows both the patient's desires and the analyst's authentic participation to find a home.

8

The Dialectics of Hope

And so I dare to hope,
Though changed, no doubt, from what I was when first
I came among these hills; when like a roe
I bounded o'er the mountains, by the sides
Of the deep rivers, and the lonely streams,
Wherever nature led: more like a man
Flying from something that he dreads than one
Who sought the thing he loved.
—William Wordsworth, "Lines"(Tintern Abbey)

I begin this chapter on the interplay between the hopes and dreads of analyst and analysand with two brief vignettes providing glimpses into ongoing analytic work from the wonderfully privileged vantage point of supervisory consultations.

A young man in his twenties begins treatment because he is confused about his sexual orientation. He is attracted to both men and women. In bed with a woman, he becomes very anxious and sexually dysfunctional. He has no performance problems with men, but feels deeply conflicted about being with a man, and his few homosexual experiences are always with men he does not like or enjoy in any way besides sexually. He wants analysis to help him understand and resolve both his attraction to men and his performance anxiety with women. He works hard, and important understandings are gained over a period of a year or so. There have been significant changes in his life; however, his paralysis regarding his sexual orientation remains, and the analyst starts to have the experience of spinning her wheels.

As this deepening stalemate is inquired into, it begins to become apparent that the patient really does not want anything resolved. If he chose as sexual partners men whom he likes, he might become deeply involved and have to confront what he dreads is true about him—that he is gay. He wants to avoid this at all cost. If he gets involved with a woman and really works to overcome his performance anxiety, he might find out either that women do not deeply excite him, therefore confirming his dread of being gay, or that women do deeply excite him, therefore requiring him to renounce his interest in men, which he can not really imagine himself doing. So the best solution is to remain immobile, and the best way to justify immobility is to refrain from acting until analysis itself resolves his sexual orientation.

There are also deep, concealed gratifications in the attention lavished on his indecisions by the female analyst, with whom he remains a seemingly asexual, preoedipal little boy. Analysis is ostensibly about helping him move; analysis becomes in fact a vehicle for him to stay where he is. Of course, all this was largely unconscious. His conscious intent is for resolution of his sexual identity. His deeper hope is to remain suspended in boyhood under the protective care of an omnipotent parent. Important analytic work had been done, but in the limiting context of the perpetuation of the patient's original hope for a timeless, presumably presexual childhood.

An extremely competent and professionally accomplished married woman in her thirties seeks treatment because of her disappointing relationships with men. She experiences her husband as weak, submissive, and bumbling. He does not excite her. She has occasional affairs with men who are strong, dominant, and controlling. They frighten her. She can have orgasms only through use of a vibrator, which she uses both alone in masturbation and also with men. She can reach orgasm only if they use the vibrator to stimulate her. She fears she is addicted to the vibrator and is afraid she will never be able to love a man or enjoy sex without mechanical aids.

Over the course of several years with a male analyst, considerable understanding had been gained and a great deal of important work had been done. She feels much better about herself in many respects, and her relationships both with the husband and with one of the lovers have become enriched. She enjoys sex much more, sometimes even without the vibrator. Yet she still feels stuck, caught between wimpy men and dangerous men. She has a strong erotic transference to the analyst, which he has worked with in a skilled and effective fashion; many important links to early childhood experiences and relationships have been uncovered. But she is still stuck.

In a supervisory consultation, I found myself listening to the process notes the analyst presented with considerable pleasure and admiration. This analytic dyad worked very well together. His interpretations were finely crafted: they were balanced; they contained different conflictual elements of the patient's experience, juxtaposed with each other in an evenhanded way. I began to notice that the interpretations even had a kind of cadence to them. "On the one hand, duh-duh, duh-duh-duh, duh-duh, and, on the other hand, duh-duh, duh-duh-duh, duh-duh." Each interpretation was perfectly symmetrical, with both sides of the conflict represented evenly. The patient's conflictual feelings were played back to her in an elegant, delicately balanced construction that was at the same time both powerful and carefully controlled. I began to imagine that the interpretations themselves had become a perfect phallic object, a kind of humming analytic version of the vibrator, very potent but delicately regulated, in the way no flesh-and-blood man could ever be. The analysis had become a form of sexual play to which she was addicted in the way she had previously been addicted to her vibrator. This was clearly an advance, but one that was constrained and limited because it was organized along the lines of the patient's deep hope for a perfect, omnipotently controlled, object.

At the beginning of treatment the patient is hurting and wants things to be better. He is hopeful enough that things can be better to put himself through the hardships, both emotional and financial, of beginning treatment, of entering the odd and unique relationship we call psychoanalysis. What exactly does the patient hope for? Do the patient's hopes derive from mature expectations or infantile longings? Does he want realistic help or magical help? Do the patient's hopes have anything much to do with what the analyst thinks she is offering? Are patients' hopes part of the problem or part of the solution?

PERSPECTIVES ON HOPE

Within psychoanalytic theorizing there have been two fundamentally different approaches to hope. One regards hope as essentially regressive and interfering with mature and rewarding experience; the other regards hope as essentially progressive and facilitating of a richer experience.

Traditionally hope has been linked with fantasy and illusion as essentially regressive tendencies. This was consistent with the broad framework provided by classical drive theory in which experience is dichotomized in terms of gratification versus frustration of infantile drive derivatives. The hopes that bring the patient into treatment are those derived from the longing for gratification of infantile sexual and/or aggressive impulses. These hopes are embedded in primary process thinking and wish fulfillment and are at considerable remove from reality. More mature, secondary process thinking, in contrast, is predicated upon the renunciation of fantasy and illusion and adherence to the reality principle. If, for Freud, religion is the institutional embodiment of infantile hopes and illusions, science is the institutional embodiment of rationality and sober judgment. There is no hope involved.

Among the few psychoanalytic contributions on hope, Harold Boris (1976) has provided a thought-provoking and powerful version of this traditional view of hope as regressive. Following Klein and Bion, Boris reasons that infants come prewired with "preconceptions," images of what they need, and these become the objects of their desire. Desire itself tends to be highly plastic, peremptory, and polymorphous. Hope entails a commitment to preconceptions, a priori, ideal images. Desire is insistent and extremely undiscriminating. Hope is choosy and demanding. When the ideal object and the actual object are closely related, hope and desire work well together. When there is too great a gap between the ideal object and actual, possible objects, a crucial and "fundamental antagonism" develops between hope and desire: "where preconceptions and actuality are too far apart, hope comes into being as separate from desire and in fact serves as a restraint upon desires more fundamental, in my view, than anxiety, the defences or other stuctures of the mind" (1976, p. 144).

In these circumstances (which define most serious psychopathology), Boris reasons, the waiting required by hope suffocates the possibility for the spark of desire and its fulfillment. The actual object is never the right object; the time is never now. Real satisfaction is always sacrificed in the hope of eventual fulfillment at some future time. To Boris, the analytic process represents the relinquishment of hope and the precipitation of a crisis of despair. Only in the living through of that crisis do genuine desire and satisfaction become possible.[1]

A second and sharply contrasting approach to hope has been developed within the traditions of psychoanalytic theorizing that emphasize developmental arrests. Here hope is regarded not as suffocating desire but as seeking a psychological space in which genuine desire may become possible, in which the self can find a "new beginning."

This approach is represented within the tradition of Freudian ego psychology in the work of Erik Erikson. Erikson locates hope within human experience in earliest infancy: "The oral stages . . . form in the infant the springs of the *basic sense of trust* and the *basic sense of mistrust* which remain the autogenic source of both primal hope and of doom throughout life" (1950, p. 80). Although Erikson regards hope as originating in infancy, he clearly does not see hope as limited by infantile wishes or longings, as something to be renounced as development and maturation proceed. Hope, in Erikson's view, is extremely constructive and growth-enhancing,[2] "the first and most basic" of the "'vital virtues' to connote certain qualities which begin to animate man pervasively during successive stages of his life" (1968, p. 233).

Winnicott also viewed hope as progressive. This approach appeared first in his discussion of "antisocial tendencies" in difficult-to-manage adolescent disturbances. Rather than regard "acting out" as an expression of instinctual impulses, requiring control and the reinforcement of boundaries, Winnicott took the surprising position that such behaviors were an expression of hope.

> *The antisocial tendency implies hope* . . . over and over again one sees the moment of hope wasted, or withered, because of mismanagement or intolerance . . . the treatment of the antisocial tendency is not psycho-analysis but management, a going to meet and match the moment of hope. (1956b, p. 309)

Winnicott saw the same optimistic longing in the most disturbing symptomatology of psychotics.

> The regression represents the psychotic individual's hope that certain aspects of the environment which failed originally may be relived, with the environment this time succeeding instead of failing in its function of facilitating the inherited tendency in the individual to develop and to mature. (1965, p. 128)

Winnicott had a tendency to introduce his extremely innovative contributions with reference to nonneurotic psychopathology and therefore outside of psychoanalysis proper. (See Greenberg and Mitchell, 1983, chap. 7.) Over time, the contributions broadened in their implications, and it became clear that Winnicott had introduced a novel vision of the analytic process itself. He came to see regression as a central feature of the therapeutic action of analysis, and regression has everything to do with hope: "The organization that makes regression useful ... carries with it the hope of a new opportunity for an unfreezing of the frozen situation" (1954, p. 283).[3] Infantile hopes, for Winnicott, do not represent a defensive or pathological demand for illusory satisfactions. Infantile hopes represent a self-healing return to the point at which psychological growth was suspended. Infantile hopes and longings do not need to be renounced but rather reanimated and brought to life, so they can grow and develop into more mature hopes through a natural, organic maturational process.

Winnicott's point of view should not be understood as a call for a simple acceptance of the patient's initial, conscious definition of her own hopes. Winnicott's development of the concepts of the true and false self grew out of his effort to disentangle the patient's wishes and hopes that represent a longing for a more genuine, more personally authentic experience from those that are a shallow adaptation to what seems to be required from the outside.

Kohut's concepts of narcissistic transferences and self-object needs closely parallel Winnicott's approach. Kohut also provides a way of rethinking the significance of infantilism and what appear to be excessive demands on the analyst and everyone else. Rather than instinctual wishes to be renounced, they are missed developmental needs to be warmly received and understood. The patient is groping toward self-cure, by trying to extract from others what was missing early in his development. Like Winnicott, Kohut feels the patient knows what he needs, regardless of what the analyst may think he knows. Kohut also stresses the importance of hopes in maturity and throughout development. There is an enduring need for ideals and idealization that vitalizes self experience. Rather than smothering desire, Kohut regards hope as perpetually flaming its embers.[4]

THE ANALYST'S HOPES

If discussions of the patient's hopes are rare in the psychoanalytic literature, discussions of the analyst's hopes have been virtually nonexistent until recently. The analyst's hopes are embedded in the service she offers—a form of treatment, a way of practicing, a set of techniques. We tend not to speak or write much of the analyst's hopes as such, because that sounds too personal somehow. The analyst is portrayed as a professional, providing a generic service that helps when applied properly. But we all know that it is much more personal than that, that the analyst's hopes for her patients are embedded in and deeply entangled with her own sense of herself, her worth, what she can offer, what she has found deeply meaningful in her own life. The more we have explored the complexities of countertransference, the more we have come to realize how personal a stake the analyst inevitably has in the proceedings. It is important to be able to help; it makes us anxious when we are prevented from helping or do not know how to help. Our hopes for the patient are inextricably bound up with our hopes for ourselves.

What is the relationship between the hopes of the patient and those of the analyst? If one thinks about hope casually, coordinating the patient's hopes with the analyst's hopes does not seem to be much of a problem. The patient longs to get better; the analyst wants to make the patient better. The patient hopes for change; the analyst knows how to facilitate change. It all ought to work fairly smoothly. But the few writers who have explored the place of hope within the analytic process more seriously have found it to be one of the most problematic and challenging aspects of the analytic relationship. The central problem is that the patient's and analyst's hopes are often quite different, and sometimes have very little to do with each other.

Consider the hopes of the obsessional patient beginning treatment. He is not interested in giving up his life's work of controlling everything that happens in his own experience and that of those around him. In fact, he is likely to be hoping that analysis will help bolster his skills at control, which he probably feels have been slipping. The analyst's hopes are likely to be very different—more oriented toward enabling the patient to experience life in a richer and very different fashion, which becomes possible only when he relaxes his efforts to omnipotently control his experience. Of course, the analyst does not say anything like: "Look, I understand that you are hoping I will help you repair and perfect your obsessional approach to living, but I can help you give all that up and find a much fuller and more meaningful life." If the analyst did say something like that, the patient would likely leave, and rightfully so. The patient would have no idea, no real possibility for grasping, what the analyst is talking about. To sign up under those conditions would be to commit to a conversion process, not analysis. It takes years for even well-intentioned analytic candidates to begin to really grasp what analysis is, how it expands the very underlying structure of experience and subjectivity, the very generation of personal meaning. The patient cannot possibly begin to grasp this and probably will not for quite some time.

So the analyst, in good faith, merely says something on the order of: "Let us begin an inquiry into your experience, and we will see what we find." But this extremely vague and nonspecific agreement upon which the work begins should not fool us into missing the necessarily broad and fundamental discordancy at the beginning of treatment between the patient's hopes and the analyst's. This is a problem not only with the obsessional patient who is looking for more effective techniques of control but also with the narcissistic patient who is looking to repair a diminishing sense of perfection, the hysterical patient who is looking for a replacement for failed "happy ideas" (Sullivan 1956), and so on.

Friedman (1988) has argued that there has always been a central paradox at the very heart of the psychoanalytic process. The patient's hopes, based on infantile longings, bring her into treatment and invest the analyst with powerful transferential significance. The analyst uses the power invested in him through the transference to help the patient. Yet a central part of the cure is the interpretation of that very transference and the dissolving of the transferential fantasies that impart authority to the analyst. The hopes embedded in the transference grant the analyst the platform he needs to do his work, but the main project of the work is the dismantling of the platform. This is a paradox indeed.[5]

Perhaps the most popular current device diverting attention from Friedman's paradox is the concept of "developmental arrest," or "developmental strivings," which makes it possible to believe that there is an arrested, truer self in the patient just waiting to unfold that both patient and analyst hope to find. The problem is that there is no good reason to assume that the initial sense of self the patient longs to be and the analyst's sense of who the patient might usefully become have much in common. The very vagueness of these concepts enables them to soften the discordance between the patient's and the analyst's hopes with which every treatment necessarily begins. The patient and analyst both surely want something to be different and better; both want the patient to have an experience of living that is richer and fuller. But it is not clear that there is much congruence between the patient's original ideas of what that would entail and the analyst's; rather, as the work proceeds, it generally becomes apparent how different those visions really are.

THE ANALYTIC CRUNCH

Most analyses have long stretches of time when the patient and the analyst are working more or less comfortably together. These are times when the discordancy between the patient's and the analyst's hopes is in the background, or perhaps when there is enough overlap between the two sets of hopes to move the work forward. The word comfortably is not quite right. Anxieties and dreads always lurk in any authentic analysis; it never quite gets comfy. But there are often stretches in which there is a good feeling of working together. We saw this in both vignettes with which I began this chapter. The patient is using interpretations to grow and expand his experience in useful ways. He is allowing the analyst to help him. The analyst has a sense she is doing her job well. But every experienced analyst has learned to be somewhat watchful, if not wary, of these good stretches. The patient is letting you help him, but always in his own particular fashion, and it often takes quite some time to find out exactly what that fashion is.

John Lennon is credited with saying, "Life is what happens when you are making other plans." This could be tailored for our purposes to read "The essential features of the transference and countertransference are what happens when you think you are simply being an analyst." Being the analyst is never simple; when it seems to be, there is something wrong. It was an appreciation of this that led Winnicott to develop his rich contributions on true and false self. When the patient appears to be simply receiving help from the analyst, there is something in the form through which the help is being internalized that itself is problematic and needs to be understood. (An appreciation of this concept might be used to distinguish the crafts of psychoanalysis and psychotherapy.)

Most analyses also have periods of crisis and impasse. These are often times when the underlying discordancy between the hopes of the patient and those of the analyst is exposed and can no longer be avoided. These are the times when it has become clear that the analysis itself has become the problem, and they reflect the broadest meaning of the term transference neurosis. These dark times in analysis are often described as analytic "stalemates" or "impasses."[6]

Webster's gives two definitions for "stalemate"; one is: "any situation making further action impossible." The analytic process is a form of action, and things should be moving, going somewhere, we tend to feel. When things are stalemated, stuck, deadlocked, there is something wrong. The other definition of "stalemate" is: "in chess, the position of the king when so situated that, though not in check, he cannot move without being placed in check, there being no other available move; it results in a draw." The analytic process can be viewed as being like a chess game, a mock war. Freud introduced this metaphor in 1913, in the context of his essentially adversarial view of the analytic process. What is the analyst's king, that extremely vulnerable but indispensible piece without which there is no game? I think we would have to say the analyst's king is "understanding," and that ultimately the analyst's understanding necessarily comes to be attacked from all sides.

In the preimpasse phase of many analyses, the patient suspends her doubts and destructiveness in relation to the analyst's understanding, pays deference to it, one might say. The analyst's understanding is often protected by a certain degree of idealization. This enables the patient to use it and grow, but also often enables her to avoid deeper levels of dread and despair. If we reverse perspectives for a moment, we might ask, "Why should the patient value and allow herself to internalize and use the analyst's understanding?" Does not the analyst, like all parents, inevitably make false promises, both intended and unintended? The very interpretations of the analyst pose a dire threat. Harold Searles (1979) has written about this difficult-to-acknowledge facet of the analytic situation:

> the dedicated therapist does not see how much ambivalence the patient has about change, even change for the "better." He does not see that the patient has reached his present equilibrium only after years of thought and effort and the exercise of the best judgment of which he is capable. To the patient, change tends to mean a return to an intolerable pre-equilibrium state, and the imposition upon him of the therapist's values, the therapist's personality, with no autonomy, no individuality, for him. He resents the therapist's presumption in assuming that the patient is pitiably eager to be rescued, and in assuming, equally humiliatingly, that the intended help is all unidirectional, from therapist to patient. (pp. 74–75)

Kleinian theory has shed considerable light on just how dangerous a hopeful attitude toward the analyst's understanding can be, and this has important implications for patient's relationship to interpretations. The recurrent Kleinian metaphor is always the baby at the breast, and Kleinians portray that situation, no matter how blissful at times, as necessarily also always harrowing. Babies are little and defenseless; bodily needs can be painful and overwhelming. The deep gratitude babies feel for a good feed is, necessarily, always shadowed by anxiety in relation to their completely dependent position vis-à-vis the breast that delivers such goodness. The greater the goodness, the more dependent and vulnerable babies feel. The more irreplaceable the object, the more dangerous is the baby's own destructiveness toward the object when it is frustrating. Gratification itself creates, paradoxically, a kind of psychological tension, a longing for relief from the vulnerability and powerlessness that the goodness of the object generates. Envious spoiling, the destruction not of the bad object but of the good object (which the Kleinians see as the source of the deepest psychopathology), provides precisely such relief. Similarly, hope in the paranoid-schizoid position (what Boris means by hope) is easy, a longing for a magical, omnipotently controlled, easily exchangeable object. Hope in the depressive position requires great courage, a longing for an all-too human, irreplaceable object, outside of one's control.[7]

It is not only at the breast that gratification is dangerous, deepening dependency and vulnerability at the very moment of pleasure and enrichment. Life itself is extremely fragile. The other whom one loves, who provides exclusive, irreplaceable satisfaction, will die, may abandon, and inevitably periodically disappoints and betrays. To love in a committed fashion, over time, is to hope; and to hope is to impart value in an inevitably uncertain future. Both love and hope are extremely risky; a genuine hopefulness about the analytic process is not possible in any real way at the beginning but is something attained only through struggle; it takes great courage. Current psychoanalytic literature is becoming increasingly sophisticated regarding just how difficult and dangerous it is for a patient to use an interpretation in a personally meaningful, truly hopeful fashion. To keep an analyst's offer of hope alive long enough to be useful and genuinely nourishing requires the precarious suspension of the complementary, comfortably foreclosing processes of idealization and envy. The analytic use of an interpretation engenders hope, rewards courage, and, in time, makes it more possible to sustain hope and desire long enough to generate authentic growth and development.

The criterion of "analyzability," as noted in chapter 1, is often defined as the patient's capacity to hear the analyst's interpretations primarily as interpretations. Whatever else these interpretations are—attacks, seductions, pleadings, abandonments—the patient must cede some authority to the analyst's interpretive understanding. I find such a criterion very dubious; it seems to me that it demands from the patient a deference that cannot possibly be wholly geniune.

The patient's subjective world is organized like a prism whose facets refract and disperse entering illumination into customary and familiar wavelengths. The analyst, from the beginning, would like to reach the patient directly, would like his understanding to expose for consideration the very structure of the patient's prism of subjectivity itself. This is not possible for the patient. The light that the analyst shines on the prism invariably enters it and is dispersed into familiar categories of experience: old dreads, old longings, old hopes. For the patient to be able to hear the interpretation as an interpretation—that is, as the analyst consciously intends it (it is likely to have other, darker unconscious meanings for the analyst also)—the patient would already have to be able to recognize an analytic interpretation as something different from anything in his previous experience. No patient starts out being able to do this. The patient comes to learn and really grasp what an analytic interpretation is by discovering what it is not. It is something truly different from anything he has encountered before. He does not know that until he has given up trying to use interpretations and analytic understanding in all the old ways.

Times of crisis, when the patient directly focuses his dread, despair, and destructiveness on the analyst's understanding, tend to be difficult for the analyst. It is a mistake to think of this difficulty as reflecting experiences that belong solely to objects within the patient's world or to the patient himself. The analyst is not simply containing fragments of the patient's experience. The analyst is really being attacked in relation to her capacity to understand—every analyst's greatest resource and also point of greatest vulnerability.

Whether they are conscious and explicit or unconscious and silent, the patient's despairing attacks on the process, attacks on the analyst's understanding, deprive the analyst of the comfort, the faith that enables him to do the work, the belief that understanding is possible and that it matters. This tends to, and should, precipitate a genuine crisis for the analyst, who is brought face to face with authentic doubts about and with the limits of his understanding. Understanding does not provide much solace for, among other things, real loss, grief over lost opportunities, irreconcilable conflicts, and, ultimately, death. The analyst's understanding, no matter how powerfully transformative and also comforting it may be in some respects, is incapable of warding off or providing restitution for these losses, conflicts, and limitations. Their meanings may change in some ways over the course of an analysis, but the actuality of human pain, conflict, and suffering imposes constraints on the range of possible meanings. That realization is painful—necessarily so—for both patient and analyst.

The dread and despair that the analyst sometimes feels in relation to the attacks on understanding is not simply a reenactment of an assigned role. The value and hopes that we analysts place on our understanding are an important part of what drew each of us into the field in the first place. To be confronted with the limitations of that understanding, our helplessness in the face of some of the deepest sources of human suffering, is cause for dread indeed.[8] The analyst's investment in her own therapeutic powers probably inevitably always functions partly to help the analyst heal herself. Helping the patient is a vehicle for regulating her own sense of helplessness, and the helplessness of her own internal objects, projected into the patient.[9]

A central consequence of the analyst's personal stake in the efficacy of his own understanding is that periods of impasse in analyses are likely to disrupt the analyst's own personal equilibrium, awakening the analyst's own dreads, and challenging the analyst's hopes not only for the patient but for himself as well.

An important feature in the the emergence from stalemates is the analyst's ability to regain her equanimity despite the collapse of understanding, her ability to survive the destructiveness of the patient's dread and despair without withdrawing. Sometimes, when language itself has proved treacherous and corrupt, the analyst can say nothing; affirmation through continued presence is the only solution. As one of Winnicott's patients put it, "The only time I felt hope was when you told me that you could see no hope, and you continued with the analysis" (1960, p. 152).

Therefore, some of the most important work done during impasses and stalemates is in the countertransference, in the analyst's struggle to regain his own sense of the meaning and value of his understanding, despite its limitations. By finding again and redefining his own realistic sense of hope, the analyst is more able to find a voice in which to speak to the patient that is different from the voices of the patient's past, offering their perpetually enticing and perpetually disappointing false promises.

In a way, a stalemate in understanding resides at the heart of every analysis. The movement that is regarded as a sign that things are going well is always partially a distraction from the patient's deepest dreads and despairs about what the analyst has to offer. Sometimes although analyst and patient never reach that dead center at the heart of the work, very useful gains are attained nevertheless. Sometimes that despair is reached and lived in and through in a single, extended crisis, out of which a different sort of hope is generated. In other analyses, the crises that redefine and transform hope are encountered in small, episodic minicrises. The following series of sessions in the treatment of a young woman provides an example of the gradual, incremental transformation of hope.

ILLUMINATION AND THE DARKNESS OF THE MOON

Sarah, a dancer in her early thirties, entered treatment with a sense of inhibition and internal struggle in both her professional and her romantic life. She is the extremely talented, only child of a successful and celebrated performing artist. The career of the father, a dancer turned choreographer, was the centerpiece around which family life was organized. The demands of his "genius" were complexly intertwined with numerous infantile claims. He dominated his seemingly willing wife and daughter with a mixture of brilliant intellectual and artistic power and intense, brittle fragility.

Because her relationships with men were often so troubled and painful, ending in abandonment and a sense of having been betrayed, Sarah sought a female analyst, collecting names from friends. In that process, she had been given my name; although a man, she was told I was kind. She thought it might be useful if she could work with a man in a constructive way. She felt reasonably comfortable in our initial consultations, and treatment was begun on a once-a-week basis. Second sessions were often scheduled, but there was no regular second appointment. I strongly recommended more frequent sessions. Yet, although she had trouble explaining why, it seemed very important to her not to have two regular appointments per week.

We came to appreciate how deeply embedded the frequency issue was with her sense of her own boundaries and her conflicts about submission and surrender. Sarah longed for a more benign but still powerful and dominant paternal figure. Her project—finding a better father—was something I saw as part of the problem, not part of the solution. A central part of my problem and challenge in the countertransference was to find a way to be with her that was neither malignantly nor benignly paternal. The issue of the session frequency was merely the beginning of a long series of such opportunities. If I insisted on greater frequency, I may have been able to get her to agree; however, we would have enacted a surrender to my presumably greater knowledge. If I accepted the single session, I was enacting the other side of the countertransference, demonstrating that I was different from the dominant father—a better father.

Undoubtedly, a central feature of the countertransference was preset in the particular piece of my reputation she had happened across. She could have heard a great deal else about me besides that some people thought I was kind. Many people have other opinions. It was as if she came to me with a promise from me that I had not made. She longed for and dreaded both the bad father and the good father. I came advertised as a good father who would help her ward off the conflictual longing for the bad father.

It should be noted that I found her extremely appealing as a patient/daughter. She made it very easy for me to feel fatherly in a way I found quite pleasing and reassuring, and she had many qualities that I could only hope my own much younger daughters might have when they reached her age. There was something very compelling and enticing about the opportunity she offered me to play out the role of a kindly and very helpful father to a very special daughter.

The third alternative was clearly to be neither a bad father nor a good one, but her analyst. But, as always, this was a lot easier said than done. I raised questions about the meaning of the frequency of the sessions; I interpreted what I felt were some of the dynamic issues. But she ended up feeling the same, and I still had to choose which way to go. I chose to accept the frequency she was comfortable with as the lesser of two evils, knowing in my bones that it was, even if arguably the lesser, still an evil with consequences we would have to discover and contend with.

Considerable progress was made over a year or so, leading to the events I will describe here. Sarah had been offered an extremely important opportunity to audition for a celebrated dance company that would have greatly enhanced her career. As was her habit, she had "run through" the dance with her father and, as was often the case, ended up feeling crushed by his predictably harsh criticism. She was particularly upset because the actual audition was only two weeks away, and she felt further exposure to his criticism would undermine her confidence and chances for success.

These father/daughter coaching sessions had been a subject of considerable analytic inquiry. They tended to have a sadomasochistic quality. In fact, when the father was particularly upset about something in his own life, he would insist that Sarah perform for him. It seemed as if his domination of her through criticism had a calming effect on him. In allowing herself to be subdued by him, she was, in some sense, offering herself in masochistic love to him. This project, however, was now in stark conflict with her concerns about her own performance. She respected him greatly, got a greal deal from his criticism and hoped-for seal of approval. Yet she felt very shaky. She wanted to resist his brilliant but critical scrutiny but could not find a way.

I wondered why she could not simply refuse to rehearse for him until after the audition, insisting on the importance of a protected space for her own creative process. As we explored why this obvious device had never occurred to her, it became clear that the only claims for creative space that had ever been made in the family were the father's. Making such claims on her own behalf was a powerful symbolic act. However, she reported in the next sesion that she had been able to do so. (I wondered about the implications of her making the claim for her own space under my protective guidance: Was it her claim, or mine, or an indeterminate amalgam?)

She was still quite concerned, because in a tryout with some friends, she found herself involved in an internal argument with her father, fending off his criticisms, at the very same time she was performing. She finally stopped in the middle of the rehearsal and screamed at her father, as if to insist that he get out of her head. Having "lost it" in rehearsal, however, she feared "losing it" in the actual audition. I told her I thought she had not so much lost something as found something, an inner freedom to find her own distinctive voice and shape her own creative process.

This was the last regularly scheduled session before her audition. We were now faced with the question of whether to schedule an additional session. Sarah was conflicted. She felt she might benefit from seeing me but was concerned about having things "churned up" at a time when it was important for her to feel calm and centered. It was apparent to both of us that there were strong resonances between the coaching with her father and the analytic work with me. It seemed very important that she decide whether she could use a session, whether it would feel as if it was in her genuine interests. I found myself in the now-familiar position of trying to avoid iatrogenically fueling her rage through reenactments of her sadomasochistic interactions with her father yet also trying to avoid undercutting her rage by going out of my way to be benevolent. I suggested the following: We would schedule a tentative appointment, and she could let me know whether she felt she could use the time in a way that felt comfortable to her. This suited her. She said she could let me know in a few days, which would be several days before the appointment in question.

I did not hear from her on the day she indicated she would call. I knew this was bound to be a complicated decision and was not surprised. I did have the option of filling the time with another patient, but I decided not to. I thought Sarah might decide belatedly to use the time, and I thought it would be good if I had it available to give to her. I did not feel particularly benevolent in making this decision; I had felt very squeezed for time I needed to do personal bookkeeping and all sorts of other chores. I could certainly use the time well if Sarah decided not to come. Although I did not tell her, I hoped she would come, and there was a slightly manic device along the lines of sour grapes in the thoughts of the better use to which I would put my time if she did not. She finally called the afternoon before the scheduled appointment. She said that she was aware that she was late in calling; if I had otherwise filled the hour, I should let her know and she would understand. However, if it was still open, she would like to use it.

She began the session the next day by suggesting that there had been, in fact, a great struggle about whether to come for the session. She realized that the whole problem of agendas was very important and difficult for her. She also noted that there were certain aspects of the arrangements for the audition on the following day that were troublesome to her and that she wanted to discuss. I asked her to tell me a bit about her struggle about whether to come for the session. She began speaking about agendas, interactions with men, and very quickly plunged into a detailed and very disturbing story of submission and betrayal with an early boyfriend, new in its circumstances, familiar in its theme.

I began to get more and more uncomfortable. I knew that it was important that Sarah feel this session was ruled by her agenda, which was not to get "churned up" before the audition. I also knew she wanted to talk about the arrangements for the audition. Yet she had become very involved in the story she was recounting. I felt that she would experience my interrupting the story as an intrusion, an imposition of my agenda upon her. I also felt quite sure that the story itself could usefully be considered an allusion to her experience of our relationship (Gill, 1982). But I felt that to make such a transference interpretation at this point could only be disruptive. There seemed to be no way for me to help her maintain her agenda that did not feel like a demand that she submit to mine. In my efforts to figure out how to help her avoid getting churned up, I was getting very churned up indeed. The position I felt boxed into was making me angry at her, and I felt there was no way to interpret what was happening without using the interpretation as a retaliatory act. It occurred to me that in certain ways she could herself be quite controlling, perhaps rather like her father. I wondered whether there had been a reversal of roles, with me now having an experience not unlike her own helplessness vis-à-vis the father.

Finally, about ten minutes before the end of the session, I did interrupt; I told her that there were only ten minutes left and that I was mindful of her having said she wanted to speak of the arrangements for the audition. She thanked me and told me of her concerns, which, of course, were also thematically related to the issues at hand—power and submission.

I was looking forward to the next session with eagerness and apprehension. I was very interested to know how the audition went, and whether what seemed to me to be my clumsiness in the prior session had had any negative effects. She began by reporting having been quite upset by the previous session. Despite her interest in keeping her own concerns in focus, she felt she had succumbed to my interest in her "resistance" to coming for the session and my agenda concerning her feelings about our relationship.

We explored her experience of my interest in her resistance and our relationship, and I asked her about what she felt might have motivated my insistence on pursuing these areas. She said she thought I might have been angry at her for delaying so long in calling me, thereby showing what I might have regarded as a disrespect for my time. Perhaps my inquiry, like her father's coaching, had a punative quality—I was reasserting my dominance and punishing her for being insufficiently solicitous of me. This connected up with previous explorations of her often quite discerning perceptions concerning my preference for being in control.

After considerable discussion of these aspects of her thoughts and fantasies, I told her about my experience of the previous session. Although it was certainly true that I am interested in the issues of agendas and the way they figure in our relationship, and that there are times when I surely get quite pushy about it, I was not aware of feeling any special sense of urgency in getting her to speak of that last time. It was true that she gave me something of a choice, and I chose to ask about the struggle over the sessions rather than her concern about the arrangements for the audition. I then described how problematic I felt it was to figure out how to help her reassert her own priorities once she was into the story she was telling me. She acknowledged that she did feel hurt when I interrupted her ten minutes before the end of the session. It felt like the many times her parents seemed uninterested in her doubts and pain. She had been quite angry at me (for the first time since the treatment began) for my imposing my agendas upon her in that session, both my original agenda about our relationship and my interruption of her toward the end of the session. However, she soon decided that my previous good record was more than enough for her to feel that my motives must have been benign, that I must have her best interests at heart.

From the beginning of our work I had noted how careful she was to portray me both to herself and to me as someone with only extremely pure and noble qualities. I pointed out to her that her effort to maintain the image of me as benign, despite her experience of the last session, was a repetition of her long-standing pattern of protecting men as she felt more and more betrayed in her submission to them. She agreed.

I then asked her more about the delay in calling me and her sense that I might have been retaliating for that. She said she had decided that it was crucial for her to take her time on this important decision, even if it inconvenienced me. But that is also why she feared I might be angry. I suggested that her putting me off was analogous to her claiming of her own creative space to practice and her kicking her father out of her head during her rehearsal. It was an act of independence that was difficult and also a bit frightening. She agreed. On the other hand, there was, arguably, a provocativeness in not calling. She might have called just to keep me posted on her difficulty in deciding. Perhaps I had sensed some provocation or interpreted her independence as a provocation, without realizing it.

I then wondered whether she had not become frightened at the act of defiance and felt a subsequent inclination to find some way to reestablish the connection with me along old lines. Perhaps she was looking for an opportunity in the subsequent session to find something of mine to defer to, an agenda with which to comply.

Sarah seemed quite struck with this idea and reported a further, substantiating bit of information. Before she finally called, she had the fleeting thought that I probably had given the time to someone else. In some sense, the situation was a test of my caring for her, particularly a test of my attitude toward her independence. When she found I had held the time open for her, she felt both very pleased and very guilty. She felt quite certain that this guilt had made her eager to find something to which she could defer in the subsequent session, reestablishing her position as a dutiful daughter and my position as a grand and benign father. We agreed that we were both struggling to find some way to connect with each other outside the old patterns, but that it was, as yet, unclear as to how we might do that more fully.

Several weeks later, following further work on various aspects of these issues, Sarah brought in a dream that struck both of us as a vivid representation of what we were struggling with.

There is a hazy early part of the dream which I do not remember, but has something to do with a man who has gone. Then I am walking at night, turn a corner, and become suddenly aware that something terrible and frightening has happened with the moon. The illumination of the moon has somehow become separated from the moon itself. The light has become detached from the dark sphere of the moon, which is only very dimly visible.

We developed the following understanding in our joint associations and speculations about the dream. She always felt her value to be an extension of her parents' splendor, both in her dealings with others and in her inner sense of herself. There has been a re-creation in her transferential relationship with me of the hope for security and illumination through the reflected glory and purity she attributes to me. In her recent experiences (both in and outside analysis), she has begun to feel herself as separate from that reflected glory. In the disillusionment in old hopes, new possibilities have begun to open up. Like the moon, she does not as yet generate her own light and heat; there is a sense of darkness and void that is frightening. But the faint outline of the dark sphere of the moon coincides with her own experience that the darkness is also an opportunity for something more self-generated and deeply personal to emerge.

IMAGINATION AND THE DIALECTICS OF HOPE

I find it most helpful to think of the patient's hopes in analysis, particularly at the beginning, as neither purely regressive (in Boris's sense of hope as smothering the possibility for desire) nor purely progressive (in Balint's sense of hope as a "new beginning" or Winnicott's notion of a knowing, natural self-healing process). The patient's initial hopes lend themselves to being understood and used in many different ways. Like most else in human experience, they are fundamentally ambiguous and provide the potential for many different forms of organization. What is most therapeutic is the analyst's ability to find opportunities for new growth embedded in old hopes, to see in the patient's hope a dialectical relationship between the static and familiar and the longing for something fuller and more rewarding. Old hopes, as Wordsworth suggests, are born from dread. They are solutions to situations that no longer exist. As we saw in the previous chapter, the hopes and wishes generated from old traumas are not infallibly helpful guides to what is currently useful: "A profound confusion of wish and need is one of the hallmarks of injury. The need is very real but the psychological injury leaves the person unequipped to recognize what was/is really needed" (Russell, 1993). To become more serviceable as a basis for generating personal meaning, old hopes require transformation within the interaction between analysand and analyst.

Consider Robert's initial hopes for analysis as providing him with a guaranteed guide for living (his desperate and necessary faith in his mother) and a magical entry into manhood (his longing for his father). Were these hopes gratified? Were they renounced? In some sense they were gratified. Different features of the analytic perspective and my personal application of it did become a serviceable guide for living. There were important ways in which he did find a father in me, a father who could respect and help reveal to him his own potency, his own manhood. Yet, in another sense, Robert's hopes were abandoned, at least in their original forms. He needed to learn that no one, including his mother or an analyst, has a surer guide to living than the one that he himself generates through reflecting on his own experience. And he needed to learn that no other man can bestow on him a manhood that he can and must fashion for himself. The dichotomy between gratification and frustration, derived from classical drive theory, does not do justice to the process. Transformation, metamorphosis—these seem more suitable terms.

Some of most popular clinical concepts become popular, I believe, not necessarily because of their accuracy (always difficult to ascertain), but because they provide a compelling, more hopeful way for the analyst and analysand to think about and live through difficult, uncomfortable clinical situations.[10] Kohut's empathic stance makes it possible for the analyst to respond to noisy, otherwise insufferable demands not as pathological self-absorption but as a striving for narcissistic equilibrium. Winnicott's distinction between developmental needs and instinctual wishes makes it possible for the analyst to respond to entitlement not as an incessant claim for infantile fulfillment but as a self-healing return to points of parental failure. The contemporary Kleinian notion of projective identification makes it possible for the analyst to regard the often intolerable anxiety, boredom, and terror that accompanies work with very disturbed patients not as a cause for alarm and escape but as evidence of the patient's unconscious efforts to communicate features of dissociated experiences or early life. I am not suggesting that any of these widely applied clinical concepts is necessarily wrong or inaccurate, but rather that one of their greatest values lies in the imaginative yield they open up for the analyst to find new possibilities in old conditions.[11]

In a very broad sense, psychopathology might well be considered a failure of imagination, a life that is stuck because old constraints foreclose the possibility of new experiences, new states of mind. The analyst can sometimes envision other ways of being and being-with, other forms through which the patient's experience, both past and present, might be organized and developed. And that imaginative reshaping opens up new possibilities for the patient, both in thought and in action. (The input from a supervisor, consultant, or colleague, of course, opens up the possibility of further imaginative constructions.)

One of the major implications of this understanding of the way clinical concepts operate is that the new possibilities, the new meanings are not simply in the patient but in the interaction between patient and analyst. New words, spoken by the analyst and lived in by the patient, can break up old, familiar states of mind and also can create new states of mind. In response to interpretations or questions, some patients say, "I just cannot think about that." Sometimes I have found it useful to ask them to see what happens when they try. It is as if the new thoughts threaten to take them someplace they have never quite been before, and the fears connected with that novelty are important to understand. Consider a brief example.

A man who had been in analysis quite a few years was intoning his familiar lament about the hopelessness for intimacy between himself and his wife. They were both too traumatized as children, he believed, too brittle, too "sensitive." The evening before he had been waiting eagerly for her return from her own career activities, late in the evening (not unusual for New York City working couples). He was happy to see her and hoped for an intimate, possibly sexual, hour or two between them. She came home distracted and grumpy, which he felt was her usual state. She had things she had to get done before settling down and focusing on being with him. He waited, feeling increasingly ignored by her. By the time she was ready to relax, he was no longer interested in being with her. It was hopeless, he felt. A woman less afraid of intimacy would make a more suitable wife for him; a man more able to sustain deprivation and insult would make a more suitable husband for her. They were hopeless together.

We had been over this ground many times before and had approached the issues in many different ways. This time I found myself trying to imagine how he might deal with his skittish wife more successfully. I asked him what he thought would happen if, instead of waiting patiently and absorbing what he felt was her insulting neglect, he told her right away that he was happy to see her, wanted to spend some time with her, was aware that she probably had things to take care of, and would be happy to do what he could to help her speed her chores. All this was actually true to his feelings, although it had never occurred to him to say anything like this to her.

I was less interested in suggesting a different course of behavior to him than in helping him imagine and think himself into a different way of being so that we could find out why such a way of being had not occurred to him. There was, of course, an implied directive in this intervention that violates the classical ideal of analytic nondirectiveness.[12] I think there are always implied directives (both conscious and unconscious) in both analytic interpretations and silences. The analyst is a continual coparticipant in the process and the meanings generated from it. What seems most important to me is the use of the intervention primarily to facilitate the inquiry, rather than effect behavioral change itself, and the effort to include in the inquiry the impact of the analyst's participation.[13]

After thinking about it for a while, he responded with amazement. He said that it was as if I were telling him that an approaching tornado would be best responded to by walking over to a nearby fence and balancing on it with one foot. As he thought himself into a different stance with his wife, he realized to what extent he in fact did experience her moods as acts of nature rather than something he might have any sort of impact on. As he thought his way into a different, more "successful" sequence of events with her, he became aware of a sense of loss in relation to his own deeply felt hurt and hopelessness. His characteristic response to these situations with his wife was to sit for a long time, alone, in the dark. There was something about the impossibility of it all that was extremely important to him; it secured him in his sense of who he was, in his complex connection to his extremely depressed and remote mother, in his omnipotent sense of control over a bleak but predictable world. My suggestion of another approach to his wife opened up the possibility of a different sort of world, a world in which he was not yet at all sure he could or wanted to live. We subsequently explored at considerable length the pervasiveness and depth of his sense of loss connected with any fundamental movement toward intimacy between him and his wife.

This particular intervention was effective in opening up new possibilities for this patient, both experientially and behaviorally. It could not have been analytically helpful (apart from possible behavioral change) early in the treatment; a great deal of work in clarifying dynamic aspects of both his relationship with his wife and his relationship with me had preceded the session in question. Part of what seemed to work was a reformulation of his situation and his past in a less foreclosed, more open fashion. What happened was not the emergence of something lying dormant in him but something quite new created in the interaction between his underused resources and my ability, at that point, to imagine another form of experience and interaction.

Friedman (1988) describes the process through which interpretation operates in a way that closely matches my experience of it.

> But it is not necessary for the therapist to know exactly what he is encouraging. It is sufficient that he treats the patient as though he were roughly the person he is indeed about to become. . . . The patient will explore being treated in that way: He will fill in the personal details himself. The exact meaning to the patient of the therapist's response, the exact nuance of his new self or new view, is something only he can experience, because part of its meaning comes from how it fits with all the rest of his life, which only he has lived. (p. 130)

I read Friedman to mean (this is not quite explicit) that the patient is about to become roughly the sort of person that the analyst is treating him as partly because the analyst is treating him precisely as that sort of person. Again, there is no purely autonomously generated meaning in analysis. Analytically useful forms of meaning and hope do not lie preformed in the patient; they are generated when the analyst has found a way to inspire personally meaningful forms of growth and expansion from the inside out.

There are other situations in which language itself becomes an obstacle and seems to block off new avenues of experience. Then the analyst's capacity to conceive of a world beyond the patient's use of language becomes crucial. Consider this example.

An extremely talented and accomplished writer in her late thirties enters treatment out of a sense of being "stuck," both in her relationships and in an inability to feel any deep sense of pleasure or joy in living. I experienced her as extremely engaging and lively, but I felt a sadness when in her presence that I had trouble connecting with her own conscious emotional state, which always seemed upbeat, to the point of being a bit pressured.

She had suffered enormous, devastating losses as a young child. Her mother died suddenly when she was one and a half years old. She was cared for by her father and her father's mother, but the grandmother also died when my patient was four. She was subsequently cared for by her father and her father's sisters.

The sense of loss in those early years must have been extraordinary. She lost those to whom she had been most deeply attached; those who remained also had sustained profound losses and must have been quite depressed. The father had enormous difficulty speaking about emotions.

He was a plucky survivor and would speak of "pulling the curtains" on feelings that were too upsetting. But he would slip into very deep, episodic depressions, which continued his whole life, and from which his only child would attempt to rescue him, often quite effectively. I had the sense that she was extremely resourceful and constitutionally strong, probably born with that difficult-to-describe but very crucial quality that the technical term "ego strength" refers to. She had had to become a parent to herself, a premature adult, to survive her psychologically orphaned state.

Memories of an early, repetitive dream and an early visceral experience emerged not long into the treatment. The dream, probably belonging to the years following her grandmother's death, involved a large, odd, egg-shaped object that was moving slowly down an incline, like a slide in a children's playground. The egg was made of concrete, but there was an intense sort of uncertainty about it. It was unclear whether it would remain on the slide or fall off, and, if it fell off, whether it would remain intact or shatter disastrously. It seemed both heavy and impassive, yet, at the same time, extremely brittle and vulnerable.

As a sort of waking counterpart to the dream, she remembered an odd recurrent feeling state from those years. She would feel a great heaviness in everything, as if she, her body, and everyone else were made of concrete. As with the dream, the feeling state seemed to combine a numbing sense of density with a feeling of intense fragility, as if everything could shatter in a moment.

Important analytic work was accomplished over the course of the first two years. She became aware that she suffered from a chronic feeling of dread, a perpetual sense of things building up. The content differed from time to time: debts, bookkeeping, deadlines, obligations, an urgent sense of running out of time. We began to realize that the content of whatever pressure she was feeling at any particular time was less important than her way of maintaining a haunted tone to her life, a sense that she had been neglecting something that was building up to a precarious degree. She began to realize that the tension created by her characterological procrastination resonated with the feeling of the childhood dream, as if she never could allow herself to be free of its grip.

Another interesting discovery also seemed related to the dream and the memory. She now recalled that she had been quite ill in those years after the grandmother's death. She was told that it was extremely important for her to rest for extended periods of time, that the germs which had been making her ill were still lying dormant in her body and might break out to reinfect her if she did not get sufficient rest. Although she had never previously made the connection, we speculated that the notion that only immobility could forestall a disastrous internal explosion was probably one source for the imagery of the dream and the memory. But we both had the sense that there was more involved.

In the third year of the analysis, she felt quite hopeless for an extended period over several months. We had worked on the many ways in which she set up her life to enable her to avoid unpleasant, discouraging feelings. She now felt much more aware of what troubled her, but also overwhelmed and defeated. Words, which before had been her greatest ally in keeping her going, feeling active, and working on things, now seemed only to serve as a means for expressing her hopelessness and despair. She often found herself feeling at a "loss for words."

My experience was now quite different. The sadness that I initially felt in her presence now seemed very connected with what she was speaking about. I also felt quite defeated at times, as if there were nothing to do, nothing to say, as if a heaviness had settled on my office that enveloped the two of us. We began to realize that we were now both living in the affective world of the early dream and bodily experience. It seemed crucial for us to both feel a sense of utter futility and dread. There was simply "no way out." She was very worried that I would abandon her, let her "slip away," replace her with other patients who could make better progress. She seemed always startled by indications of my commitment to her: willingness to schedule missed sessions, flexibility in fees, or anticipations of the treatment continuing for quite some time. We began to realize that her early experience with her father loomed as a backdrop for the connection between us. Would I be able to tolerate her hopelessness? Would I "pull the curtains," abandoning her to save my own mental equilibrium? Could I tolerate being with her without words that could take us someplace?

She began to have a series of dreams that seemed thematically connected with the childhood dream. She was shut inside small houses; there were scenes of natural beauty outside, but her windows were boarded up. There were odd monsters: a sea creature, coming up from the depths, with a "sort of face" that looked almost human; shapeless, battling monsters that ended up, somewhat tamed, in the backseat of her car, empowering her in a vague way. I began to have the sense that the egg was opening up, that she was allowing into her experience the threatening, formless feelings that had been encased within the egg, never before fully felt, never symbolized, never integrated into the rest of her self-organization.

Eventually the slide returned, this time with her on it.

I dreamed of a group of people in a landscape of high hills. The ground was hard and cracked, like baked earth or stone. There was a slide—some of the people were going down. I decided I would also; there was a sense of daring or danger about the decision. The ride is very fast, and shoots back up at the bottom, returning her to where she started.

These dreams, accompanying the sense of futility that enveloped her experience and my own for a period of months, proved a turning point. Language returned in a much less pressured way, and other things besides despair seemed worth speaking about again. Feelings were fuller, and both pleasure and pain were experienced with a greater intensity. The capacity to imagine something constructive growing out of a full immersion in the futility and senselessness of her pain carried her through this phase of the analytic process to richer forms of experience.

T. S. Eliot struggled with the transformation of hope in a different context.

> I said to my soul, be still, and wait without hope
> For hope would be hope for the wrong thing. . . .
> Wait without thought, for you are not ready for
> thought:
> So the darkness shall be the light, and the stillness
> the dancing. ("East Coker," 1963, p. 186)

Similarly, the hope that the patient brings to the analysis and the hope that drives the motion of the work is always partially "hope for the wrong thing." The patient's initial hopes are always a complex blend of wishes and needs, hopes fashioned from pain, frustration, longing, laced with restoration, magical transformation, and retribution. According to the Greek myth, Zeus put hope in the very bottom of Pandora's box, beneath greed, vanity, slander, envy, and the other dark realms of human experience. Sometimes, hope for the right thing can be reached only through an immersion in prolonged and harrowing dread.

ENDINGS

Of all the odd features of the analytic relationship, the ending of it is the oddest of all. It is a very strange good-bye, for both analysand and analyst. The technical term termination suggests the somber finality, so difficult to grasp in a relationship not interrupted by death or growing estrangement. The king's instrutions to the White Rabbit in *Alice in Wonderland* have always captured for me the feeling of abruptness and arbitrariness of termination: "Begin at the beginning and go on till you come to the end: then stop."

The problem, of course, is deciding when the end has been reached. The analytic literature provides probably less illumination on this question than on any other aspect of psychoanalysis. Terms like "complete analyses" or "natural terminations" are used not infrequently. These terms had some meaning in the early decades of analysis, when the process lasted several months and was expected to reach certain prescribed dynamic issues. In today's analytic world, with its plethora of theories and its staggering proliferation of different ways of thinking about mind, these terms have little real meaning. (The concept of a "complete" analysis is now most often found in its negative form as a term of abuse, as in "He is obviously incompletely analyzed.")

In fact, terms such as complete and natural serve to conceal what has become painfully apparent about the ending of analysis—its inevitable incompleteness and unnaturalness. Ending is necessary, if the analytic work is not to become a static alternative to a fully lived life. But there is always more to learn; there are always ways in which the analyst and the analytic process could continue to enrich experience.

Why ever stop? Apart from considerations of time and money (very real considerations), analysis, by its very nature, demands a suspension of choice and responsibility. No matter what is happening in the analysand's life, there is always the sense that things may be different when the analysis is over. No matter what is happening at the moment, there is the sense that one will deal with it in one's session the next day. One of the startling realizations upon leaving analysis is the sense that one is now fully responsible for one's life. The suspension that analysis provides, useful, necessary, enriching, is now over.

Analysis must end not only because the therapeutic suspension (or regression) it provides becomes constraining if indefinitely perpetuated. Ironically, the very dyadic nature of the analytic relationship comes eventually to constrain the full exploration of the analysand's personal experience. The shared consciousness between analysand and analyst, if things have gone well, has opened up domains and forms of experience not available before. But, at some point, the analysand has to take back the analysis and to make it fully his own. If the analysand is to do so, the analyst must be able to become reconciled to the limits of her own participation and understanding, to feel comfortable both with what she has been able to do and also with what she has not been able to do. The patient's fullest hopes, both the rational and the irrational, are never fully realized; that can be painful and the occasion for real grief on the part of both analyst and analysand. But an analysis that has gone well is also the occasion for genuine hope on the part of the analysand, and a renewal of faith in the analytic method for the analyst.

I noted in chapter 3 that a full appreciation of the metatheoretical revolution demands a very different approach to termination. The understandings generated in analysis are seen as co-creations of analysand and analyst, generated in the complex encounter between the analysand's experience and ideas and the analyst's experience and theoretical perspectives. It is crucial for the analyst to anticipate, with the analysand, that the analysand will grow past the understandings they have generated together. To assume that that understanding is "complete," the analysand "fully analyzed," is to fix the latter forever in a conflict between personal growth and loyalty to the analyst. To anticipate and welcome change, change beyond the analyst's participation and, perhaps, capacity to understand, is to free the analysand to both treasure the analytic work that has been done and remain open to the ways in which it will inevitably be transcended.

The ending of a book about psychoanalytic experience and psychoanalytic ideas has something in common with ending the psychoanalytic process with a patient. It is a commonplace for writers to report a depressive experience upon completion of a book. That state may have a particular quality for writers of clinical theory. It is hard enough to have to declare any book finished. While you are working on it, it is open, alive, still pregnant with unrealized possibilities. Once it is sent by the publisher to the printer, it is finished, fixed, unalterable.

The particular wrinkle for the author of clinical theory is that while the book has stopped, work goes on. He sees his patients the next day, and the inadequacy of the theory to capture new features of the clinical experience soon becomes inescapable. He notices something new, or something old in a new way. He realizes that in writing about one thing, he has neglected other important things. Books of psychoanalytic theory are less fixed structures, less like buildings, and more like action photos, snapshots of a process that, if it remains alive, is continually changing.

In ending with a patient, my deepest hope for the impact of our work is that it be valued without being sanctified, that it finds a place in her experience without superimposing a set of constraints on the ongoing personal generation of her experience. I have come to think of the relationship between psychoanalytic theory and clinical practice in a similar way, and therefore have similar hopes for readers of psychoanalytic books, mine and those of others. Einstein's attitude toward theory in physics captures for me the obvious limits yet enduring value of psychoanalytic theory: "One thing I have learned in a long life: that all our science, measured against reality, is primitive and childlike—and yet it is the most precious thing we have" (quoted in Ferris, 1988, p. 15).

NOTES

INTRODUCTION

1. Schliemann has been described as the "quintessential nineteenth-century hero" (Fleishman, 1992, p. 34). Peter Gay (1988) suggests that Freud envied Schliemann above all others and hoped to become "the Schliemann of the mind" (p. 326). In a letter to Wilhelm Fliess in the early 1890s, Freud compares analytic success in uncovering an early childhood memory to the discovery of Troy: "[The memory] answers all requirements and into which all left-over riddles flow; it is everything at once, sexual, unconscious, natural, etc. I scarcely dare to believe it properly. It is as if Schliemann had dug up Troy, considered legendary, once again" (quoted in Gay, 1988, p. 172).

CHAPTER 1

1. This is James Strachey's original translation from Freud's "*Wo Es war, soll Ich werden.*" There have been many recent arguments in favor of a different translation, including "Where it was, there I shall become." (See, for example, Lear, 1990, pp. 168–69; Loewald, 1980, p. 280*n*)

2. Hans Loewald's work and recent contributions by Arnold Modell, Fred Pine, Joseph Sandler, Roy Schafer, and others have pointed to the latent supportive, "holding" substructure of the analytic situation and relationship, and the conditions of safety that it provides. Clearly, classical analysis can be practiced in a warm and engaging fashion. As Merton Gill (1982) and Samuel Lipton (1977) have argued, all indications are that Freud often practiced in just that way.

3. The equation of the patient's reality with subjectivity and the analyst's reality with objectivity played a prominent role in what might be considered "classical" interpersonal psychoanalysis as well. Irvin Hoffman (1987b) has pointed to this equation in Harry Stack Sullivan's view of the therapeutic process as involving a clarification of "parataxic distortions." Fromm was similarly a devoted believer in the powers of rationality and identified neurosis with immaturity and lack of productivity. These ideas are markedly different from those of many contemporary interpersonal authors, such as Edgar Levenson and Merton Gill, who tend to characterize their epistemology in terms of "perspectivism." (This shift will be taken up in greater detail in chapter 2.)

4. Freud also became increasingly interested in "character pathology," where the problem was not a discrete, ego-alien symptom but the structure of the personality as a whole. But the types of character pathology with which Freud was concerned (1916, pp. 311–36)—such as those "wrecked by success," "the exceptions," and "criminals from a sense of guilt"—were personalities who were poorly adapted to their society, whose conflicts over their sexual and aggressive impulses interfered with productive functioning.

5. Fromm drew heavily on the literature of existential philosophy and existential psychology. These disciplines and their applications in existential psychoanalysis have had a great deal to say about personal meaning, subjectivity, and authenticity, much of which has been rediscovered and reworked in a particularly psychoanalytic fashion in the analytic literature of recent decades. What contemporary psychoanalytic theorists have been able to contribute is a study of meaning and subjective experience in the evolving context of object relations, both in childhood and in the analytic situation.

6. As Gerald Fogel, in his evaluation of Loewald's contribution, puts it:

> the "classical" neurotic patient becomes irrelevant, no longer exists in Loewald's paradigm. . . . Although a variable pre-oedipal core that varies in its accessibility to analysis may be more common in our time, many so-called "difficult" patients may appear less so as these former difficulties with theory become clarified. (1989, p. 428)

7. The term meaningful here refers to a sense of personal value, importance, and devotion, not to semiotic significance or intelligibility. The shift in modern psychoanalysis from rational explanation to personal meaning cannot be explained away by arguing that Freud's drive concepts always referred to both causal explanation and meaning or "un-

derstanding" (for example, as is stated by such writers as Habermas and Ricoeur in their reinterpretations of Freud).

8. Charles Taylor (1991, p. 48), who approaches these issues from an extremely cogent and illuminating philosophical perspective, argues that selfhood—identity and the need for recognition—was not absent in premodern times, but that it was provided by social structures and, hence, was unproblematic.

9. Sterba notes the necessity for him to become involved in "attacking that part of the ego which was using the patient's unhappy experience with the physician in her childhood to obstruct the analysis" (1934, p. 368) as well as "counteracting part of the super-ego's opposition" (p. 368) in which she was defending herself against the erotic feelings toward the analyst because they represented her conflictual underlying erotic fantasies toward her father.

10. In her fascinating autobiographical account of her experiences in Vienna in the 1930s, Esther Menaker (1989) describes a conversation with her analyst, Anna Freud, about this very question. Menaker recalled an appendectomy at age seven with anesthesia, but without any explanations or preparations. Anna Freud responded that at that time, "children were generally treated as creatures who would be unable to understand the complex world of adult reality, and so no attempt was made to tailor explanations to the limitations of their comprehension." She then recalled a similar experience of her own, an appendectomy at the same age. By way of preparation she had been told by her father (Sigmund Freud) that she was going to have her picture taken (Menaker, 1989, pp. 35–36).

11. This view has been developed with great thoughtfulness by William Grossman, who argues that

> *the problem of the "self" in analysis is a matter of tactics and technique. Problems of analysis of self-material have been mistakenly regarded as showing the inadequacy of Freudian drive and ego-psychological theory. Rather than a theoretical difficulty, the trouble was a lack of systematic consideration of what goes into the art of the analyst—what Lowenstein called "dosage, timing and tact". . . Mechanical, insensitive or poorly timed interpretations of drive and conflict, sometimes "wild analysis," do not refute theory but expose its misapplications.* (1982, pp. 931–32)

12. Taylor (1991) argues that the "ideal of authenticity" pervades modernity. A common commitment to such an ideal underlies the great diversity of recent contributions to the analytic literature. Both the importance of and

the problems with the concept of authenticity will be taken up in chapter 5.

13. Ogden's contributions represent the culmination of an important tradition of analytic work with schizophrenic patients (see Boyer and Giovacchini, 1967, Rosenfeld, 1987, Searles, 1979, 1986) that has focused increasingly on the importance of both subjectivity and intersubjectivity in a way that has had an important impact on analytic theorizing and practice with all patients.

14. The progressively radical sequence through which Kohut's innovations were introduced is instructive. In their original form, Kohut's (1971) theoretical and technical contributions concerned patients with "narcissistic personality disorders," considered nonanalyzable in the traditional classical manner. These were patients who suffered a more fundamental disturbance than ordinary neurotic patients, with their conflicts between drive-based impulses and defenses. Six years later Kohut (1977) realized that his innovations pertained not only to more disturbed patients; rather, they offered an alternative frame of reference for understanding and working with all patients. Now "disorders of the self" are understood to underlie all forms of psychopathology, including classical neurosis.

15. Jonathan Lear (1990), drawing heavily on Loewald's vision and reworking of Freud, has recently proposed an interpretation of psychoanalysis as evolving into a science of subjectivity: "Psychoanalysis did not begin with this self-understanding: it had to discover this about itself" (p. 22).

16. Winnicott and Kohut provide an interesting counterpoint to Loewald. They offer a view of the self as unfolding in the responsive presence of others, in contrast to Loewald's view of the self as built up out of layers of interactions with others. Bion and Lacan provide further alternatives with respect to the route to authentic subjectivity; both seem to point to a liberating process of being sprung from dulling familiarities of language and enculturation (Sass 1988).

17. Michael Eigen is one of the few contemporary writers to describe the radically innovative project shared by the more visionary recent analytic authors. He has written about the way in which Winnicott, Bion, and Lacan

> express the subject's struggle to live faithfully, together with impediments to this endeavour. Their central concern is the subject's radically reorienting relations to lived truth as it moves through vicissitudes of meaning. . . . If one reads these authors carefully, one discovers that the primary object of creative experiencing is not mother or father but the unknowable

ground of creativeness as such. . . . *This is a radically new enterprise within psychoanalysis proper. . . . The wholling tendency expressed here is a differentiated one. It is not primarily based on mastery or control, although circumspection comes into play. It grows most basically through a faith in a spontaneous play of experiencing and meaning which aims to express and unfold what is most real for the subject, his emotional truth or way of being a subject, who one is.* (1981, pp. 428–31)

18. Gill (1983, p. 213) has quipped that "an analyzable patient is a patient with whom the analyst can maintain the illusion of neutrality."

CHAPTER 2

1. This division between theory and metatheory is a heuristic device to help distinguish and explore recent analytic contributions. We shall see in the next chapter that, as is always the case, the real world is never as tidy as our concepts. Contributors to the development of theory have implicit metatheoretical positions; contributors to the development of metatheory often have made implicit contributions to theory.

2. Loewald (1974) has noted this essential feature of Freud's vision:

   Freud does not appear to have recognized that the objective reality of science is itself a form of reality organized (although not created in a solipsistic sense) by the human mind and does not necessarily manifest the culmination of mental development or represent any absolute standard of truth, as he assumed. (p. 364)

3. It is important to note a recurrent finding in virtually all empirical studies of the effectiveness of psychotherapy and psychoanalysis (very difficult research to do). Although analysts have traditionally put great weight on what they know and tend to regard accurate and well-timed interpretations as the key therapeutic agent in the analytic process, the research tends to find that patients do not remember interpretations or grant them much importance in themselves. Rather, it is the quality of the therapeutic relationship that seems most important. This suggests that what the analyst knows may be less important than what the analyst does with what he believes. This issue will be taken up in detail in chapter 3.

4. *If one must demonstrate ability to understand and carry out a*

"psychoanalytic process" in order to become an analyst, some rather clear concept and explicit statement of that process should exist. It does not, to this point. This unfortunate situation has to do with our habit of accepting theory as description, with our failure to develop a methodology of evidence. It may also reflect the erosion of scientific unity and professional identity . . . we need to make use of formal research methods—replicable data, research design, and measurement of process and outcome. (Compton, 1990, p. 596)

5. *If metapsychology is dying from inconsistency, let it be reborn into a vital psychoanalytic science by the effort to account for our original and always most stimulating data, the transactions of the psychoanalytic hour. And . . . let it be transfigured into an effort to achieve . . . intermediation . . . between psychoanalysis and the biological sciences of the human organism. (Holt, 1981, p. 141)*

6. This is a very different problem from the increasingly important question of the effectiveness of psychoanalysis in improving the quality of life, productivity, and physical as well as mental health. The substantiation of the utility of psychoanalysis in relation to our current concerns with cost-effectiveness and health care is related to but distinct from the question of the truth value of the analyst's ideas about what is happening (whether the treatment itself is effective or not).

7. See Spezzano (1993) for an extremely incisive discussion of the nature of psychoanalytic knowledge and a very effective response to critics who suggest that psychoanalytic concepts must be grounded in extra-clinical empirical data.

8. Consider the recent debate between Daniel Stern and Fred Pine on the theoretical concept of "symbiosis," the centerpiece of Margaret Mahler's developmental theory, which dominated the psychoanalytic imagination for several generations. Mahler's vision was based on the widely accepted premise that the infant lives in a blurry, confused world and cannot distinguish self from other people or significant others from each other. Stern draws on an impressive array of data from current infant research suggesting that the infant is much more capable of perceptual and cognitive discriminations than anyone ever imagined. The infant seems to be able to distinguish very deftly among different important people in his environment and has quite a clear sense of the distinction between himself and his mother. These data, Stern argues, disprove the assumptions underlying Mahler's account that the psychological birth of the child occurs only gradually, much later, out of a symbiotic merger with the mother. Rather, Stern

argues, the infant is involved from the beginning, in a dialectic between separateness and contact. Symbiotic fantasies, as they appear in clinical work with adults, are retrospective displacements of fantasies of later childhood (after language and symbolization have developed) back onto infancy, where they never happened.

It appears as if empirical data have sorted out truth and falseness among competing psychoanalytic concepts. Yet Pine, a collaborator of Mahler's, has fashioned a very compelling response to Stern's theory. It is hard to substantiate the notion of symbiosis as a global phase, Pine allows, but there is no way to disprove the claim that the infant experiences "moments" of symbiotic merger. Just because the infant *can* discriminate between self and others does not suggest she is doing so all the time. Symbiotic merger, precisely the experiences Mahler granted such crucial developmental import, may not occupy the infant all the time, but they may still be the primary shapers of the child's experience.

The Stern/Pine dispute provides a case study on the relation between psychoanalytic theorizing and empirical findings. There is no question that the data generated by infant research have had an important impact on ongoing theorizing. They have prompted new ideas, such as those developed by Stern, and forced an innovative reshaping of preexisting ideas, in Pine's revisions. But empirical research has not and cannot serve as a final adjudicator between the truth claims of Mahler's versus Stern's theories of child development.

9. At points Schwaber seems to acknowledge that the analyst's participation is essential, that the patient's experience cannot be known outside the analyst's participation. Yet what she emphasizes is the importance of listening for the patient's perception of the analyst's participation so as to eliminate the latter as a contaminant in the otherwise pure expression of the patient's point of view. As the impact of the analyst's input is peeled back, the centrality of the patient's own subjective point of view emerges.

> It may be the case that if, in a particular moment, the analyst's model becomes clearly recognisable, it is evident that the analyst has moved away from the immediacy of the patient's inner experience. In contrast, an interpretation which derives more closely from within the patient's, rather than the analyst's vantage point, may not be as likely to reveal a particular theoretical preference. (1990a, p. 34n.)

10. Levenson's (1992) emphasis on the "manifest" content of the patient's dreams and other communications and Bion's (1967) notion of

the analyst proceeding with "neither memory nor desire" place a similar faith in the possibility of a theory-free grasp of the patient's experience from an interpersonal and Kleinian perspective, respectively. Their approaches suffer from some of the same difficulties as Schwaber's.

11. Lawrence Friedman (1988) has offered an incisive critique of the claim by the proponents of the phenomenological strategy that they are merely exploring the patient's experience. He argues that the patient's experience does not come prepackaged by the patient but is inevitably organized within the conceptual schemes provided by the analyst's theories. The phenomenologists display an allergic attitude toward theory in general: If our concepts cannot be presented as Truth, perhaps we can dispense with concepts altogether. They are forced to choose between disclaimed theory or being unable to say anything useful at all (either to the analytic community or to their patients):

> *psychoanalysis is threatened by a general impatience with all theoretical perspectives—by the belief that we can go where psychoanalysis was leading without a compass and get there faster if we unload our conceptual baggage. . . . A good way to get lost is to go everywhere.* (Friedman, 1988, p. 276)

12. Friedman, whose work I have found a treasure trove of new and provocative thoughts, conflates complexity with ambiguity. This allows him to arrive at the surprising (and I think erroneous) conclusion that the complexity of Freudian theory embodies the principle that the patient's mind is rich with potentials that may be correctly interpreted in many equally valid ways. Friedman's reading of Freud as a constructivist, as accounting for the impact of the analyst's theory on the data found, is extremely atypical and difficult to support. Friedman is the constructivist who makes a more constructive use of Freud. Freud himself compared the input of the analyst on the analytic process to the impact of the male on gestation. The analyst, like the sperm, starts the process going but has little role after that: "On the whole, once begun, it goes its own way and does not allow either the direction it takes or the order in which it picks up its points to be prescribed for it" (Freud, 1913, p. 130).

13. Hoffman (1992) makes the important distinction between the more authoritarian, simpler positivism of Freud and his contemporaries and the more "open-minded positivism" of many authors today (for example, Pine, 1991). For the latter, reality may never be grasped fully, and there are many different truths that enable us to grasp a piece of it. Nevertheless, these authors still believe that relevant psychoanalytic

realities (the patient's experience) are something that exists in a unique, preformed fashion in the patient, that our theoretical truths enable us to approach, even if only asymptotically. From a hermeneutic/constructivist framework, reality becomes fully formed only through someone's approach to it, through a human effort to understand it. Therefore, the analyst's concepts do not grasp or uncover the patient's realities; they inevitably become part of the realities that are being understood.

14. Since the time of Schliemann (Freud's hero), archaeologists have realized that determining precisely what it was that he unearthed is very complicated and difficult. Schliemann assumed he simply uncovered the Homeric "Priam's city," late Bronze Age Troy of around 1250 B.C. Actually, it is now believed that Schliemann was digging in a layer of remnants of a much earlier settlement (dating to about 2400 to 2200 B.C.): "Today the archaeologists talk of nine principal layers with 45 'phases'" (Fleischman, 1992, p. 34). It is difficult to sort out what is what, and, interestingly, the greatest difficulty was created by Schliemann himself who dug a deep trench through the middle of everything, looking for Priam's treasure. In line with current philosophy of science, we would have to say that the act of observation itself irreversibly altered the data being observed. As with psychoanalytic understanding, it seems as if each age to some degree reinvents its own Troy.

15. Donnel Stern (1987, 1990, 1991) has made important contributions along lines similar to Hoffman's.

16. Charles Taylor (1989) has made a similar point in his philosophical analysis of self. "The self is partly constituted by its self-interpretations. . . . But the self's interpretations can never be fully explicit. Full articulacy is an impossibility. . . . We clarify one language with another, which in turn can be further unpacked, and so on" (p. 34).

17. Sass and Wolfolk (1988) have argued that, from a hermeneutic perspective, the value of good interpretations is not in a correspondence with some external, objective truth but rather in a correspondence of coherences, the tendency of analyst and analysand to organize experiences in similar ways.

18. This strategy for learning about the patient has had two sources: Harry S. Sullivan's concept of participant-observation, as developed by subsequent interpersonalists (for example, Edgar Levenson, Darlene Ehrenberg), and Melanie Klein's concept of projective identification, as developed by subsequent neo-Kleinians (Wilfred Bion, Betty Joseph, Heinrich Racker).

19. Racker (1968, p.170) sounded this warning, which has been repeated by subsequent authors who emphasize the constructive use of the ana-

lyst's experience. (See, for example, Hoffman, 1983, p. 416.)

20. The empirical solution (one day research will tell us which theory is best) and the phenomenological solution (anything goes, as long as the patient, the ultimate arbitor, says so) help define these twin dangers by solidly embracing them. The empirical ideal represents a "lapsed positivism" (I am borrowing this phrase from Brunner, 1993) and the phenomenological ideal embraces a theoretical relativism.

21. See Taylor (1991) for another compelling argument against the conclusion that anything goes. He demonstrates that any meaningful understanding of the ideal of authenticity must operate within what he calls "horizons of significance" that preclude a slide into subjectivism and "soft relativism."

22. Charles Spezzano (1993) has recently argued for a "relational model" of inquiry in psychoanalysis very similar in tone and principles to Bernstein's approach.

CHAPTER 3

1. Schwaber (1983, p. 381) and Stolorow (1986) have pointed out that although Kohut's early concern was with the "empathic stance" at the core of psychoanalytic methodology, he arrived at a genetic-developmental theory to which he attributed the same absolute, positivistic scientific status as earlier analytic theorists had claimed for their developmental theories.

2. There are considerable differences in the degree of complexity that "containing" or "holding" is understood to entail. Bion, for example, envisions containment as a complex mental function in which the mother/analyst receives, organizes, and reorganizes mental content projected into her by the child/analysand. In this view, the analyst's interpretations are an important feature of the process. Other descriptions of containing or holding (for example, M. Balint, 1968, and E. Balint, 1991) stress interpretive restraint on the part of the analyst, a specifically noninterpretive being-with the analysand in a nonverbal, often inchoate, perhaps ultimately unknowable, experience. Both ways of approaching holding are to be found in Winnicott's work.

3. Bollas (1987, p. 206) suggests that Winnicott meant for "his interpretations . . . to be played with—kicked around, mulled over, torn to pieces—rather than regarded as the official version of the truth."

4. Friedman (1988) attributes the recent popularity of the concept of "empathy" in psychoanalytic circles to its role in allowing clinicians the illusion that the particular lines of development in the patient are simply inherent in the patient and inevitable all along. It allows the clinician to be blind to the impact of her own participation and the conceptual grid that her own theory provides.

If a therapist has a wish for a change that seems so inevitable that it looks not like a change but like an elucidation of what is already present, he will not want to see himself as entering a field of various potential responses. A theory of the mind will actually interfere—though not so much with his vision as with his liberty. He wants to see potential as already actual so that he can surreptitiously foster integration and imagine that what he accomplishes has been thrust on him. (p. 420)

Friedman argues further that the central project of postclassical theorizing (a great deal of what I have termed the revolution in theory) has been a reaction against the complexities of Freudian theory and the substitution of a holistic vision in its place. The true or core self is regarded as something that simply emerges or unfolds in a properly empathic or facilitating environment. In such a perspective, interpretation and theory itself tend to be devalued, as experience-distant and irrelevant to the simple emergence of the patient's authentic subjectivity.

A rebellion against abstraction is in progress, and a longing for concrete items. By and large, what the revisionists do is to palm the discarded abstractions that are necessary for understanding, and use them (without credit) in isolating their concrete items and in talking about those items. (p. 252)

In contrast to Friedman, I believe that there has been much more to postclassical theorizing than merely a reactive rebellion against the complexities of Freudian theory. Rather, I have argued that postclassical theories constitute a revolution, a new and important emphasis on personal meaning rather than rational insight and control. But, like Friedman, I believe that in the rebellion against classical rationalism, the importance of (rational) theory in the generation of personal meaning has often been minimized and devalued.

5. Benjamin (1991) has sounded a warning along these lines. Gill and Hoffman, major contributors to this line of theorizing, are well aware of the dangers of an overzealous search for the analyst's contribution and warn against it. (See Gill, 1984, and Hoffman, 1991.) In contrast to the antitheoretical bias found in some authors involved in the metatheoretical revolution, Hoffman has often anchored his contributions to the theory of analytic process in Racker's object relations theorizing (for example, Hoffman, 1983).

6. See Kohut (1984, chap. 7) and Schafer (1983, chap. 5) for elaborations of this sort of approach to resistance.

7. Lachmann (1990) has recently argued that the self-psychological approach needs to be broadened precisely in terms of this issue.

8. Thus, Warren Poland decries those who see various psychoanalytic models as competing with each other, in contrast to those more helpful theorists who "strove to integrate."

> *Many of the "interpersonalists" in the middle of the century, like many in new schools now, saw themselves as their generation's revolutionaries. Then, like now, new conceptions which might have enriched analytic understanding often served to screen out unconscious forces.* (in Jacobs, 1991, p. xii)

9. This is a common but very serious misreading. Kuhn argues that the choice between paradigms is not purely a question of logic or evidence, because different paradigms are concerned with different problems and have their own logical and evidential signature. But this does imply that Kuhn thinks choice between paradigms is irrational. "Kuhn always intended to distinguish forms of rational persuasion in argumentation that take place in scientific communities from those irrational forms of persuasion that he has been accused of endorsing" (Bernstein, 1983, p. 53). uuhn regards work within the paradigms themselves, in either normal or evolutionary science, as necessarily rational, if they are to be considered scientific. This is not "a model of rationality that searches for determinate rules which can serve as necessary and sufficient conditions" but "a model of practical rationality that emphasizes the role of exemplars and judgmental interpretation" (Bernstein, 1983, p. 57).

10. For example:

> *Psychoanalysis, Freud once said, is a cure through love. On the manifest level, Freud meant that psychoanalytic therapy requires the analysand's emotional engagement with the analyst and the analyst's empathic understanding of his patient. But the latent content of this remark, which Freud only gradually discovered, and then through a glass darkly, is that psychoanalysis in its essence promotes individuation.* (Lear, 1990, p. 27)

CHAPTER 4

1. The key concept in Harry Stack Sullivan's "interpersonal psychiatry," developed in the 1930s and 1940s, was the "self-system." The object relations theory developed in the 1940s and the 1950s by Fairbairn uses the traditional term ego, but his libidinal ego and antilibidinal ego were a far cry from Freud's use of the term and more properly termed "selves." Winnicott, who has had an enormous impact on contempo-

rary psychoanalytic thinking, was concerned, more than anything else, with the authenticity versus falseness of self-experiences. Melanie Klein's seminal work implicitly shifted from a framework based on impulses as the fundamental units of mind to selves (good and bad) as the basic units, a shift that became explicit in the neo-Kleinian work of Racker and current Kleinian- (and Winnicottian-) inspired writers like Ogden. Finally, the contributions of the most important writers within more mainstream psychoanalytic thought, like Loewald and Schafer, have been concerned most fundamentally with various aspects of the concept of the self. And the self has been the central domain of Kohut and post-Kohut self psychologists.

2. It has been noted that Freud used no term systematically that is easily translated into "self." Freud's *ich,* and Strachey's Latinate translation into "ego," sometimes refers to the person as a whole, sometimes to a specific function or set of functions. From this perspective, Freud had no use for another term, since there is no "self" as such, only the person and specific functions of the person.

3. The self also has been a major focus in virtually all contemporary intellectual disciplines: philosophy (Taylor, 1989), social and cognitive psychology (Curtis, 1991), literary theory, and politics. My concern here is exclusively with the self in psychoanalysis.

4. For example, David Rapaport (1957) defines structure as a "relatively stable (having a slow rate of change) characteristic configuration that we can abstract from the behavior observed" (p. 701).

5. In the discussion that follows I am indebted to Schafer (1976, 1983, 1992) for his critique of spatial metaphors and his rethinking the nature of mind in his work on action language and narrative. However, Schafer tends to present his contributions as merely extensions and clarifications of preexisting Freudian theory, in a clearer, less muddled, less scientized form. I believe that thinking about mind in temporal as well as spatial terms (encompassing action and narrative) leads to a quite different understanding of mind, self, psychopathology, and the analytic process than Freud ever envisioned. I am thus extending some of Schafer's original insights in ways he himself did not pursue.

Although he has abandoned drive theory metapsychology, Schafer has always been loath to replace it with a systematic alternative, such as, for example, a comprehensive relational metapsychology. (See Mitchell, 1988.) Consequently, many of his emphases (for example, on sexuality and aggression) seem arbitrary and not persuasively grounded or justified. In his early contributions (1968, 1976), Schafer found little use for the concept of the "self," which he regarded as an illusory derivative of infantile experience employed in the service of disclaiming action. In his latest contributions (1992), Schafer has seemingly reluctantly granted the self a central place in the development of "narrative" accounts of the actions that constitute experience. Yet because he does not envision self in the context of a relational matrix, Schafer's "self" narratives have an oddly cognitive and arbitrary tone. A key difference between his approach and mine is that Schafer envisions a single narrator of multiple selves who seemingly operates outside of relational configurations; I envision multiple narratives told always from a perspective deeply embedded in an affectively charged relational context. This makes relationships with others not as easy simply to rewrite as Schafer seems to suggest. Schafer similarly (and in my view mistakenly) grants the analyst total narrative freedom and control by placing the analyst outside the transference/countertransference interaction. (See Hoffman's [1992] critique of Schafer as a "limited constructivist.")

6. Matisse, as a painter, described the same contrast from the other side. The artist should avoid narrative description, he argued. His "work of art must carry within itself its complete significance and impose that on the beholder even before he recognizes the subject matter" (quoted in Elderfield 1992).

7. I am indebted to Neil Altman (personal communication) for this analogy and for helping me work out my thinking about the dialectical relationship between spatial and temporal accounts of self.

8. I am borrowing this example from a discussion of self from a somewhat different angle in Polly Young-Eisendrath and James Hall (1987).

9. *The person's self is the history of many internal relations. . . . there is no one unified mental phenomenon that we can term self. . . . The concept of self should refer to the positions or points of view from which and through which we sense, feel, observe and reflect on distinct and separate experiences in our being. One crucial point of view comes through the other who experiences us.(Bollas, 1987, pp. 9–10)*

10. Daphne Socarides and Robert Stolorow (1984) argue that splitting in the child may be derived from the parents' perception of the child as "split" and discontinuous (p. 71). Ogden (1989) has suggested that demands for allegiances by a parent may greatly affect the possibility for containing and integrating "masculine" and "feminine" dimensions of the self. And Harold Searles (1986) has pointed out how "disharmoniously-wedded parents have counterparts (however much

exaggerated or otherwise distorted) in comparable poorly-married parental introjects" (pp. 195–96).

11. Van der Kolk (1989) has recently reviewed studies pointing to the underlying physiology of attachment. Networks of endorphin releasers are laid down in the early months of life in the context of attachment to caregivers with different styles of caregiving. One could extend this line of thought to speculate about whether different versions of self developed in different important early relationships correspond to subtle but important differences in physiological function.

12. Both Ogden (1989) and Jay Greenberg (1991) have recently argued that the patient at the end of analysis has a richer, more varied, but not necessarily more homogeneous experience.

13. Theorists coming from traditions in which the self is viewed in spatial terms as integral, continuous, and layered sometimes criticize object relations theorists and interpersonal theorists for lacking a theory of psychic structure. Kernberg (1980, p. 42), for example, drawing on metaphors from Freudian ego psychology, sees Melanie Klein's theory as lacking for precisely this reason. Yet this is not simply an omission. Kleinian theory presupposes a much more fluid, temporal vision of mind as shifting from one self-organization to another, not the stable, layered self of Kernberg's ego psychological model.

14. This kind of approach both to mind and self has interesting parallels in many other areas of contemporary science: in Lewis Thomas's (1974) biology, in which the individual is viewed as a symbiotic community of organisms; in Gerald Edelman's (1987) "neural Darwinism," in which networks of neurons with different patterns of organizing the external world compete for dominance; in Michael Gazzaniga's (1985) neuroscience, in which the brain is pictured as a social organization composed of modules; and in Marvin Minsky's (1985) artificial intelligence, in which the mind is understood to be composed of collections of quasi-independent agents.

15. The exclusivity and simplicity in which Kohut sometimes presents his injunction for the analyst to empathize with the patient's subjective point of view (which he generally equates with this positive developmental striving) have led to some confusion about how this applies to the patient's multiple, conflictual, and unconscious points of view. Does the analyst remain attuned and empathic only with what the patient consciously experiences and wants? What about the analyst's response to experiences and needs that are unconscious and disclaimed? Suggestions have appeared in recent self-psychological literature that when the analyst interprets unconscious content or confronts the patient with ideas that are discrepant with what the patient thinks or

feels, this response is truly "empathic" as well, because it reflects an empathy with what the patient "really" needs. In this way, empathy is being defined post hoc in terms of what turns out well, and the original meaning of the empathic attitude as a resonance with and confirmation of the patient's own consciously felt experience of her own subjective point of view has been totally lost. These recent lines of development in self psychology sometimes seem to be approaching a notion of multiple subjectivities, multiple versions of the self. ⁻

16. Daniel Stern (1985) argues that a "sense of a core self" is built up out of what he describes as "self-invariants," involving experiences of agency, coherence, affectivity, and continuity, combining together to create a sense of one's own subjective perspective.

17. In a similar vein, William Grossman (1982) argues that what he calls the "self-concept" is a fantasy, but a fantasy that plays a central role in organizing experience and guiding behavior.

18. The neurophysiologist Horace Barlow (1987) argues that:

> the infant brain must build a model of what it is interacting with. . . . Thus the content and validity of introspection can be enlarged, but only by social experience leading to the incorporation of models of other people's minds. . . . Thus consciousness becomes the forum, not of a single mind, but of the social group with whom the individual interacts. (p. 373)

19. There are important similarities between the temporal view of mind presented here and the view of mind developed over the centuries in eastern philosophy and meditation. In the Buddhist notion of "mindfulness," for example, mind is explored as process, with apparently substantial selfness revealed as transitory and illusory. (See, for example, Epstein, 1990.) In the more psychoanalytic perspective developed here, self-organizations, even if shifting, multiple, and rife with reified spatial metaphors, are regarded as extremely durable, important, and worthy of detailed investigation. Whereas the Buddhist ideal involves a letting go of content and a surrender to process, the analytic ideal involves a dialectic between an exploration and immersion in content and a freedom to move past it in the flow of experience. This dialectic is very much what Winnicott had in mind in his discussions of "play."

The struggle to find the best way to grasp the dialectic between continuity and discontinuity is also an important theme in western philosophy and can be traced back to the pre-Socratics. Heraclitus' river is never the same from moment to moment, yet it remains the same river; the flame of the candle changes constantly, yet it retains the same form.

20. Could we equate the experience of self as integral and continuous with consciousness and the organization of self into multiple and discontinuous patterns with the unconscious? No. Multiple organizations of self are not infrequently experienced simultaneously in consciousness ("I am of two minds about it"). Conversely, the experience of the self as integral and continuous sometimes can be inaccessible to consciousness. There are people who experience themselves as dealing with each interpersonal situation as a threat requiring a particular adaptation. It may be only after a considerable time in analysis that an experience of self emerges that suggests a continuity and consistency across those different adaptations.

Similarly, we cannot simply equate the concept of self as integral and continuous with "subjectivity" and the concept of self as multiple and discontinuous with "objectivity" or observable, patterned variations in behavior. There often is an objective integrity and continuity to the way a person functions across different relational contexts (apparent to an external observer), apart from his own subjective experience of that continuity. It is often of extreme analytic importance and utility for the patient to realize that while he has experienced himself as dealing with various people in different ways, each on his or her own terms, he actually has been acting in a quite repetitive, stereotyped fashion. Conversely, the multiple, discontinuous configurations that may, in an objective sense, constitute patterns of behavior also are important components (either consciously or unconsciously) in the fabric of subjective experience.

Finally, we cannot simply equate the distinction between multiple and discontinuous selves and an integral and continuous self with the distinction in Freudian ego psychology between self-representations and ego. Although the traditional terms can be reworked in this way (both Fast, 1990, and Greenberg, 1991, independently have recently proposed just such a reworking), what I have been describing is different both connotatively and denotatively from the way these terms have been used traditionally. The term *representation* has a cognitive connotation; representations are conceptual images of certain types of experience on a more abstract, cognitive plane. The multiple versions of self I have been describing are more than representations. They are not ideas in the mind; nor are they aspects of the person—feelings, impulses, or values. They are dynamic versions of the person herself; they embody active patterns of experience and behavior, organized around a particular point of view, a sense of self, a way of being, which underlie the ordinary phenomenological sense we have of ourselves as integral. (See also Grotstein, 1977.) Each version does all the things generally attributed to the "ego."

The sense of self as integral and continuous certainly can be encompassed within the term *ego*, but it has a very different place in contemporary theorizing than "ego" does in classical ego psychology. In the latter, the major dynamic scene of the action is in structural, drive-related conflict. The conscious and preconscious sense of self, assignable to the ego, is an epiphenomenon of unconscious conflict resolution. In postclassical theorizing, the self-forming process is a central dynamic scene of the action in its own right and has conscious, preconscious, and unconscious dimensions. As we have seen in chapter 1, the engagement of the patient in a fashion that will help generate and confirm a sense of continuity of personal experience has become an essential feature of contemporary psychoanalytic technique.

21. This is language in what Sullivan (1938) terms the "syntaxic" mode, established through the process of "consensual validation": "the words have been stripped of as much as possible of the accidents of their personal history in you, and it is by that process that they come to be so peculiarly impersonal" (p. 213).

22. In this analytic mode, language serves the purpose of conveying what Kohut (1984) termed, in defining empathy, "vicarious introspection": "the capacity to think and feel oneself into the inner life of another person" (p. 82).

23. Loewald (1976) was interested in embellishing precisely these qualities of language that Sullivan aimed at stripping away: "The emotional relationship to the person from whom the word is learned plays a significant, in fact crucial, part in how alive the link between thing and word turns out to be" (p. 197).

24. Racker (1968) captures this dialectic between unity and multiplicity in the relationship between the analyst and analysand as the analytic process deepens and the patient becomes more able to use the analyst's input:

> With this greater activity and freedom the analyst includes himself more in the psychoanalytic process, and likes to do so; thus, the transference and countertransference experiences become more intensely mobilized and enriched. His passivity gives place to a greater interchange of roles with the patient, analyst and patient oscillating to a higher degree between listening and speaking, between passivity and activity, between femininity and masculinity; and thus the infantile psychosexual conflicts are analyzed as they are manifested in these aspects of the analyst-patient relationship. (p. 180)

CHAPTER 5

1. It is important to note that the slogan "return to Freud" often serves more as a rhetorical device than a genuine preservation of Freud's original concepts. The "Freud" who is returned to is often one fashioned along contemporary lines. Consider, for example, the striking differences between Freud's drives, embedded in nineteenth-century biology and Newtonian physics, and Lacan's version of Freud, embedded in twentieth-century structural linguistics. This is why Schafer (1992) suggests that "'Back to Freud!' is perhaps the greatest rhetorical ploy of all. The advisor is saying 'Back to my Freud; repress the rest'" (p. 152).

2. Chodorow (1980) suggests that "the central core of self is, internally, a relational ego, a sense of self-in-good-relationship" (p. 427).

3. In most realms of contemporary thought impacted upon by "post-modernism," the traditional polarity between nature and nurture has been thrown into question. The assumption of either separate "drives" or an autonomous "culture" is no longer tenable. In fact, the very concept of "nature" (as well as "culture") held at any particular historical time is best viewed itself as a construction.

4. For this reason, I do not find helpful Bollas's (1993) claim that "each infant is born with a personality." Surely genetic differences in constitution and temperament are crucial, but "personality" for me presupposes an interpersonal field wherein genetic and environmental factors are forged into interactive patterns and character structure.

5. These issues concerning early development are an exact parallel to the issues discussed in chapter 2 regarding the analyst's inevitable impact on the development of the patient's self experience in the analytic process.

6. An interesting variant of the developmental strategy has been developed recently by Malcolm Slavin and Daniel Kriegman (1989), who have proposed a new paradigm for psychoanalysis derived from evolutionary biology and broad considerations concerning genetics and adaptation.

   They suggest that Freud's concept of endogenous instinctual drives, representing peremptory, aggressively self-interested, asocial, exclusively personal needs, can be thought to refer to that aspect of the personality that shapes and maintains the self as individual versus the self as embedded in a relational matrix: "In the drives we have a mechanism that guarantees access to some types of motivation that *arise from non-relational sources and are, in a sense, totally dedicated toward the promotion of our individual interests*" (p. 37).

A close reading suggests that Slavin and Kriegman alter Freud's notion of "drives" in order to make it work within their larger scheme:

> *Drives, and the structural model of drive-defense conflict, assume a subsidiary role within a larger, relationally designed and configured psyche. But, to the extent that the classical agenda is read as a "narrative of conflict," it captures certain major, significant features of the relational world and the inherently "divided" way we are adapted to it.* (p. 47)

"Drives" relocated and reset into a relationally configured psyche are no longer Freud's "drives," prewired, endogenous pressures whose meaning is represented within the mind unmediated by the semiotic, metaphoric meaning systems of the relational world. Once again, the effort to portray a part of the psyche as separate from, prior to, and sheltered from the interactive, mutually regulatory structures of the relational matrix proves problematic.

7. Bollas (1987) argues that there is no purely generic "holding environment"; the particularities of the individual mother's handling of the baby become the existential medium of the baby's world and are structured into the developing child's personal idiom.

8. Sullivan's (1953) basic motivational distinction between the need for interpersonal security and needs for satisfaction reflects this duality. More recently, both Greenberg (1991) and Spezzano (1993) have made the conflict between self-development, self-expression, or self-reaction on the one hand and the safety provided by affiliation on the other the centerpiece of their motivational theories.

9. Farber (1976, chap. 12), from which the second epigraph at the beginning of this chapter is drawn, provides a wonderful account of the deceptiveness of revelatory models of insight. Similarly, Masud Khan (1963) alerts us to the elusiveness of the "true" self and chides Guntrip for having fallen prey to the seductive "danger of romantization of a pure self system" (p. 304).

10. Winnicott (1968) suggests that the capacity to "use" the other is a precondition for fully passionate experience.

11. For example, Greenberg (1991) notes: "David Rapaport made a great deal of the importance of the drives in protecting people from passive submission to external pressures. He wrote that our innate drive endowment guarantees autonomy from the environment; it provides our ultimate 'safeguard from stimulus-response slavery'" (p. 39).

12. The ideal balance between self-definition and membership in a social unit varies from culture to culture—consider, for example, the contrast between our more individually oriented western tradition and the supraindividual units of eastern traditions—and from individual to individual, with probable roots in temperament.

13. Loewald (1978) defines the self as "an atonement structure," shaped in a context of inevitable generational conflict, and repeatedly depicts the richest form of experience as one that overcomes the compulsive separation between self and other, inside and outside, on different levels of organization. Philip Bromberg (1991) has similarly noted the fluidity of the relationship between internality and externality in health and their forced separation in serious forms of psychopathology.

    Most people take their own subjective states of interiority for granted, and can routinely accept the fact that there is more to them than meets the eye as a mental state that joins them to the rest of mankind without intrinsic emotional isolation. They can be both in the world and separate from it as a unitary experience that blends selfhood and relatedness. Others, more developmentally fragmented, protect their subjective interiors as a lifelong task of emotional survival, while paying the price of never-ending efforts at self-validation, or desperate aloneness. (p. 400)

14. Thus, Taylor (1991) argues against what he calls the "monological ideal." Our identities are always defined "in dialogue with, sometimes in struggle against, the identities our significant others want to recognize in us. And even when we outgrow some of the latter—our parents, for instance—and they disappear from our lives, the conversation with them continues within us as long as we live" (p. 33).

15. Bromberg (1991, p. 417*n*) points to the danger of "adult-erating" the patient if the experiential reality of the self as preverbal baby is not acknowledged and worked with in its own terms. Emmanuel Ghent (1991) makes a similar point about the subjective reality of the patient's experience of self as baby.

16. Daniel Stern (1985) suggests that what he calls different "senses" of self—emergent, core, intersubjective, and verbal—are not passed through sequentially in stages but coexist together in adult experience. Ogden (1989) argues that what he terms the "autistic-contiguous" mode of experience, involving a basic kinesthetic sense of sensory continuity and embodiment, operates in a continual, dialectical interplay with paranoid-schizoid and depressive modes of organizing experience.

17. Certain people feel that, at a point in their childhood, time stopped in any personally meaningful sense. When such patients regress to that developmental fixation point, they can experience a reanimation of time (Joseph Newirth, personal communication).

18. This represents an essential narrowing of Sullivan's interpersonal theory, from which it is derived. Sullivan took great pains to describe ways in which interactions are structured through "personifications" of self and others.

19. This position is also found in some versions of self psychology (such as Goldberg) but not in others, where there is an increasing focus on interaction (for example, in the "intersubjective perspective" of Stolorow and his collaborators).

20. Some more progressive contemporary Freudians (for example, Jacobs, 1991), while still committed to a one-person perspective, allow for the importance of different degrees of interaction and the analyst's more personal experience, while all the time affirming the central priority of the one-person framework.

21. See Mitchell (1980) for an extensive treatment of the relationship between the intrapsychic and the interpersonal in Sullivan's contributions. There I suggest that it is most useful to regard people as simultaneously self-regulatory and field-regulatory. See Beatrice Beebe and Frank Lachmann (1992) for a similar approach.

22. James Fosshage (1992) has recently argued for a more interpersonal approach to countertransference combined with an essentially self-psychological perspective.

23. The concern with what the analyst is feeling also becomes a key factor in approaches drawing on Klein's concept of projective identification, particularly as amended by Bion. Here the patient communicates largely through unconscious fantasies of placing sectors of her experience into the analyst's mind; the analyst knows about these processes largely through their impact on the analyst's own experience. Bollas and other members of the British Independent group have reworked Bion's contributions on projective identification together with Winnicott's (1949) important contribution on "objective countertransference."

24. The importance of the analyst's offering herself to be used as an object by the patient as developed by the British Independent group has been an important counterpoint to the emphasis on the analyst's establishment of her own personal subjectivity in analytic interaction in American interpersonal psychoanalysis.

25. See Michael Tansey and Walter Burke (1989) for a helpful effort to sort out the useful from the not so useful in the analyst's experience.

CHAPTER 6

1. They also introduced the concept of drive neutralization, through which the aggressive drive becomes stripped of its primitive, propulsive qualities and used by the ego for its conflict-free operations.

2. While Hartmann and other Freudian ego psychologists use the concept of "neutralization" to portray the development of the self out of modulated and de-aggressivized energy, Klein sees primitive aggression as with us always.

3. The importance of the question of justification in the polarization of psychoanalytic positions around the issue of an aggressive drive is dramatically illustrated by the positions taken on this question by Kernberg (1984) on the one side and Stolorow, Brandschaft, and Atwood (1987) on the other. Each side regards the other theory as not just wrong but as exacerbating the patient's problems and leading to the worst possible mishandling of the patient's aggression.

   Kernberg sees the rejection of instinct theory in favor of a theory of environmental failure by self psychology and many versions of object relations theory as equivalent to a rejection of the biological basis of human development. They lead, in Kernberg's view (1984, pp. 187–89), to an inevitable neglect of the clinical importance of aggression and unconscious conflict, particularly in terms of understanding the transference. Through his eyes, aggression is not a response to a situation, but an unjustified, distorted, prestructured set of proclivities brought to a situation. The abandonment of the theory of an aggressive drive leads to a failure to interpret these proclivities, causing the non-drive analyst to coddle the patient in a very nonanalytic fashion.

   Stolorow, Brandschaft, and Atwood (1987) do not regard the intense aggression of the "borderline" patients Kernberg describes as an intrinsic feature of the dynamics of these patients. Rather, they see this rage toward the analyst as a justified reaction to the analyst's misunderstanding of them. In this view, Kernberg's postulation of an aggressive drive is not only wrong, but it also leads the clinician to mistreat the patient, producing the very aggression that is assumed to be there to start with!

4. Gill (1991) has argued that defining an action as assertion or hostility is a construction of the observer, not an inherent property of the affect itself. I do not believe it is entirely a matter of construction. Sex and hunger are different organismic states. They can each be interpreted in many different ways, and sometimes confused with each other—but they begin as different phenomena. I believe assertion and aggression, while obviously more closely related, are based on distinctly different organismic states.

5. Grotstein (1982) argues for a reinterpretation of Klein's notion of a biologically rooted Death Instinct operating along the same lines, grounded in a phylogenetically developed reaction to natural dangers to the species. "To the aggressive instinct, one could see an inherent preconception of the predator, that is, the hereditary, phylogenetic enemy of the species.... Bowlby (personal communication) believes that all animal species, including human, have some awareness of being prey and predator ... and that stranger anxiety is the human form of predator fear" (p. 201).

6. This is consistent with Lichtenberg's recent work on affect, in which he argues that aggression is an inborn response with a very specific, adaptive function: "[It is] ... an aversive response available from birth as an indicator of distress within the caregiver-infant unit; it signals the need for a response from the caregiver" (1989, p. 168).

7. Grotstein makes a similar point, arguing that "via phenomenological inference ... unpleasure by its very nature is experienced as the invasion of the self by a cruel 'not me'" (1982, p. 204).

8. Schafer argues that much of the ordinary language of experience is derived from preverbal, infantile bodily experience, with all of the mistakes and misunderstandings of infantile thought. It is precisely these misunderstandings that are illuminated through the analytic process, allowing the patient to own and assume agency over a subjective world previously disclaimed and experienced as given and immutable. The great irony is that traditional psychonanalytic language portrays mind in precisely those same kinds of terms, as a collection of spaces filled with things and substances. The concept of an aggressive drive, which accrues spontaneously, builds up more and more pressure, demands discharge, feels cathartic when discharged, causes a toxic kind of sickness if dammed up—the very concept of an aggressive drive, in this view, derives from a reified anal metaphor: "It does not go too far to suggest that, however austerely this conceptualization may be expressed, it implies an archaic, animistic, usually excremental model of aggression" (1976, p. 282). Thus, Schafer, consistent with the perspective developed here, abandons Freud's notion of drive as a propulsive force yet grants aggression a central role in the early shaping and definition of the child's sense of self.

9. Minsky (1985) provides a fascinating argument for the adaptive, evolutionary function of affects such as anger as anchored in their role in motivating behavior. An author who has trouble getting down to writing, for example, conjures up an image of a rival working on similar material. The competitive anger that is generated fuels activities that now take on a greater priority.

10. Many theorists and clinicians who think of themselves as believing in Freud's drive theory actually understand aggression as operating in the fashion I have been developing here, as innate but lacking the self-propelling quality Freud (and Hartmann) considered crucial. (See, for example, Pine, 1990, pp. 84–85.) Because this revised version of drive is not distinguished sharply from Freud's version of drive, the two very different concepts become conflated and attributes of each are drawn upon without awareness of their incompatibility.

11. Ogden (1989) has described this inevitable deep dread in both analysand and analyst in vivid terms.

> *The patient unconsciously holds a fierce conviction (which he has no way of articulating) that his infantile and early childhood experience has taught him about the specific ways in which each of his object relationships will inevitably become painful, disappointing, suffocating, overly sexualized, and so on. There is no reason for him to believe that the relationship into which he is about to enter will be any different. . . . Everything that the analysand says (and does not say) in the first hours can be heard in the light of an unconscious warning to the analyst concerning the reasons why neither the analyst nor the patient should enter into this doomed and dangerous relationship.* (pp. 181–82)

12. Both Kleinians and self psychologists often neglect what are to me crucial dimensions of the analytic situation. In locating negative transference in an aggressive drive, Kleinians often miss the justifiable reasons for the patient's aggression in a subjectively experienced endangerment in the analytic situation. On the other hand, to assume that intense, chronic aggression in the analytic situation is an iatrogenic consequence of bad theory and/or bad technique fails to deal adequately with the degree to which the patient's style of response to endangerment, with its biological and temperamental origins and its embeddedness in a firmly established world of bad objects, precludes the development and enrichment of relations with others.

13. Along similar lines, Ogden (1989, 1992b) suggests that the paranoid-schizoid position and the depressive position are more usefully thought of in a healthy dialectical relationship with each other. (He also adds a third, more primitive organization, the autistic-contiguous position.) To live always in the paranoid-schizoid position is to be wracked and torn by impossible demands for a pure love and pure hate. But to live always in the depressive position, even if it were possible, would be to fade into the muted, gray tones of am-

bivalence. One would see good and bad in everyone; fairness would prevail. Kohut suggests that idealization (even if greatly unrealistic) can play a positive, enriching role in the lives of healthy adults. Similarly, Ogden points to the way in which the pure loving and hating of the paranoid-schizoid position can serve as the wellsprings of passion, breaking apart the measured balance of ambivalence and integration when they have become stale and constraining.

CHAPTER 7

1. Many do not seem to be bothered by guilt in this regard. The most extraordinary expression of this arrogant and elitist attitude I have ever heard was by a speaker arguing against the necessity and/or merits of altering the analytic frame. Defending classical theory of technique in all circumstances, he told the following joke: A young woman hung around the stage door following a theatrical performance starring a famous male actor. She told him of her admiration for him, and one thing led to another. The next morning, the woman told the actor that she was poor and hungry, and asked for money to buy some bread. The actor gave her a ticket to that evening's performance. She explained again that she was hungry and that the ticket was of little use to her. He replied, "If you wanted bread, you should have fucked a baker."

2. Winnicott's distinction between classical neuroses and false-self disorders, Kohut's (1971) distinction between classical neuroses and disorders of the self, the distinction between structural conflict and developmental arrests (Stolorow and Lachmann, 1980)—all work the same way.

3. Stolorow and George Atwood (1992) might consider this traditional approach as suffering from what they call the "myth of the isolated mind."

4. Winnicott (1956a) speaks of the mother failing the child, incrementally and usefully, as she emerges from her primary maternal preoccupation and reclaims herself.

5. As Daniel Stern (1985) points out,

> any change in the infant may come about partly by virtue of the adult interpreting the infant differently and acting accordingly. Most probably, it works both ways. Organizational change from within the infant and its interpretation by the parents are mutually facilitative. The net result is that the infant appears to have a new sense of who he or she is and who

*you are, as well as a different sense of the kinds of interactions
that can now go on.* (p. 9)

6. Ghent (1992) has written beautifully about the complex and often paradoxical relationship between benign and malignant features of the patient's longings, in which legitimate needs are often defensively "black-
washed" into coercive "neediness." Similarly, Peter Shabad (1993) has
described the ways in which early pain and loss are often sustained by
being organized and perpetuated into self-defeating demands.

7. These include: splitting, projective identification, dissociative frag-
mentations into true and false selves, the importance of early parental
responsiveness, and the devastating impact of child abuse.

8. See Davies and Frawley (1993) for an excellent review of and contribution to contemporary work with survivors of childhood sexual
abuse that explores these reenactments and reversals of the abuse in
the analytic relationship.

9. See Aron (1992) and Burke (1992) for a very helpful dialogue on the
implications of the mutual but asymmetrical nature of the analytic relationship.

10. Consider the response of a contemporary analyst to a patient in the
stalemating kind of despair that Ferenczi was struggling with:

> *At this point the analyst, who had felt all along that she was
> being dragged towards a deadly abyss, told the patient about it
> saying "I'm afraid I can't help it either, I'm willing to walk
> with you up to the edge of the abyss and, as we have been
> doing all along, try to see things together, but I shall not jump
> down with you. I will be very sorry indeed if you do . . . but I
> shall let you go by yourself . . . this is your choice and I cannot
> prevent it."* (Mehler and Argentieri, 1989, p. 300)

11. For a vivid presentation of this point of view and some very interesting clinical material, see Roth and Segal (1990).

12. Samson and Weiss (1986) see situations like this as representing unconscious tests of an analyst's ability, unlike an incestuous parent, to
resist illicit overtures.

13. Casement's (1991) writings are rich with instructive examples of the
analyst's struggle to find and meet the patient's needs yet generate and
maintain a deep analytic process:

> *when a patient is prompting the analyst to depart from classi-
> cal technique, particularly if it is being rigidly adhered to, this
> need not always be seen as seductive or manipulative. The pa-
> tient may be searching for a more viable balance between the*

similarities in the analytic relationship (that represent trauma)
and a sufficient difference (that alone can provide the neces-
sary security for the analysis to continue). It is the balance
here that matters. (p. 272)

Employing Winnicott's (1954) distinction between "libidinal demands" and "unmet needs" (p. 273), Casement sometimes decides
that meeting the patient's desires and demands is crucial and sometimes refusing to meet them is crucial. I disagree with Casement's traditional assumption that these reflect different states in the patient, to
be decided through the correct diagnosis. But his discussion of the
process through which he decides what to do, both in his own mind
and in collaboration with the patient, is a model for effective analytic
work in finding, with the patient, a positive, constructive way to construe what is happening, whether a maintenance of or departure from
the frame. Casement tends to feel that the decision arrived at was determinative; my suspicion is that the thoughtful and caring way in
which he engages his patients about these decisions was probably
more important. See Anthony Bass (1993) for an interesting overview
of Casement's work in the context of larger developments in thinking
about the analyst's participation.

14. See Stuart Pizer (1992) for a cogent discussion of the place of negotiation in daily clinical work.

CHAPTER 8

1. Boris's view of hope as regressive and inhibiting, while derived from
the instinct theories of Freud and Klein, is not wedded to drive theory;
it is also implicit, for example, in Fairbairn's (1952) object relations
theory. Boris derives ideal imagoes from a priori preconceptions, but
one could just as easily derive them, as does Fairbairn, from actual experience. Fairbairn's "exciting object" is formed from fragments of
real experience with parents, and the enticements of the exciting object engender perpetual hope in the libidinal ego, a continual yearning
for illusory, false promises. It is the hope for the exciting object that
keeps the internal object world a closed system. Only in the transference, when some other form of connection becomes possible, are the
adhesive, secretly hopeful, ties to bad objects finally renounced.

2. Robert Coles (1970) stresses the progressive features in Erikson's understanding of hope.

He explicitly and in detail affirmed what could be called the
existential and philosophical aspects of psychoanalytic theory.

> *That is, each of the "stages". . . results in something, leads*
> *somewhere. The struggles that inevitably characterize all*
> *growth can generate utterly reliable talents as well as in-*
> *tractable "problems" . . . Hope is . . . "the ontogenetic basis*
> *of faith, and is nourished by the adult faith which pervades*
> *patterns of care."* (p. 273)

See also Fromm (1968) and Ernest Schachtel (1959) for similar approaches to the place of hope in psychological development.

3. See Bollas (1987), Pine (1985), and Casement (1990) for applications of Winnicott's concepts of regression to environmental failures as features of the analytic process in general.

4. Given the sparseness of references to hope in the psychoanalytic literature, it is interesting that Melanie Klein, who explored and emphasized the darkest realms of human experience, speaks of hope frequently. Klein became interested in hope in the 1930s, in connection with the introduction of her concept of the "depressive position," where hope is "based on the growing unconscious knowledge that the internal and external object is not as bad as it was felt to be in its split off aspects" (1975, p. 196). This is very different from the hope that Boris was speaking about, which is hope in the paranoid-schizoid position, hope that preserves idealization, omnipotence, and splits experience. Klein is speaking of a more mature version of hope that is generated through the capacity to sustain an integrated, textured experience of oneself and others, despite loss and vulnerability: "It can be observed in the analysis of both adults and children that, together with a full experience of depression, feelings of hope emerge" (Klein, 1975, p. 75n)

5. Lawrence Friedman (1988, chap. 2) suggests that psychoanalytic theory has generated various devices for enabling us to avoid facing that paradox head on, including: Freud's concept of the "unobjectionable positive transference" (it is not necessary to interpret a part of the patient's infantile hopes, which we can exploit for our claims to authority); Herman Nunberg's more explicit injunction to parlay the patient's transferential hopes into an addiction to the analyst that will make his power irresistible; and the widely employed concept of the "working" or "therapeutic alliance," in which it is arbitrarily assumed that there really is a part of the patient, even if in germinal form, that happens to share the analyst's sense of reality, values, and goals.

6. See, for example, G. Friedman (1991), Mehler and Argentieri (1989), and Rosenfeld (1987).

7. Harold Searles (1979, chap. 21) also distinguishes between more

fragmentary, often latently sadistic and controlling forms of hope from more mature and realistic hope.

8. Ferenczi (1988) has provided some of the most powerful statements of the analyst's unavoidable anguish (or defensive detachment) in such situations.

> *I try not to let the discouragement of my patients infect me, although it may cost me a great deal of effort to hold out against the incessant reproaches and accusations. One cannot help feeling inwardly hurt—at least I cannot—when after years of work, often quite exhausting work, one is called useless and unable to help, just because one cannot provide everything, to the full extent, that the poor suffering person needs in his precarious position.* (p. 55)

9. As Harold Searles (1979) has put it, "the therapist's dedication becomes, as seen from this vantage point, an anxious, deeply ambivalent effort to both make contact with and keep safely at a distance the projected components of his self" (p. 80). And Racker (1968) suggests that "The analyst may . . . seek to suffer now, through his analytic 'children,' what he had made his own parents suffer, either in fantasy or in reality. The transference is, in this aspect, an unconscious creation of the analyst" (p. 177).

10. Charles Spezzano (personal communication) has suggested in this connection that "the failure of each theory to make clinical work unconfusing keeps alive a constant hunger and receptivity to new theory of any kind; this will never cease to be true."

11. L. Friedman (1988) has made a similar point about Kohut's contributions:

> *It must be an impressive experience for a patient to have his pathology consistently given its progressive rather than its regressive significance—to be told that his immaturity is not a hammock but a launching pad, his incompleteness a purple heart from deprivation, not a badge of indolence, greed, and cowardice.* (p. 385)

12. Kenneth Frank (1992, 1993) has thoughtfully explored the place of explicit cognitive-behavioral interventions in contemporary psychoanalytic technique.

13. This view is in marked contrast to the more traditional one-person assumption that analysts can, in fact, remain uninvolved in the patient's evolving process. Owen Renik (1992), for example, has recently stated this credo:

If an analyst presents explanations to his patient, does the ana-
lyst not run the risk of imposing understanding, rather than fa-
cilitating the patient's autonomous development of his own
understanding. We consider neutrality, the effort to avoid sug-
gestion and compromise of the patient's autonomy, to lie at
the heart of our clinical work. (p. 176)

In my view, the patient never develops his understanding independently from the analyst's participation. The patient's experience is always something unformed in the patient, emerging and shaped in one
particular way among many possible ways in the interaction with a
particular analyst. As I suggested in chapter 5, autonomy and authenticity do not depend on a fantasied independence of the subject's experience from its interactive matrix but on the use to which jointly derived meanings, values, and understandings are put. The patient's experience is always in need of construction and elaboration. There is
no reason to believe that a patient's lone attempts to construct and
elaborate meanings is any more authentic or even really any more independent of the analyst's unintended participation than an elaboration explicitly arrived at jointly with the analyst. What is crucial, in
my view, is not an effort to purge the patient's understandings from
the analyst's participation but continually to reflect upon the ways the
patient is positioning himself vis-à-vis and employing the analyst's
participation.

REFERENCES

Abend, S. 1986. "Countertransference, Empathy and the Analytic Ideal: The Impact of Life Stresses on Analytic Capability." *Psychoanalytic Quarterly* 55:563–75.

Arlow, J. 1985. "The Concept of Psychic Reality and Related Problems." *Journal of the American Psychoanalytic Association* 33:521–35.

Aron, L. 1991. "Working Through the Past—Working Toward the Future." *Contemporary Psychoanalysis* 27:81–109.

———. 1992. "Interpretation as Expression of the Analyst's Subjectivity." *Psychoanalytic Dialogues* 2, no. 4:475–508.

———, and I. Hirsch. 1992. "Money Matters in Psychoanalysis." In *Relational Perspectives in Psychoanalysis,* ed. N. Skolnick and S. Warshaw. Hillsdale, NJ: Analytic Press.

Atwood, G., and R. Stolorow. 1984. *Structures of Subjectivity: Explorations in Psychoanalytic Phenomenology.* Hillsdale, NJ: Analytic Press.

Balint, E. 1991. "Commentary." *Psychoanalytic Dialogues* 1, no. 4: 423–30.

Balint, M. 1968. *The Basic Fault: Therapeutic Aspects of Regression.* London: Tavistock.

Barlow, H. 1987. "The Biological Role of Consciousness." In *Mindwaves,* ed. C. Blakemore and S. Greenfield. Oxford, U.K.: Basil Blackwell.

Bass, A. 1992. "Review Essay: *Psychotic Anxieties and Containment,* by Margaret Little," *Psychoanalytic Dialogues* 2, no. 1:117–31.

———. 1993. "Review Essay: *Learning from the Patient,* by Patrick Casement," *Psychoanalytic Dialogues* 3, no. 1:151–67.

Bateson, C. 1987. "The Revenge of the Good Fairy." *Whole Earth Review* Summer:34–38.

Beebe, B., and F. Lachmann. 1992. "A Dyadic Systems View of Communication." In *Relational Perspectives in Psychoanalysis,* ed. N. Skolnick and S. Warshaw. Hillsdale, NJ: Analytic Press.

Benjamin, J. 1988. *The Bonds of Love: Psychoanalysis, Feminism and the Problem of Domination.* New York: Pantheon.

———. 1991. "Commentary." *Psychoanalytic Dialogues* 1, no. 4:525–34.

———. 1992a. "Reply to Schwartz." *Psychoanalytic Dialogues* 2, no. 3:417–24.

———. 1992b. "Recognition and Destruction: An Outline of Intersubjectivity." In *Relational Perspectives in Psychoanalysis,* ed. N. Skolnick and S. Warshaw. Hillsdale, NJ: Analytic Press.

Berlin, I. 1991. *The Crooked Timber of Humanity: Chapters in the History of Ideas.* New York: Knopf.

Bernstein, R. 1983. *Beyond Objectivism and Relativism: Science, Hermeneutics, and Praxis.* Philadelphia: University of Pennsylvania Press.

Bion, W. R. 1967. "Notes on Memory and Desire." In *Melanie Klein Today,* vol. 2, ed. E. Bott Spillius. London: Routledge.

———. 1990. *Brazilian Lectures.* London: Karnac.

Bollas, C. 1987. *The Shadow of the Object: Psychoanalysis of the Unthought Known.* New York: Columbia University Press.

———. 1991. *The Forces of Destiny: Psychoanalysis and Human Idiom.* London: Free Association Press.

———. 1993. "Interview." *Psychoanalytic Dialogues* 3, no. 4, in press.

Boris, H. 1976. "On Hope: Its Nature and Psychotherapy." *International Review of Psycho-Analysis* 3:139–50.

Boyer, L. B., and P. L. Giovacchini. 1967. *Psychoanalytic Treatment of Schizophrenic, Borderline and Characterological Disorders.* New York: Jason Aronson.

Brenner, C. 1982. *The Mind in Conflict.* New York: International Universities Press.

———. 1987. "A Structural Theory Perspective." *Psychoanalytic Inquiry* 7, no. 2:167–72.

Bromberg, P. 1983. "The Mirror and the Mask: On Narcissism and Psychoanalytic Growth." *Contemporary Psychoanalysis* 19, no. 2:359–87.

———. 1988. "Interpersonal Psychoanalysis and Self Psychology: A Clinical Comparison." In *Self Psychology: Comparison and Contrast,* ed. D. Detrick and S. Detrick. New York: Analytic Press.

———. 1991. "On Knowing One's Patient Inside Out." *Psychoanalytic Dialogues* 1, no. 4:399–422.

Brunner, J. 1993. "Loyal Opposition and the Clarity of Dissent." *Psychoanalytic Dialogues* 3, no. 1:11–20.

Burke, W. 1992. "Countertransference Disclosure and the Asymmetry/Mutuality Dilemma." *Psychoanalytic Dialogues* 2, no. 2:241–71.

Casement, P. 1991. *Learning from the Patient.* New York: Guilford.

Chodorow, N. 1980. "Gender, Relation, and Difference in Psychoanalytic Perspective." In *Essential Papers on the Psychology of Women,* ed. Claudia Zanardi. New York: New York University Press, 1990.

Coles, R. 1970. *Erik H. Erikson: The Growth of His Work,* Boston: Little, Brown.

Compton, A. 1990. "The Psychoanalytic Process." *Psychoanalytic Quarterly* 59, no. 4:585–98.

Cooper, A. 1987. "Changes in Psychoanalytic Ideas: Transference Interpretation." *Journal of the American Psychoanalytic Association* 35, no. 1:77–98.

Curtis, R. 1991. *The Relational Self.* New York: Guilford.

Cushman, P. 1991. "Ideology Obscured: Political Uses of the Self in Daniel Stern's Infant." *American Psychologist* 46, no. 3:206–19.

Davies, J., and M. Frawley 1992. "Dissociative Processes and Transference-Countertransference Paradigms in the Psychoanalytically Oriented Treatment of Adult Survivers of Childhood Sexual Abuse." *Psychoanalyatic Dialogues* 2, no. 1:5–36.

———. 1993. *Treating the Adult Survivor of Childhood Sexual Abuse: Psychoanalytic Perspectives.* New York: Basic Books.

Dennett, D. 1991. *Consciousness Explained.* Boston: Little, Brown.

Dimen, M. 1991. "Deconstructing Differences: Gender, Splitting and Transitional Space." *Psychoanalytic Dialogues* 1, no. 3:335–52.

Eckardt, M. 1982. "The Theme of Hope in Erich Fromm's Writing." *Contemporary Psychoanalysis* 18, no.1:141–52.

Edelman, G. 1987. *Neural Darwinism: The Theory of Neuronal Group Selection.* New York: Basic Books.

Ehrenberg, D. 1992. *The Intimate Edge.* New York: W.W. Norton.

Eigen, M. 1981. "The Area of Faith in Winnicott, Lacan and Bion." *International Journal of Psycho-Analysis* 62:413–33.

Elderfield, J. 1992. *Henri Matisse: A Retrospective.* New York: Museum of Modern Art.

Eliot, T. S. 1963. *Collected Poems: 1909–1962.* New York: Harcourt, Brace and World.

Epstein, M. 1990. "Beyond the Oceanic Feeling: Psychoanalytic Study of Buddhist Meditation." *International Journal of Psycho-Analysis* 17:159–66.

Erikson, E. 1950. *Childhood and Society.* New York: W.W. Norton.

————. 1968. *Identity: Youth and Crisis.* New York: W.W. Norton.

Fairbairn, W. R. D. 1952. *An Object Relations Theory of the Personality.* New York: Basic Books.

Farber, L. 1976. *Lying, Despair, Jealousy, Envy, Sex, Suicide, Drugs, and the Good Life.* New York: Basic Books.

Fast, I. 1990. "Self and Ego: A Framework for Their Integration." *Psychoanalytic Inquiry* 10:141–62.

Fenichel, O. 1940. *Problems of Psychoanalytic Technique.* New York: *Psychoanalytic Quarterly.*

Ferenczi, S. 1988. *The Clinical Diary of Sandor Ferenczi,* ed. J. Dupont. Cambridge, MA: Harvard University Press.

Ferris, T. 1988. *Coming of Age in the Milky Way.* New York: William Morrow.

Fleishman, J. 1992. "I Sing of Gods and Men and the Stones of Fabled Troy." *Smithsonian* January:34.

Fogel, G. 1989. "The Authentic Function of Psychoanalytic Theory: An Overview of the Contributions of Hans Loewald." *Psychoanalytaic Quarterly* 58:419–451.

Fosshage, J. 1992. "The Analyst's Experience of the Analysand." Paper presented at the meeting of the American Psychoanalytic Association, April 4.

Foster, R. 1992. "Psychoanalysis and the Bilingual Patient: Some Observations on the Influence of Language Choice on the Transference." *Psychoanalytic Psychology* 9, no. 1:61–76.

Frank, K. 1992. "Combining Action Techniques with Psychoanalytic Therapy." *International Review of Psycho-Analysis* 19:57–79.

————.. 1993. "Action, Insight and Working Through: Outline of an Integrative Approach." *Psychoanalytic Dialogues* 3, no. 4.

Freud, S. All references are to *The Standard Edition of the Complete Psychological Works of Sigmund Freud (SE),* vols. 1–24, ed. J. Strachey. London: Hogarth Press, 1953–74.

————. 1895. *Studies in Hysteria. SE* 2.

————. 1905. "Fragment of an Analysis of a Case of Hysteria." *SE* 7:1–122.

————. 1909. "Analysis of a Phobia in a Five-Year-Old Boy." *SE* 10:3–149.

————. 1913. "On Beginning the Treatment. (Further Recommendations on the Technique of Psycho-Analysis I.)" *SE* 12:123–44.

————. 1914. "On Narcissism: An Introduction." *SE* 14:67–102.

————. 1915. "Instincts and Their Vicissitudes." *SE* 14:117–40.

————. 1916. "Some Character Types Met with in Psychoanalytical Work." *SE* 14:311–33.

————. 1918. "From the History of an Infantile Neurosis." *SE* 17:3–122.

———.1919. "Lines of Advance in Psychoanalyatic Therapy." *SE* 17:157–68.

———.1920. *Beyond the Pleasure Principle. SE* 18:1–64.

———.1923. *The Ego and the Id. SE* 19:1–66.

———.1927. *The Future of an Illusion. SE* 21:3–56.

———.1930. *Civilization and Its Discontents. SE* 21:59–145.

———.1933. *New Introductory Lectures on Psycho-Analysis. SE* 22:1–182.

———.1937. "Analysis Terminable and Interminable." *SE* 23:216–53.

———.1940. *An Outline of Psychoanalysis. SE* 23:139–207.

———,and J. Breuer. 1895. *Studies on Hysteria. SE* 2.

Friedman, G. 1991. "Case presentation." *Contemporary Psychoanalysis* 27, no. 3:483–92.

Friedman, L. 1988. *The Anatomy of Psychotherapy.* Hillsdale, NJ: Analytic Press.

Fromm, E. 1941. *Escape from Freedom.* New York: Avon.

———.1947. *Man for Himself.* Greenwich, CT: Fawcett.

———.1968. *The Revolution of Hope.* New York: Harper & Row.

———.1973. *The Anatomy of Human Destructiveness.* New York: Holt, Rinehart and Winston.

Gay, P. 1988. *Freud, a Life for Our Time.* New York: W.W. Norton.

Gazzaniga, M. 1985. *The Social Brain: Discovering the Networks of the Mind.* New York: Basic Books.

Geertz, C. 1979. "From the Native's Point of View: On the Nature of Anthropological Understanding." In *Local Knowledge: Further Essays in Interpretive Anthropology.* New York: Basic Books, 1983.

Ghent, E. 1990. "Masochism, Submission, Surrender." *Contemporary Psychoanalysis* 24, no. 1:108–36.

———.1992. "Process and Paradox." *Psychoanalytic Dialogues* 2, no. 4:135–60.

Gill, M. 1982. *The Analysis of Transference,* vol. 1. New York: International Universities Press.

———.1983. "The Interpersonal Paradigm and the Degree of the Therapist's Involvement." *Contemporary Psychoanalysis* 19, no. 2:200–237.

———.1984. "Transference: A Change in Conception or Only in Emphasis? A Response." *Psychoanalytic Inquiry* 4, no. 3:489–524.

———.1991. "Discussion of Mitchell's 'Comparing Theories of Aggression: Toward an Integration.'" Paper presented at the meeting of Chicago's Association for Psychoanalysis, November 2.

Goldberg, A. 1990. *The Prisonhouse of Psychoanalysis.* Hillsdale, NJ: Analytic Press.

Goldner, V. 1991. "Toward a Critical Relational Theory of Gender." *Pschoanalytic Dialogues* 1, no. 3:249–72.

Gould, S. J. 1981. *The Mismeasure of Man*. New York: W.W. Norton.

———.1990. *The Individual in Darwin's World*. The second Edinburgh Medal Address. Edinburgh: Edinburgh University Press.

Greenberg, J. 1991. *Oedipus and Beyond: A Clinical Theory*. Cambridge, MA: Harvard University Press.

———, and S. Mitchell. 1983. *Object Relations in Psychoanalytic Theory*. Cambridge, MA.: Harvard University Press.

Grosskurth, P. 1986. *Melanie Klein: Her World and Her Work*. New York: Knopf.

Grossman, W. 1982. "The Self as Fantasy: Fantasy as Theory." *Journal of the American Psychoanalytic Association* 30:919–38.

———. 1991. "Pain, Aggression, Fantasy and Concepts of Sado-masochism." *Psychoanalytic Quarterly* 60:22–52.

Grotstein, J. 1977. "The Psychoanalytic Concept of Schizophrenia. I. The Dilemma." *International Journal of Psycho-Analysis* 58:403–25.

———.1982. "The Spectrum of Aggression." *Psychoanalytic Inquiry* 22, no. 2:193–212.

———.1987. "Making the Best of a Bad Deal: A Discussion of Boris's 'Bion Revisited.'" *Contemporary Psychoanalysis* 23, no. 1:60–76.

Guntrip, H. 1969. *Schizoid Phenomena, Object Relations, and the Self*. New York: International Universities Press.

Habermas, J. 1968. *Knowledge and Human Interests*. New York: Beacon.

Harris, A. 1991. "Gender as Contradiction." *Psychoanalytic Dialogues* 1, no. 2:197–224.

———. 1992. "Aggression: Pleasures and Dangers." Paper presented at a conference entitled "Aggression: Contemporary Controversies," sponsored by the Association for Psychoanalytic Self Psychology, February 29.

Hartmann, H., E. Kris, and R. M. Loewenstein. 1949. "Notes on the Theory of Aggression." *Psychoanalytic Study of the Child* 3/4:9–36.

Hinde, R. 1977. "Study of Aggression: Determinants, Consequences, Goals, and Functions." In *Determinants and Origins of Aggressive Behavior*, ed. J. DeWit and W. Hartup. The Hague: Mouton.

Hoffman, I. Z. 1983. "The Patient as Interpreter of the Analyst's Experience." *Contemporary Psychoanalysis* 19:389–422.

———. 1987a. "The Value of Uncertainty in Psychoanalytic Practice." *Contemporary Psychoanalysis*, 23 no. 2:205–15.

———. 1987b. Discussion of "The Intrapsychic and the Interpersonal" by Stephen Mitchell. Meeting of the Chicago Association for Psychoanalytic Psychology, December 5.

———.1991a. "Discussion: Toward a Social-Constructivist View of the Psychoanalytic Situation." *Psychoanalytic Dialogues* 1:74–105.

———.1991b. "Reply to Benjamin." *Psychoanalytic Dialogues* 1:535–44.

———.1992. "Some Practical Implications of a Social-Constructivist View of the Psychoanalytic Situation." *Psychoanalytic Dialogues* 2:287–304.

Holt, R. 1981. "The Death and Transfiguration of Metapsychology." *International Review of Psycho-Analysis* 8, pt. 2:129–44.

Jacobs, T. 1991. *The Use of the Self.* New York: International Universities Press.

Jacobson, E. 1964. *The Self and the Object World.* New York: International Universities Press.

Joseph, B. 1989. *Psychic Equilibrium and Psychic Change.* London: Tavistock/Routledge.

Jung, C. 1933. *Modern Man in Search of a Soul.* New York: Harvest.

Kaplan, D. 1985. "Cultural Affairs." *Contemporary Psychology* 30:290–91.

Kennon, G. 1989. *Sketches from a Life.* New York: Pantheon.

Kermode, F. 1985. "Freud and Interpretation." *International Journal of Psycho-Analysis* 12:3–12.

Kernberg, O. 1980. *Internal World and External Reality.* New York: Jason Aronson.

———. 1984. *Severe Personality Disorders.* New Haven: Yale University Press.

Khan, M. M. R. 1963. *The Privacy of the Self.* New York: International Universities Press.

Klein, M. 1975. *Envy and Gratitude and Other Works: 1946–63.* New York: Delacorte.

Kohut, H. 1971. "The Analysis of Self." New York: International Universities Press.

———. 1972. "Thoughts on Narcissism and Narcissistic Rage." *The Psychoanalytic Study of the Child* 27:360–400.

———. 1977. *The Restoration of the Self.* New York: International Universities Press.

———. 1984. *How Does Analysis Cure?* Chicago: University of Chicago Press.

Konner, M. 1982. *The Tangled Wing: Biological Constraints on the Human Spirit.* New York: Holt, Rinehart and Winston.

Kristeva, J. 1992. *The Samurai.* New York: Columbia University Press.

Kuhn, T. 1962. *The Structure of Scientific Resolutions,* 2nd ed. Chicago: University of Chicago Press.

Lachmann, F. 1990. "On Some Challenges to Clinical Theory in the Treatment of Character Pathology." In *The Realities of Transference: Progress in Self Psychology,* vol. 5. Hillsdale, NJ: Analytic Press.

Lakoff, G. and M. Johnson. 1980. *Metaphors We Live By.* Chicago: University of Chicago Press.

Laplanche, J., and J. B. Pontalis. 1973. *The Language of Psychoanalysis.* London: Karnac.

Lear, J. 1990. *Love and Its Place in Nature.* New York: Farrar, Straus and Giroux.

Levenson, E. 1983. *The Ambiguity of Change.* New York: Basic Books.

———. 1992. *The Purloined Self.* New York: Contemporary Psychoanalysis Books.

Lichtenberg, J. 1983. *Psychoanalysis and Infant Research.* Hillsdale, NJ: Analytic Press.

———. 1989. *Psychoanalysis and Motivation.* Hillsdale, NJ: Analytic Press.

Lipton, S. 1977. "The Advantages of Freud's Technique as Shown in His Analysis of the Rat Man." *International Journal of Psycho-Analysis* 58:255–74.

Little, M. 1985. "Winnicott Working in Areas Where Psychotic Anxieties Predominate: A Personal Record." *Free Associations* 3:9–41.

Loewald, H. 1960. "On the Therapeutic Action of Psycho-Analysis." *International Journal of Psycho-Analysis* 58:463–72.

———. 1974. "Psychoanalysis as an Art and the Fantasy Nature of the Analytic Situation." In *Papers on Psychoanalysis.* New Haven, CT: Yale University Press, 1980.

———. 1976. "Primary Process, Secondary Process and Language." In *Papers on Psychoanalysis.* New Haven, CT: Yale University Press.

———. 1978. "The Waning of the Oedipus Complex." In *Papers on Psychoanalysis.* New Haven, CT: Yale University Press.

———. 1980. *Papers on Psychoanalysis.* New Haven, CT: Yale University Press.

———. 1988. *Sublimation.* New Haven, CT: Yale University Press.

McDougall, J. 1985. *Theaters of the Mind: Illusion and Truth on the Psychoanalytic Stage.* New York: Basic Books.

Malcolm, J. 1980. *Psychoanalysis: The Impossible Profession.* New York: Vintage.

Mann, T. 1927. *The Magic Mountain.* New York: Knopf.

———. 1934. *Joseph and His Brothers.* New York: Knopf.

Mehler, J., and S. Argentieri. 1989. "Hope and Hopelesness: A Technical Problem?" *International Journal of Psycho-Analysis* 70, pt. 2:295–304.

Menaker, E. 1989. *Appointment in Vienna.* New York: St. Martin's.

Meyerson, P. 1981. "When Does a Need Become a Wish?" *Contemporary Psychoanalysis* 17, no. 4:607–26.

Minsky, M. 1985. *The Society of Mind.* New York: Simon and Schuster.

Mitchell, S. 1980. "The Intrapsychic and the Interpersonal: Different Theories, Different Domains, or Historical Artifacts?" *Psychoanalytic Inquiry* 8, no. 4:472–96.

———. 1988. *Relational Concepts in Psychoanalysis: An Integration.* Cambridge, MA: Harvard University Press.

Modell, A. 1984. *Psychoanalysis in a New Context.* New York: International Universities Press.

Ogden, T. 1986. *The Matrix of the Mind: Object Relations and the Psychoanalytic Dialogue.* New York: Jason Aronson.

———. 1989. *The Primitive Edge of Experience.* New York: Jason Aronson.

———. 1991. "An Interview with Thomas Ogden." *Psychoanalytic Dialogues* 1, no. 3:361–76.

———. 1992a. "The Dialectically Constituted/Decentered Subject of Psychoanalysis. I. The Freudian Subject." *International Journal of Psycho-Analysis* 73, pt. 3:417–26.

———. 1992b. "The Dialectically Constituted/Decentered Subject of Psychoanalysis. II. The Contributions of Klein and Winnicott." *International Journal of Psycho-Analysis* 73, no. 4:613–26.

Oremland, J. 1991. *Interpretation and Interaction: Psychoanalysis or Psychotherapy?* Hillsdale, NJ: Analytic Press.

Parens, H. 1979. *The Development of Aggression in Early Childhood.* New York: Jason Aronson.

Person, E. 1980. "Sexuality as the Mainstay of Identity: Psychoanalytic Perspectives." *Sigma* 5, 605–30.

Pine, F. 1985. *Developmental Theory and Clinical Process.* New Haven, CT: Yale University Press.

———. 1990. *Drive, Ego, Object, Self.* New York: Basic Books.

Pizer, S. 1992. "The Negotiation of Paradox in the Analytic Patient." *Psychoanalytic Dialogues* 2, no. 2:215–40.

Poland, W. 1991. "Foreword." In *The Use of the Self* by T. Jacobs. New York: International Universities Press.

Polanyi, M. 1958. *The Study of Man.* London: Routledge and Kegan Paul.

Racker, H. 1968. *Transference and Countertransference.* New York: International Universities Press.

Rangell, L. 1988. "The Future of Psychoanalysis: The Scientific Crossroads." *Psychoanalytic Quarterly* 57, no. 3:313–40.

Rapaport, D. 1957. "A Theoretical Analysis of the Superego Concept." In *The Collected Papers of David Rapaport,* ed. M. Gill. New York: Basic Books.

Remnick, D. "The Struggle for Light." *New York Review of Books* Apr. 16, 1990:3–4.

Renik, O. 1992. "Prologue." *Psychoanalytic Inquiry* 12, no. 2:175–81.

Ricoeur, P. 1970. *Freud and Philosophy: An Essay on Interpretation.* New Haven, CT: Yale University Press.

Riviere, J. 1952. "On the Genesis of Psychical Conflict in Earliest Infancy." In *Developments in Psycho-Analysis.* ed. J. Riviere. London: Hogarth.

Rorty, R. 1979. *Philosophy and the Mirror of Nature*. Princeton, NJ: Princeton University Press.

Rosenfeld, H. 1987. *Impasse and Interpretation*. London: Tavistock.

Roth, P., and H. Segal. 1990. "A Kleinian View." *Psychoanalyatic Inquiry* 10, no. 4:541–49.

Rothstein, A. 1983. *The Structural Hypothesis: An Evolutionary Perspective*. New York: International Universities Press.

Russel, P. 1993. "Commentary." *Psychoanalytic Dialogues* 3.

Ryle, G. 1949. *The Concept of Mind*. Chicago: University of Chicago Press.

Samson, H., and J. Weiss. 1986. *The Psychoanalytic Process: Theory, Clinical Observation and Empirical Research*. New York: Guilford.

Sartre, J-P. 1958. *Existential Psychoanalysis*. Chicago: Gateway.

———. 1981. *The Family Idiot: Gustave Flaubert*, vol. 1. Chicago: University of Chicago Press.

Sass, I. 1988. "The Self and Its Vicissitudes: An 'Archaelogical' Study of the Psychoanalytic Avante-Garde." *Social Research* 55, no. 4:551–607.

———, and R. Woolfolk. 1988. "Psychoanalysis and the Hermeneutic Turn: A Critique of *Narrative Truth and Historical Truth*." *Journal of the American Psychoanalytic Association* 36:429–54.

Schachtel, E. 1959. *Metamorphosis*. New York: Basic Books.

Schafer, R. 1968. *Aspects of Internalization*. New York: International Universities Press.

———. 1976. *A New Language for Psychoanalysis*. New Haven, CT: Yale University Press.

———. 1978. *Language and Insight*. New Haven, CT: Yale University Press.

———. 1983. *The Analytic Attitude*. New York: Basic Books.

———. 1992. *Retelling a Life*. New York: Basic Books.

Schwaber, E. 1983. "Listening and Psychic Reality." *International Review of Psycho-Analysis* 10, pt. 4:379–92.

———. 1990a. "The Psychoanalyst's Methodological Stance." *International Journal of Psycho-Analysis* 71, pt. 1:31–36.

———. 1990b. "Interpretation and Therapeutic Action." *International Journal of Psycho-Analysis* 71, pt. 2:229–40.

Schwartz, D. 1992. "Commentary." *Psychoanalytic Dialogues* 2, no. 3:411–16.

Searles, H. 1979. *Countertransferance and Related Subjects*. New York: International Universities Press.

———. 1986. *My Work with Borderline Patients*. Northvale, NJ: Jason Aronson.

Shabad, P. 1993. "Resentment, Indignation, Entitlement: The Transformation of Unconscious Wish into Need." *Psychoanalytic Dialogues* 3, no. 4, in press.

Shane, M., and E. Shane. 1980. "Psychoanalytic Developmental Theories of the Self: An Integration." In *Advances in Self Psychology*, ed. A. Goldberg. New York: International Universities Press.

Silverman, M. 1985. "Countertransference and the Myth of the Perfectly Analyzed Analyst." *Psychoanalytic Quarterly* 54, no. 2:175–99.

———. 1987. "Clinical Material." *Psychoanalytic Inquiry* 7, no. 2:147–67.

Simon, J., and W. Gagnon. 1973. *Sexual Conduct*. Chicago: Aldine.

Slavin, M., and D. Kreigman. 1989. "Beyond the Classical-Relational Dialectic in Psychoanalysis: A New Paradigm from Contemporary Evolutionary Biology." Paper presented at Division 39 (Psychoanalysis) of the American Psychological Association, Boston.

Snow, C., and C. Ferguson 1977. *Talking to Children: From Input to Acquisition*. Cambridge, U.K.: Cambridge University Press.

Socarides, D., and D. Stolorow. 1984. "Affects and Selfobjects." In *Annual of Psychoanalysis*, vol. 12/13. New York: International Universities Press.

Spence, D. 1982. *Narrative Truth, Historical Truth*. New York: W.W. Norton.

———. 1987a. "Turning Happenings into Meanings: The Central Role of the Self." In *The Book of the Self: Person, Pretext and Process*, ed. P. Young-Eisendrath and J. Hall. New York: New York University Press.

———. 1987b. *The Freudian Metaphor: Toward Paradigm Change in Psychoanalysis*. New York: W.W. Norton.

Spezzano, C. 1993. *Affect in Psychoanalytic Theory and Therapy: Towards a New Synthesis*. Hillsdale, NJ: Analytic Press.

Sterba, R. 1934. "The Fate of the Ego in Analytic Therapy." Reprinted in *The Evolution of Psychoanalytic Technique*, ed. M. Bergmann and F. Hartmann. New York: Basic Books, 1976.

Stern, Daniel. 1985. *The Interpersonal World of the Infant*. New York: Basic Books.

Stern, Donnel B. 1987. "Unformulated Experience." *Contemporary Psychoanalysis* 19:71–99.

———. 1990. "Courting Surprise." *Contemporary Psychoanalysis* 26:452–78.

———. 1991. "A Philosophy for the Embedded Analyst." *Contemporary Psychoanalysis* 27:51–80.

Stolorow, R. 1986. "Critical Reflections on the Theory of Self Psychology: An Inside View." *Psychoanalytic Inquiry* 6, no. 3:387–402.

———, and G. Atwood. 1992. *Contexts of Being: The Intersubjective Foundations of Psychological Life*. Hillsdale, NJ: Analytic Press.

Stolorow, R., B. Brandschaft, and G. Atwood. 1987. *Psychoanalytic Treatment: An Intersubjective Approach*. Hillsdale, NJ: Analytic Press.

Stolorow, R., and F. Lachmann. 1980. *Psychoanalysis of Developmental Arrests.* New York: International Universities Press.

Sullivan, H. 1938. "The Data of Psychiatry." In *The Fusion of Psychiatry and the Social Sciences.* New York: W.W. Norton, 1964.

———. 1950. "The Illusion of Personal Individuality." In *The Fusion of Psychiatry and the Social Sciences.* New York: W.W. Norton, 1964.

———. 1953. *The Interpersonal Theory of Psychiatry.* New York: W.W. Norton.

———. 1956. *Clinical Studies in Psychiatry.* New York: W.W. Norton.

Sulloway, F. 1983. *Freud: Biologist of the Mind.* New York: Basic Books.

Tansey M., and W. Burke. 1989. *Understanding Countertransference: from Projective Identification to Empathy.* Hillsdale, NJ: Analytic Press.

Taylor, C. 1989. *The Sources of the Self: The Making of the Modern Identity.* Cambridge, MA. Harvard University Press.

———. 1991. *The Ethics of Authenticity.* Cambridge, MA: Harvard University Press.

Thomas, L. 1974. *The Lives of a Cell: Notes of a Biology Watcher.* New York: Bantam.

Van der Kolk, B. 1989. "The Compulsion to Repeat the Trauma." *Psychiatric Clinics of North America* 12, no. 2:389–411.

Wachtel, P. 1987. *Action and Insight.* New York: Guilford Press.

Waelder, R. 1936. "The Principle of Multiple Functioning: Observations on Over-determination." *Psychoanalytic Quarterly* 5:45–62.

———. 1960. *The Basic Theory of Psychoanalysis.* New York: International Universities Press.

Wallerstein, R. 1988. "One Psychoanalysis or Many?" *International Journal of Psycho-Analysis* 69, pt. 1:5–22.

Winnicott, D. 1945. "Primitive Emotional Development." In *Through Paediatrics to Psycho-Analysis.* London: Hogarth, 1958.

———. 1949. "Hate in the Countertransference." In *Through Paediatrics to Psychoanalysis.* London: Hogarth, 1958.

———. 1954. "Metapsychological and Clinical Aspects of Regression within the Psycho-Analytic Set-up." In *Through Paediatrics to Psycho-Analysis.* London: Hogarth, 1958.

———. 1956a. "Primary Maternal Preoccupation." In *Through Paediatrics to Psycho-Analysis.* London: Hogarth, 1958.

———. 1956b. "The Anti-Social Tendency." In *Through Paediatrics to Psycho-Analysis.* London: Hogarth, 1958.

———. 1958. "The Capacity To Be Alone." In *The Maturational Process and the Facilitating Environment.* New York: International Universities Press, 1965.

———. 1960. "Ego Distortion in Terms of True and False Self." In *The*

Maturational Process and the Facilitating Environment. New York: International Universities Press, 1965.

———. 1963. "Communicating and Not Communicating Leading to a Study of Certain Opposites." *The Maturational Process and the Facilitating Environment.* New York: International Universities Press, 1965.

———. 1965. *The Maturational Process and the Facilitating Environment.* New York: International Universities Press.

———. 1968. "The Use of the Object and Relating Through Identifications." In *Playing and Reality.* Middlesex, England: Penguin, 1974.

———. 1986. *Holding and Interpretation: Fragment of an Analysis.* New York: Grove.

Wolf, E. 1991. "Discussion." *Psychoanalytic Dialogues* 1, no. 2:158–72.

Young-Eisendrath, P., and J. Hall. 1987. "Ways of Speaking of Self." In *The Book of the Self: Person, Pretext, and Process,* ed. P. Young-Eisendrath and J. Hall. New York: New York University Press.

INDEX